OP   6⁵⁰

The Almanac of
American Letters

The Almanac of
American Letters

RANDY F. NELSON

William Kaufmann, Inc.

LOS ALTOS, CALIFORNIA

Library of Congress Cataloging in Publication Data

Nelson, Randy F   1948–
    Almanac of American letters.

    Bibliography: p.
    Includes index.
1. American literature—History and criticism
—Anecdotes, facetiae, Satire, etc.   2. Authors,
American—Biography—Anecdotes, facetiae, satire,
etc.   I. Title.
PS92.N37   810'.9   80–27571
ISBN 0–86576–008–X

10 9 8 7 6 5 4 3 2 1

First Edition

Printed in the United States of America

Designed by Al Burkhardt

For Susan, Miles, Ian

Contents

Preface

Although the formal literary chroniclers gag at Matthew Arnold's definition of history (one "vast Mississippi of falsehood"), they sometimes imply that the story of American letters does somehow *flow* from period to period, every literary moment being a transition into another. One can sense even among students in English classes nowadays a conviction that there has always been a sort of collective stream of unconsciousness connecting William Bradford to Horatio Alger to Truman Capote.

Heaven help us, such history is bunk! The real narrative of American letters doesn't flow as much as it lurches: in fact the very notion that there is a narrative to be recounted may itself be a fiction. Rather than reading *the* story of American literature one might be well served by reading the disparate stories of American literature. Rather than reading a formal history, one might try sampling a scrapbook.

This volume is not an exercise in the correction of ideas, as Bernard DeVoto called one of his histories: it is, simply, an almanac, a book of juxtapositions. Here the momentous and the trivial lie (Arnold notwithstanding) side by side. It's a book of charts, dates, biographies, statistics, and essays. It is incomplete and irreverent, and it aspires to be a supplement to whatever real literary history is being written now.

There is of course already a vast collection of fine writing on American literature, and this present book should be taken only as a special kind of reader's guide to this library. In the following pages are some stories behind the stories—some anecdotes, odd facts, blistering quotations, and, in all, enough information to suggest that when one re-searches an old topic he can be instructed and astonished and entertained by what needs rediscovering from time to time. There are, alas, no amazing new discoveries in this book; but there are some amazing old discoveries, enough to make the bibliography the most important chapter of *The Almanac of American Letters*.

Randy F. Nelson
Davidson, 1980

Acknowledgements

I began this book in graduate school as an entertainment for friends and finished it for my students at Davidson: along the way I have been helped by a great number of those friends and by many of my students. Susan McCloskey, Cindy Blanton Tomiszer, Jill and Steve Messner, Cherie and Bruce Olsen, and Judith and Steve Marsh all supplied advice and encouragement when I needed them.

Mary Earnhardt, Ann Callahan, Joan Wilkins, and Rosalie Sailstad typed lectures of mine which were later revised into sections of this text. Louise Thompson typed the hundreds of pages of manuscript which went to the publisher. My thanks to them all.

Leland Park, Mary Beaty, and Violet Weisner supplied information on sources and reference materials for this book. They are no longer surprised by my strange requests; and for that, as well as for their help, I am grateful. Thanks should go also to Richard Ludwig of the rare books and manuscripts division of Firestone Library at Princeton University, to the staff of the Berg Collection of the New York Public Library, and to the curators of rare books and manuscripts at the Houghton Library of Harvard University. Also I thank Carey S. Bliss, Curator of Rare Books at the Huntington Library, for his expert advice.

Peter Andrews gave me permission to reprint his excellent article from *Horizon*, and I am deeply appreciative.

Susan Nelson did editorial work at various stages of manuscript preparation: I appreciate her moral support throughout the ordeal and her advice on organizing and revising the material. Mike Hamilton improved the galleys immensely with his suggestions, and to my great benefit Hansford Epes and Charles Lloyd put the entire text under their careful eyes for a time. Thank you.

I express my gratitude also to proofreaders Ann McMillan, Jane Cain, Larry Cain, Mary Bolding, Bill Bolding, Judith Marsh, and Steve Marsh.

Most of all, though, I appreciate the efforts of two good boys, Miles and Ian Nelson: they donated some of their time to this book too and have taught me lessons in perspective.

The Almanac of
American Letters

Facts and Figures

§ | *Introduction*. While most literary historians fondly discuss what they call the "development" of ideas, few of them are willing to risk refutation by citing the exact amounts, precise listings, or definite dates of those longest, shortest, best, worst, most, least, first, last, largest, or smallest phenomena of the national letters. Here's the antidote, an entire chapter—a Guinness booklet—devoted to the (more or less) measurable features of American literature.

Firsts

Almost everyone thinks that the FIRST BOOK printed in America was the *Bay Psalm Book* or, more properly, *The Whole Booke of Psalmes Faithfully Translated into English Meter* (1640). It may well have been the first book, but in order for it to qualify, one must first discount William Peirce's *An Almanack for the Year 1639* which was printed a few months earlier. Also appearing earlier was a document called *The Oath of a Free-man*, a short pledge of loyalty to the government, which was published in the winter of 1638—39. There are, nevertheless, no extant copies of either the *Almanack* or the *Oath*.

The FIRST PUBLISHER in American history would have been the Reverend Jose Glover, owner of the first printing press to come to the New World. Glover sailed for Massachusetts in the summer of 1638, but he died on the voyage. His widow and children settled in Cambridge where they hired a former locksmith named Stephen Daye as the first printer.

Royall Tyler wrote the FIRST COMEDY by an American citizen; it was called *The Contrast* (1790) and was preceded only by Thomas Godfrey's more serious *Prince of Parthia* (1765). *The Prince* appeared at the Southwark Theatre in Philadelphia during 1767. The second play to be written by an American citizen was *The Father* by William Dunlap, professionally produced in 1789. This latter was also the first play to be printed in America.

The FIRST ENTIRELY AMERICAN BOOK was British. That is to say, the first book entirely bound in America, impressed on American plates, and printed on American paper was Charlotte Turner Smith's *Elegiac Sonnets and Other Poems* (1795). It was, alas, a reprint of an English edition.

The Methodists organized the FIRST DENOMINATIONAL PUBLISHING CONCERN in 1789. The Reverend John Dickins donated $600 toward starting the new company in Philadelphia and saw published within a year John Wesley's *The Christian Pattern*, an imitation of Thomas À Kempis's *Imitation of Christ*.

The FIRST BOOKSELLER in America may have been Hezekiah Usher of Cambridge. He opened his business in 1639 and later secured a monopoly for printing the laws of the General Court of the state.

The FIRST POET to achieve wide recognition in America was not Anne Bradstreet nor Edward Taylor but Benjamin Thompson, a Harvard graduate, class of '62. That's 1662. Fourteen years after graduation he turned out *New Englands Crisis, or a Brief Narrative of New Englands Lamentable Estate at Present, compar'd with the former (but few) years of Prosperity. Occasioned by many unheard of Crueltys practised upon the Persons and Estates of its united Colonyes, without respect of Sex, Age or Quality of Persons by the Barbarous Heathen thereof.* This was a thirty-one page account of King Philip's War in verse form. It was not a bestseller.

The FIRST NOVEL written in America may have been *Adventures of Alonso: Containing Some Striking Anecdotes of the Present Prime Minister of Portugal* (London, 1875), by a "Native of Maryland," possibly Thomas A. Digges. It was also the first American novel to be translated (into German). The FIRST NOVEL BY A BLACK AUTHOR was *Clotel, or the President's Daughter, a Narrative of Slave Life in the United States* by William Wells Brown. This was more or less a political instrument attacking Thomas Jefferson as a supporter of slavery: the plot concerns Jefferson's "slave daughter" by a black mistress.

The FIRST LITERARY CLUB in the United States grew out of the informal meetings of James Fenimore Cooper, Henry Brevoort, William Dunlap, Charles Wiley, Gulian Verplanck, Fitz-Greene Halleck, and James Kent in New York City during the early 1820s. It was known at first as The Lunch or the Cooper Club and then by 1825 (when William Cullen Bryant and Samuel F. B. Morse became members) as the Bread and Cheese. One voted to accept prospective members by an offering of bread; voting with cheese signified blackballing.

In 1798 the author of *Wieland* (also 1798—THE FIRST GOTHIC NOVEL in America), Charles Brockden Brown, wrote the FIRST sustained PLEA FOR what is now called WOMEN'S RIGHTS; it was *Alcuin: A Dialogue.*

Francis Hopkins (1739—91) was the country's first literary over-achiever. He wrote the FIRST SONG published in America, designed the first seal of the state of New Jersey, became the first federal judge in Pennsylvania, helped design the first American flag, wrote the FIRST widely recognized SATIRICAL POEM ("The Battle of the Kegs"), and signed the Declaration of Independence.

In 1677 appeared the FIRST AMERICAN BOOK TO BE ILLUSTRATED, which contained a map of New England done in woodcut by the printer John Foster. The book was Hubbard's *Narrative of the Indian Wars.* The FIRST PORTRAIT to appear in an American volume was that of Increase Mather, the frontispiece in some of the copies of his *Blessed Hope* (1701). Mather's *Ichabod* (1702) carried the FIRST COPPERPLATE ENGRAVING in an American book.

The FIRST LITERARY SOCIETY FOR JOINT AUTHORSHIP of a work was the Connecticut Wits (see *Organizations*). Their *Anarchiad* ran in the New Haven *Gazette* during 1786 and 1787.

The FIRST BOOK FOR THE BLIND came from Philadelphia in 1833, but it was not printed in Braille. The Pennsylvania Institution for the Instruction of the Blind used raised letters in regular type for publishing *The Gospel of St. Mark*, and blind readers decoded the words letter by letter using the tips of their fingers.

The FIRST BOOK MADE ENTIRELY BY ONE MAN did not come until 1923. It was then that Dr. Dard Hunter of Chillicothe, Ohio, brought out *Old Papermaking*. The book was 140 pages long, and every em of it was Hunter's product. He wrote the text, made the paper, cut the type, printed the pages, and bound the book. He even sold the book himself, but at that he was less of a success.

The FIRST BOOK CLUB was of course the Book of the Month Club founded in April, 1926. The first president was Robert Haas; and the first book judges were Dorothy Canfield, William A. White, Henry Seidel Canby, Christopher Morley, and Heywood Broun. Their first selection was Sylvia Townsend Warner's *Lolly Willowes, or the Loving Huntsman* which went to the 4,750 first members.

The FIRST American to have his own ENGRAVED BOOKPLATE, according to available records, was Thomas Dering. His design was printed in Boston by Nathaniel Hurd sometime during 1740.

The FIRST RARE BOOK DEALER in the New World was probably Samuel G. Drake who opened his Boston enterprise on July 10, 1830. His specialty was old books concerning the Indians.

Certainly the FIRST DETECTIVE drawn by an American author was Poe's C. Auguste Dupin, appearing in several of the author's tales in the early 1840s. But the identity of the FIRST AMERICAN MYSTERY NOVEL is something of a, well, problem. It may have been James Fenimore Cooper's *The Ways of the Hour* (1850), a courtroom drama attacking the whole notion of trial by jury. It may have been Anna Katharine Green's *The Leavenworth Case* (1878), a novel depending more on "detection" than Cooper's. Or it may even have been Mark Twain's *Pudd'n head Wilson* (1894), in which fingerprints were first used to solve the crime. It all rather depends on how one marshals the evidence.

The FIRST PRESIDENTIAL PRESS CONFERENCE in American history was a private one which took place in 1829. It was attended only by John Quincy Adams, as he swam nude in the Potomac, and a woman writer named Anne Newport Royall, who trapped Adams by sitting on the Presidential knickers until he answered her questions.

Rudolph Fisher wrote the FIRST MYSTERY peopled only WITH NEGRO CHARACTERS: it was *The Conjure Man Dies* (1932), now a collector's item.

The FIRST COMIC BOOK after the current style was *Funnies on Parade* published by Eastern Color Company of Waterbury, Connecticut, in 1933. It was seven by nine inches, this because the pages were fitted onto news sheets and folded twice. *Funnies* was not sold directly but was distributed as a gift premium used by Proctor & Gamble and the Canada Dry Company.

The FIRST COMIC BOOK TO BE SOLD DIRECTLY and regularly was *Famous Funnies*, published by Dell for ten cents a copy. The first issue was May, 1934.

The word *blurb*, familiar to all in the book trade, was first coined "officially" by writer Gelett Burgess in 1907, although it had appeared on book jackets as early as 1899. It was at a banquet of the American Booksellers' Association that Burgess defined this new verb as "to make a sound like a publisher" and then added, "A blurb is a check drawn on Fame, and is seldom honored."

§ | *The First Presses.* What follows is a chronological listing of the first printing presses set up in each of the continental United States.

State	City	Year
Massachusetts	Cambridge	1639
Virginia	Jamestown	1682
Maryland	St. Mary's City	1685 (Aug.)
Pennsylvania	Philadelphia	1685 (Dec.)
New York	New York City	1693
Connecticut	New London	1709
New Jersey	Perth Amboy	1723
Rhode Island	Newport	1727
South Carolina	Charleston	1731
North Carolina	New Bern	1749
New Hampshire	Portsmouth	1756
Delaware	Wilmington	1761
Georgia	Savannah	1762 (1st imprint, 1763)
Louisiana	New Orleans	1764
Vermont	Dresden (now Hanover, N. H.)	1778
Florida	St. Augustine	1783
Maine	Falmouth (now Portland)	1785
Kentucky	Lexington	1787
District of Columbia	Georgetown	1789
West Virginia	Shepherdstown	1790
Tennessee	Hawkins Court House (now Rogersville)	1791
Ohio	Cincinnati	1793
Michigan	Detroit	1796

State	City	Year
Mississippi	Walnut Hills (now Vicksburg)	ca. 1798
Indiana	Vincennes	1804
Alabama	Wakefield	1807
Missouri	St. Louis	1808
Illinois	Kaskaskia	1814
Texas	Galveston	1817
Arkansas	Arkansas Post	1819
Wisconsin	Navarino (now Green Bay)	1833
Kansas	Shawnee Baptist Mission	1834 (Mar.)
California	Monterey	1834 (ca. June)
New Mexico	Santa Fe	1834 (Aug. or Sept.)
Oklahoma	Union Mission	1835
Iowa	Dubuque	1836
Idaho	Clearwater	1839
Oregon	Oregon City	1846
Nebraska	Winter Quarters (now Florence)	1847
Utah	Salt Lake City	1849 (Jan.)
Minnesota	St. Paul	1849 (April)
Washington	Olympia	1852
South Dakota	Sioux Falls	1858 (before Oct. 4)
Nevada	Genoa	1858 (Dec.)
Arizona	Tubac	1858 (Dec.)
Colorado	Denver	1859 (April)
Wyoming	Fort Bridger	1863 (June)
Montana	Virginia City	1863 (after Oct. 19)
North Dakota	Fort Rice	1864

§ | *The Declaration of Independence.* The first publications of the Declaration of Independence were in these newspapers during July, 1776. All things considered, it was remarkably speedy distribution of the news.

July 6	Philadelphia	*Pennsylvania Evening Post*
July 8	Philadelphia	*Dunlap's Pennsylvania Packet*
July 9	Philadelphia	*Pennsylvanischer Staatsbote*
July 9	Baltimore	*Dunlap's Maryland Gazette*

July 10	Philadelphia	*Pennsylvania Gazette*
July 10	Philadelphia	*Pennsylvania Journal*
July 10	Baltimore	*Maryland Journal*
July 10	New York	*Constitutional Gazette*
July 11	New York	*Packet*
July 11	New York	*Journal*
July 11	Annapolis	*Gazette*
July 12	New London	*Connecticut Gazette*
July 13	Philadelphia	*Pennsylvania Ledger*
July 13	Providence	*Gazette*
July 15	New York	*Gazette*
July 15	Hartford	*Connecticut Courant*
July 15	Norwich	*Packet*
July 16	Exeter	*New Hampshire Gazette*
July 16	Salem	*American Gazette*
July 17	Worcester	*Massachusetts Spy*
July 17	New Haven	*Connecticut Journal*
July 18	Boston	*Continental Journal*
July 18	Boston	*New England Chronicle*
July 18	Newport Mercury	*Extraordinary*
July 19	Newburyport	*Essex Journal*
July 19	Williamsburg, Va.	*Virginia Gazette* (Purdie) tract; in full July 26
July 20	Williamsburg	*Virginia Gazette*
July 20	Portsmouth	*Freeman's Journal*
July 22	Watertown	*Boston Gazette*

(First British printing was in the London *Chronicle*, August 13, 1776.)

§ | *Funds.* Americans certainly are not alone in the world with their love of evaluating everything in terms of money; but they do seem to take a special joy in counting and comparing, especially when they're counting coins. The results are not all tabulated yet, but here are a few examples of what happened when readers measured American literature in dollars and decimals.

Thomas Paine actually lost money by publishing *Common Sense*. The book came out first as a pamphlet and later in an enlarged edition which sold well in America, Canada, England, France, and South America. In all printings, *Common Sense* easily topped half a million copies, yet in 1779 Paine still owed thirty-nine pounds, 11 shillings for presswork on his most famous piece.

In 1839 Edgar Allan Poe assumed the editorship of *Graham's Magazine* where he boosted circulation from 5,000 to 37,000. For his efforts Poe earned a handsome $800 a year, far more than he made in any other comparable period in his life. It was, in addition, more than the total income he realized from the ten books he published before his death.

In 1912 Richard W. Tully began losing what may have been the costliest plagiarism suit in American history. When a woman insisted that his *Bird of Paradise* was in fact a play she had written some time earlier, Tully challenged her in court. Within weeks the woman disappeared—for twelve years—although she returned in 1924 to reopen the case. This time she produced the "original" manuscript of the play and secured a judgment of $781,990.00. Tully, however, lost far more than that. He continued to fight, paying lawyers from his personal fortune. In 1930 the New York State Court of Appeals held that there was no resemblance between the two plays and reversed the findings of the lower court. Nevertheless, Tully was ruined: all of his money had gone for legal fees, and he did not write another word before his death in 1945.

Thomas Wolfe's composition of *Look Homeward, Angel* has become a legend itself. Tradition has it that he wrote standing up, using the top of his refrigerator for a desk and dropping finished pages to the floor without reading them. At the end of the day Wolfe would scoop up the pile and toss it into a crate; then at the end of a book he would mail the crate to a publisher. People who saw the manuscript of *Look Homeward, Angel* swear that stacked page on top of page it made a column three feet high. The truth, though, is that *O Lost*, as it was originally called, had 330,000 words on 1,114 pages and stood about five inches high. Naturally this amount was still far too much for an ordinary novel, and the publisher insisted on cutting the work by a third. After weeks of hard work the author resubmitted his book, now eight pages shorter than the original version: what had happened of course is that Wolfe did make the required cuts but then wrote another 100,000 words to fill in gaps. At last editor and author agreed on a reorganization of sections and to a final publication schedule. In the process they slashed 90,000 words, the equivalent of a full-length novel. For the entire completed manuscript Wolfe got an advance of $500, minus ten percent for his literary agent. Considering everything that he wrote, that amounts to about $.00104 per word.

The highest per-word rate ever paid to an author, American or otherwise, went to Ernest Hemingway in 1960. In January of that year *Sports Illustrated* gave him $30,000 for an article on bullfighting. Hemingway gave the editors 2,000 words. You figure it out.

The man most willing to pay for interesting manuscripts is Malcolm Forbes, publisher of *Forbes* magazine. It is however in his capacity as collector rather than as publisher that Mr. Forbes is willing to part with so many dollars. In 1978, for instance, he paid $85,000 for an unprinted manuscript by a completely unknown author named Robert Lewis. In fact, Lewis is no professional writer at all: he was the copilot of the plane which dropped the atomic bomb at Hiroshima on August 6, 1945. The manuscript in question was Lewis's logbook, for which Forbes paid the most money ever taken for an American autograph document. The previous high had been a mere $75,000, also paid by Forbes in 1978, for a Paul Revere autograph.

In his college years Ernest Lawrence Thayer edited the Harvard *Lampoon*, and William Randolph Hearst was one of his "employees." After they graduated, Hearst edited the *San Francisco Examiner*; and Thayer became one of *his* employees. In that capacity Thayer wrote for his humor column, one of the most famous poems in the English language , "Casey at the Bat." The verses brought him five dollars.

The greatest fine ever collected for an overdue library book was reported by Richard Dodd in December, 1968. His great-grandfather had neglected to return a treatise on febrile diseases to the University of Cincinnati Medical Library in 1823. Dodd thus inherited a bill for $22,646.

Pulitzer Prizes: Fiction.

1918	Ernest Poole	*His Family*
1919	Booth Tarkington	*The Magnificent Ambersons*
1920	No prize	
1921	Edith Wharton	*The Age of Innocence*
1922	Booth Tarkington	*Alice Adams*
1923	Willa Cather	*One of Ours*
1924	Margaret Wilson	*The Able McLaughlins*
1925	Edna Ferber	*So Big*
1926	Sinclair Lewis	*Arrowsmith*
1927	Louis Bromfield	*Early Autumn*
1928	Thornton Wilder	*Bridge of San Luis Rey*
1929	Julia M. Peterkin	*Scarlet Sister Mary*
1930	Oliver LaFarge	*Laughing Boy*
1931	Margaret Ayer Barnes	*Years of Grace*
1932	Pearl Buck	*The Good Earth*
1933	T. S. Stribling	*The Store*

1934	Caroline Miller	*Lamb in His Bosom*
1935	Josephine W. Johnson	*Now in November*
1936	Harold L. Davis	*Honey in the Horn*
1937	Margaret Mitchell	*Gone with the Wind*
1938	John P. Marquand	*The Late George Apley*
1939	Marjorie Kinnan Rawlings	*The Yearling*
1940	John Steinbeck	*The Grapes of Wrath*
1941	No prize	
1942	Ellen Glasgow	*In This Our Life*
1943	Upton Sinclair	*Dragon's Teeth*
1944	Martin Flavin	*Journey in the Dark*
1945	John Hersey	*A Bell for Adano*
1946	No prize	
1947	Robert Penn Warren	*All the King's Men*
1948	James A. Michener	*Tales of the South Pacific*
1949	James Gould Cozzens	*Guard of Honor*
1950	A. B. Guthrie, Jr.	*The Way West*
1951	Conrad Richter	*The Town*
1952	Herman Wouk	*The Caine Mutiny*
1953	Ernest Hemingway	*The Old Man and the Sea*
1954	No prize	
1955	William Faulkner	*A Fable*
1956	Mackinlay Kantor	*Andersonville*
1957	No prize	
1958	James Agee	*A Death in the Family*
1959	Robert Lewis Taylor	*The Travels of Jamie McPheeters*
1960	Allen Drury	*Advise and Consent*
1961	Harper Lee	*To Kill a Mockingbird*
1962	Edwin O'Connor	*The Edge of Sadness*
1963	William Faulkner	*The Reivers*
1964	No prize	
1965	Shirley Ann Grau	*The Keepers of the House*
1966	Katherine Anne Porter	*The Collected Stories of Katherine Anne Porter*
1967	Bernard Malamud	*The Fixer*
1968	William Styron	*The Confessions of Nat Turner*
1969	N. Scott Momaday	*House Made of Dawn*
1970	Jean Stafford	*Collected Stories*
1971	No prize	
1972	Wallace Stegner	*Angle of Repose*

1973	Eudora Welty	*The Optimist's Daughter*
1974	No prize	
1975	Michael Shaara	*The Killer Angels*
1976	Saul Bellow	*Humbolt's Gift*
1977	No prize	
1978	James Alan McPherson	*Elbow Room*

Pulitzer Prizes: Drama

1918	Jesse Lynch Williams	*Why Marry?*
1920	Eugene O'Neill	*Beyond the Horizon*
1921	Zona Gale	*Miss Lulu Bett*
1922	Eugene O'Neill	*Anna Christie*
1923	Owen Davis	*Icebound*
1924	Hatcher Hughes	*Hell Bent for Heaven*
1925	Sidney Howard	*They Knew What They Wanted*
1926	George Kelly	*Craig's Wife*
1927	Paul Green	*In Abraham's Bosom*
1928	Eugene O'Neill	*Strange Interlude*
1929	Elmer Rice	*Street Scene*
1930	Marc Connelly	*The Green Pastures*
1931	Susan Glaspell	*Alison's House*
1932	George S. Kaufman, Morrie Ryskind, and Ira Gershwin	*Of Thee I Sing*
1933	Maxwell Anderson	*Both Your Houses*
1934	Sidney Kingsley	*Men in White*
1935	Zoe Atkins	*The Old Maid*
1936	Robert E. Sherwood	*Idiot's Delight*
1937	George S. Kaufman and Moss Hart	*You Can't Take It With You*
1938	Thornton Wilder	*Our Town*
1939	Robert E. Sherwood	*Abe Lincoln in Illinois*
1940	William Saroyan	*The Time of Your Life*
1941	Robert E. Sherwood	*There Shall Be No Night*
1942	No prize	
1943	Thornton Wilder	*The Skin of Our Teeth*
1944	No prize	
1945	Mary Chase	*Harvey*
1946	Russel Crouse and Howard Lindsay	*State of the Union*

1947	No prize	
1948	Tennessee Williams	*A Streetcar Named Desire*
1949	Arthur Miller	*Death of a Salesman*
1950	Richard Rodgers, Oscar Hammerstein II, and Joshua Logan	*South Pacific*
1951	No prize	
1952	Joseph Kramm	*The Shrike*
1953	William Inge	*Picnic*
1954	John Patrick	*Teahouse of the August Moon*
1955	Tennessee Williams	*Cat on a Hot Tin Roof*
1956	Frances Goodrich and Albert Hackett	*The Diary of Anne Frank*
1957	Eugene O'Neill	*Long Day's Journey into Night*
1958	Ketti Frings	*Look Homeward, Angel*
1959	Archibald MacLeish	*J.B.*
1960	George Abbott, Jerome Weidman, Sheldon Harnick, and Jerry Bock	*Fiorello*
1961	Tad Mosel	*All the Way Home*
1962	Frank Loesser and Abe Burrows	*How to Succeed in Business Without Really Trying*
1963	No prize	
1964	No prize	
1965	Frank D. Gilroy	*The Subject Was Roses*
1966	No prize	
1967	Edward Albee	*A Delicate Balance*
1968	No prize	
1969	Howard Sackler	*The Great White Hope*
1970	Charles Gordone	*No Place to Be Somebody*
1971	Paul Zindel	*The Effect of Gamma Rays on Man-in-the-Moon Marigolds*
1972	No prize	
1973	Jason Miller	*That Championship Season*
1974	No prize	
1975	Edward Albee	*Seascape*
1976	Michael Bennett and others	*A Chorus Line*

| 1977 | Michael Cristofer | *The Shadow Box* |
| 1978 | Donald R. Coburn | *The Gin Game* |

Pulitzer Prizes: Poetry
(established 1922)

1922	Edwin Arlington Robinson	*Collected Poems*
1923	Edna St. Vincent Millay	*The Ballad of the Harp Weaver: A Few Figs from Thistles: Eight Sonnets in American Poetry. 1922. A Miscellany*
1924	Robert Frost	*New Hampshire: A Poem with Notes and Grace Notes*
1925	Edwin Arlington Robinson	*The Man Who Died Twice*
1926	Amy Lowell	*What's O'Clock*
1927	Leonora Speyer	*Fiddler's Farewell*
1928	Edwin Arlington Robinson	*Tristram*
1929	Stephen Vincent Benet	*John Brown's Body*
1930	Conrad Aiken	*Selected Poems*
1931	Robert Frost	*Collected Poems*
1932	George Dillon	*The Flowering Stone*
1933	Archibald MacLeish	*Conquistador*
1934	Robert Hillyer	*Collected Verse*
1935	Audrey Wurdemann	*Bright Ambush*
1936	Robert P. Tristram Coffin	*Strange Holiness*
1937	Robert Frost	*A Further Range*
1938	Marya Zaturenska	*Cold Morning Sky*
1939	John Gould Fletcher	*Selected Poems*
1940	Mark Van Doren	*Collected Poems*
1941	Leonard Bacon	*Sunderland Capture*
1942	William Rose Benét	*The Dust Which Is God*
1943	Robert Frost	*A Witness Tree*
1944	Stephen Vincent Benét	*Western Star*
1945	Karl Shapiro	*V Letter and Other Poems*
1946	No prize	
1947	Robert Lowell	*Lord Weary's Castle*

1948	W. H. Auden	*The Age of Anxiety*
1949	Peter Viereck	*Terror and Decorum*
1950	Gwendolyn Brooks	*Annie Allen*
1951	Carl Sandburg	*Complete Poems*
1952	Marianne Moore	*Collected Poems*
1953	Archibald MacLeish	*Collected Poems*
1954	Theodore Roethke	*The Waking*
1955	Wallace Stevens	*Collected Poems*
1956	Elizabeth Bishop	*Poems North and South*
1957	Richard Wilbur	*Things of This World*
1958	Robert Penn Warren	*Promises: Poems 1954–56*
1959	Stanley Kunitz	*Selected Poems 1928–1958*
1960	W. D. Snodgrass	*Heart's Needle*
1961	Phyllis McGinley	*Times Three: Selected Verse from Three Decades*
1962	Alan Dugan	*Poems*
1963	William Carlos Williams	*Pictures from Breughel*
1964	Louis Simpson	*At the End of the Open Road*
1965	John Berryman	*77 Dream Songs*
1966	Richard Eberhart	*Selected Poems*
1967	Anne Sexton	*Live or Die*
1968	Anthony Hecht	*The Hard Hours*
1969	George Oppen	*Of Being Numerous*
1970	Richard Howard	*Untitled Subjects*
1971	William S. Merwin	*The Carrier of Ladders*
1972	James Wright	*Collected Poems*
1973	Maxine Winokur Kumin	*Up Country*
1974	Robert Lowell	*The Dolphin*
1975	Gary Snyder	*Turtle Island*
1976	John Ashbery	*Self-Portrait in a Convex Mirror*
1977	James Merrill	*Divine Comedies*
1978	Howard Nemerov	*Collected Poems*

Nobel Prize Winners in Literature

1930	Sinclair Lewis
1936	Eugene O'Neill

1938 Pearl S. Buck
1948 T. S. Eliot
1949 William Faulkner
1954 Ernest Hemingway
1962 John Steinbeck
1976 Saul Bellow

§ | *Caldecott Medal Winners.* These are the best illustrated children's books published in the United States, chosen each year in honor of Randolph J. Caldecott (1846— 1886), a noted English illustrator.

1938	*Animals of the Bible*	Lathrop
1939	*Meil Li*	Handforth
1940	*Abraham Lincoln*	d'Aulaire
1941	*They Were Good and Strong*	Lawson
1942	*Make Way for Ducklings*	McCloskey
1943	*The Little House*	Burton
1944	*Many Moons*	Thurber (Slobodkin, illus.)
1945	*Prayer for a Child*	Field (Jones, illus.)
1946	*The Rooster Crows*	Petersham
1947	*The Little Island*	MacDonald (Weisgand, illus.)
1948	*White Snow, Bright Snow*	Tresselt (Duvoisin, illus.)
1949	*The Big Snow*	Hader
1950	*Song of the Swallows*	Politi
1951	*The Egg Tree*	Milhous
1952	*Finders Keepers*	Lipkind (Mordvinoff, illus.)
1953	*The Biggest Bear*	Ward
1954	*Madeline's Rescue*	Bemelmans
1955	*Cinderella*	Brown
1956	*Frog Went A-Courtin'*	Langstaff (Rojankovsky, illus.)
1957	*A Tree Is Nice*	Udry (Simont, illus.)
1958	*Time of Wonder*	McCloskey
1959	*Chanticleer and the Fox*	Cooney

1960	*Nine Days to Christmas*	Ets & Labastida
1961	*Baboushka and the Three Kings*	Robbins (Sidjakov, illus.)
1962	*Once a Mouse*	Brown
1963	*The Snowy Day*	Keats
1964	*Where the Wild Things Are*	Sendak
1965	*May I Bring a Friend?*	de Regniers (Montresor, illus.)
1966	*Always Room for One More*	Leodhas (Hogrogian, illus.)
1967	*Sam, Bangs & Moonshine*	Ness
1968	*Drummer Hoff*	Emberly, Barbara (Ed. Emberly, illus.)
1969	*The Fool of the World and the Flying Ship*	Ransome (Shulevitz, illus.)
1970	*Sylvester and the Magic Pebble*	Steig
1971	*A Story-A Story*	Haley
1972	*One Fine Day*	Hogrogian
1973	*The Funny Little Woman*	Hearn: retold by Mosel (Lent, illus.)
1974	*Duffy and the Devil*	Zemach, Harve (Margot Zemach, illus.)

Honor Books:

| | *Three Jovial Huntsmen* | Jeffers |
| | *Cathedral: the Story of its Construction* | Macaulay |

The 100 Most Influential American Books

(Compiled by the Grolier Club of New York City)

| 1640 | | *Bay Psalm Book* |
| 1644 | Williams, Roger | *The Bloody Tenent of Persecution for Cause of Conscience* |

1649		*Platform of Church Discipline*
1662	Wigglesworth, Michael	*Day of Doom*
1682	Rowlandson, Mary	*Narrative of the Captivity and Restauration*
1702	Mather, Cotton	*Magnalia Christi Americana*
1717	Wise, John	*Vindication of the Government of New England Churches*
1727	*New England Primer* (earliest known)	
1736	Zenger, John Peter	*Brief Narrative of Case and Trial*
1751	Franklin, Benjamin	*Experiments . . . on Electricity*
1754	Edwards, Jonathan	*Freedom of the Will*
1757	Franklin, Benjamin	*Almanac for 1758*
1768	Dickinson, John	*Letters of a Pennsylvania Farmer*
1776	Paine, Thomas	*Common Sense*
1776	Jefferson, Thomas, et al.	*Declaration of Independence*
1783	Webster, Noah	*A Grammatical Institute*
1787		*Northwest Territory Ordinance*
1787		*Constitution, The*
1788	Hamilton, Madison, and Jay	*The Federalist*
1789		*Bill of Rights*
1791	Franklin, Benjamin	*Autobiography*
1792	Thomas, Robert	*Farmers' Almanac for 1793*
1794	Rowson, Mrs. Susanna	*Charlotte. A Tale of Truth*
1796	Washington, George	*Farewell Address*

1802	Bowditch, Nathaniel	*The New American Practical Navigator*
1804	Marshall, John	*Marbury v. Madison*
1806	Weems, Mason	*Washington*
1809	Irving, Washington	*A History of New York*
1810	Thomas, Isaiah	*History of Printing in America*
1814	Lewis, Meriwether and Clark, William	*History of the Expedition to the Pacific Ocean*
1819 —20	Irving, Washington	*The Sketch Book*
1821	Bryant, William Cullen	*Poems*
1823	Monroe, James	*Annual Message, December 2, 1823*
1826	Cooper, James F.	*The Last of the Mohicans*
1827	Goodrich, Samuel	*Peter Parley's Tales About America*
1828	Webster, Noah	*An American Dictionary*
1830	Smith, Joseph	*The Book of Mormon*
1833	Beaumont, William	*Experiments and Observations on the Gastric Juice*
1834	Crockett, David	*Crockett Almanack for 1835*
1835	Simms, William Gilmore	*The Yemassee*
1836	Gray, Asa	*Elements of Botany*
1836	McGuffey, William	*The Eclectic First Reader*
1837	Hawthorne, Nathaniel	*Twice-Told Tales*
1837	Emerson, Ralph Waldo	*The American Scholar*
1840	Dana, Richard Henry, Jr.	*Two Years Before the Mast*
1840 —44	Audubon, John James	*The Birds of America*
1841 —44	Emerson, Ralph Waldo	*Essays*

1842	Longfellow, Henry W.	*Ballads*
1843	Prescott, William	*History of the Conquest of Mexico*
1843	Frémont, J. C.	*Report on Exploration of Country Lying Between the Missouri River and the Rocky Mountains*
1843	Holmes, Oliver W.	*The Contagiousness of Puerperal Fever*
1844	Moore, Clement	*Poems*
1845	Cushing, Luther	*Rules for Proceedings and Debate in Deliberative Assemblies*
1845	Poe, Edgar Allan	*Tales*
1845	Poe, Edgar Allan	*The Raven and Other Poems*
1845	Herbert, Henry W.	*The Warwick Woodlands*
1848	Lowell, James Russell	*The Biglow Papers*
1849	Parkman, Francis	*The California and Oregon Trail*
1850	Hawthorne, Nathaniel	*The Scarlet Letter*
1851	Melville, Herman	*Moby-Dick*
1852	Stowe, Harriet Beecher	*Uncle Tom's Cabin*
1854	Arthur, T. S.	*Ten Nights in a Bar Room*
1854	Thoreau, Henry	*Walden*
1855	Longfellow, Henry W.	*The Song of Hiawatha*
1855	Whitman, Walt	*Leaves of Grass*
1855	Bartlett, John	*Familiar Quotations*
1855	Bulfinch, Thomas	*The Age of Fable*
1857	Taney, Roger (and others)	*Dred Scott v. Sandford*
1858	Holmes, Oliver W.	*The Autocrat of the Breakfast Table*
1860	Stephens, Mrs. Ann S.	*Malaeska*
1862		*Emancipation Proclamation* (September 22, 1862)
1863	Lincoln, Abraham	*Gettysburg Address*

1866	Whittier, John G.	*Snow-Bound*
1868	Alger, Horatio, Jr.	*Ragged Dick*
1868	Alcott, Louisa May	*Little Women*
1870	Harte, Bret	*The Luck of Roaring Camp*
1872	Sears, Roebuck	*First Mail-Order Catalog*
1875	Eddy, Mary Baker	*Science and Health*
1876	Clemens, Samuel	*Tom Sawyer*
1878	Green, Anna Katherine	*Leavenworth Case*
1879	George, Henry	*Progress and Poverty*
1880	Wallace, Lew	*Ben-Hur*
1881	Harris, Joel C.	*Uncle Remus*
1881	Holmes, Oliver W., Jr.	*The Common Law*
1881	James, Henry	*The Portrait of a Lady*
1884	Lincoln, Mary	*Mrs. Lincoln's Boston Cook Book*
1885	Howells, Wm. Dean	*The Rise of Silas Lapham*
1885	Clemens, Samuel	*Huckleberry Finn*
1886	Burnett, Francis H.	*Little Lord Fauntleroy*
1888	Bellamy, Edward	*Looking Backward*
1890	Mahan, Alfred T.	*The Influence of Sea Power on History*
1890	James, William	*Principles of Psychology*
1890 −91		
−96	Dickinson, Emily	*Poems*
1891	Garland, Hamlin	*Main Travelled Roads*
1891	Bierce, Ambrose	*Tales of Soldiers and Civilians*
1893	Turner, Frederick Jackson	*The Significance of the Frontier in American History*
1894	Holt, Luther	*The Care and Feeding of Children*
1895	Crane, Stephen	*The Red Badge of Courage*
1899	Veblen, Thorstein	*The Theory of the Leisure Class*
1899	Markham, Edwin	*The Man With the Hoe*

Words and Symbols Unique to American Literature

§ | *Dickinson's Particular Slant.* The controversy over Emily Dickinson's dashes began in 1962 when the *Saturday Review* published an article interpreting the poet's end-line flourishes. The author of the article, Edith Perry Stamm, had studied Dickinson's manuscripts and concluded the following: lines ending with an upward-slanting dash (——) were intended to be read with a rise in the inflection of the voice; lines ending with a downward sloping dash (——) were to be read with a corresponding drop in inflection; and those lines with level dashes were to be read in a monotone—all this stemming from a theory of oral interpretation of poetry which Dickinson presumably learned while a student at the Amherst Academy.

The first reply to Stamm's argument appeared in an article by Theodora Ward published in April, 1963, again by the *Saturday Review*. Ward had examined other manuscripts of Dickinson and noted that the angled dashes also appeared in the poet's letters.

A mere trifle, countered Stamm: obviously Dickinson intended her letters to have been read and interpreted poetically. And there the argument stood for some time. At last R. W. Franklin completed his *Editing of Emily Dickinson* and added a final ingredient to the now simmering controversy. Not only did Dickinson vary the slant of her dashes from fair copy to fair copy of the same poem, but she frequently used the same kind of angled flourish in copying recipes. He then demonstrated how one should read the baking instructions for bread and cookies.

§ | *Other Letters.* In Hawthorne's day, and even in our own, few people misunderstood the significance of Hester Prynne's scarlet letter: it was but an outward and visible sign of an inner state of being, at least to the Puritan community and to generations of high school students who knew that her *A* stood for *Adultery*. There were, however, other letters used to mark lawbreakers in the Massachusetts Bay Colony during the seventeenth and eighteenth centuries. In nearly all cases the letters were cut, not embroidered, from scarlet cloth and worn on the sleeve or bosom for a year, or perhaps two or three years if the crime were severe enough. Nevertheless, there gradually came to be a consensus that the punishment itself was a cruel and unusual one, so the wearing of scarlet letters did not extend past the time of Jonathan Edwards. While the practice lasted, other entries in the alphabet of sin included *I* for *Incest*, *B* for *Blasphemy*, *R* for *Rape*, *P* for *Poisoning*, *F* for *Forgery*, *D* for *Drunkenness*, *T* for *Theft*, and *V* for *Viciousness*.

§ | *The Interabang.* In 1967 the American Type Founders Company invented a new mark of punctuation which they called the interabang. It looked like this ‽ and presumably now serves as the best punctuation for exclamatory questions such as "What the hell are *you* doing in there‽"

§ | *Hugo Gernsback.* This American Jules Verne may have the most successful record of prediction ever attempted. Surely his greatest effort was *Ralph 124C41+: A Romance of the Year* 2660, published in installments in *Modern Electrics* throughout 1911 and 1912. Besides giving a detailed account of the principles of radar more than twenty-five years before it was invented, the book also makes use of these now-realized inventions: juke boxes, vending machines, fluorescent lighting, skywriting, flying saucers, microfilm, the tape recorder, night baseball, sleep teaching devices, solar heaters and solar cells, liquid fertilizer, hydroponics, radio networks, automatic packaging machines, loudspeakers, stainless steel, and synthetic fibres such as nylon. Gernsback also donated his name to the field of science fiction itself: a "Hugo" is now an annual award given to the year's best science fiction novel. There is, though, one other word that Gernsback ushered into the American lexicon, this one much more commonly known than last year's Hugo Award winner. In 1909, after opening the world's first radio store at 69 West Broadway in New York, he published in *Modern Electrics* a speculative article which carried in its title what was then, and remains now, something of a controversy: the word was *television.*

§ | *The Beats.* The decade of the 1950s spawned its own version of the lost generation when certain down-and-outers like Allen Ginsberg, Jack Kerouac, William Burroughs, and others began calling themselves the "beat" generation. This term ignited immediately much argument between those who insisted that *beat* meant "beat up or battered" and those who understood it as "rhythmic, with the beat"—the one group seeing it as a pejorative label, the other as a code word for initiates. In truth, the word grew into all of its many connotations before the decade ended, and its meaning depended as much on the user's perspective as on the original coining of the term.

Nevertheless, one can point with some confidence to a specific anecdote revealing, if not how the beats came into being, then how they first came to be labelled. Apparently Jack Kerouac borrowed the word from a drug-ravaged derelict named Herbert Huncke. In "The Origins of the Beat Generation" the novelist recalled,

> John Clellon Holmes . . . and I were sitting around trying to think up the meaning of the Lost Generation and the subsequent existentialism and I said, "You know, this is really a beat generation: and he lept up and said, "That's it, that's right."

Holmes took the phrase to signify "being right down to it, because we all really know where we are. . . ." If this inspired reading was indeed a misinterpretation, Kerouac at least had the courtesy not to contradict it in public; and later he even took up the term "beatific" as descriptive of much that was done by beat people. Detractors, on the other hand, see Holmes as a sort of inspired idiot who completely misread Kerouac's original remark. However, the first and greatest prophet of beat-ness, Herbert Huncke himself, did not make further pronouncements on the '50s or any other decade: he faded into myth, or obscurity perhaps, somewhere in the vicinity of Times Square.

§ | *The Cabalistic I.* Rejection slips are tickets to nowhere. They are cold, formal notifications of a writer's failure and rarely offer any printed consolation along with the refusal to publish. The *New Yorker* magazine, however, has for years printed and mailed rejection slips displaying a coded "message" of encouragement. In the center of each notice loom the following lines:

> We regret that we are unable to use the enclosed material. Thank you for giving us the opportunity to consider it.
>
> The Editors.

But below and to the left of these charming words is a symbol, an *I*, either the Roman numeral one or a capital *i*. Although the mark has no explanation and no clear connection to anything else on the page, many writers have taken some consolation from their own inference that this represented, after all, the number one rejection slip. The *I* seemed to be a clue that their work had made it to the highest echelons, just barely missing publication.

Brendan Gill, author of *Here at the New Yorker*, recalls in his memoir having had a sort of perverse pride in collecting these notices in the days before he became a writer for the magazine. He reasoned that less talented writers must have been getting rejection slips marked *II* or *III*. One can imagine Gill's consternation, then, upon joining the staff and learning that not a soul there knew the origin of the cabalistic *I*. Tradition had kept it in the same position on every rejection slip mailed to every author headed nowhere. The symbol itself stands for absolutely nothing.

§ | *Plymouth Rock*. America's oldest symbol is a fraud. Still current among school children is a belief that the *Mayflower* Pilgrims landed at Plymouth Rock on December 21, 1620. In point of fact, they landed at the very tip of Cape Cod on November 11, 1620. There are absolutely no contemporary records of the rock story, and it did not become popular until the 1740s.

§ | *The New Deal*. Franklin D. Roosevelt used Mark Twain as a source for the term *New Deal*. In a letter he penned to the International Mark Twain Society on December 8, 1933, the President acknowledged lifting the phrase "from that passage in the book *A Connecticut Yankee in King Arthur's Court*, in which the Yankee declares that, in a country where only six people out of a thousand have any voice in the government, what the 994 dupes need is a new deal."

§ | *The Tycoon*. The most enterprising word-smiths of the 1920s and '30s were the writers of *Time* magazine, all of whom looted the thesaurus and ravaged foreign tongues for new acquisitions. The Greek word *kudos*, for example, became *Time* slang for honorary degrees although it now refers to recognition in a more general sense. The word *pundit*, too, was mined at Yale but minted at *Time*. However, the most famous and most frequently used and most controversial of these was the Japanese *tycoon* ("great lord"). There was a great number of readers who felt that enough was enough. One of them wrote this:

> *Time's* editor is tall and thin.
> He and Roget are next of kin,
> Thesaurus is his middle name,
> Terseness his very end and aim.

> He stalks the shy, uncommon word,
> To give the inarticulate herd
> Vocabularies wide and weird
> And potent as the Prophet's beard.

> He passes by "galloon," "simoon,"
> He scorns "monsoon," "baboon," and "loon,"
> But he's married himself to the word "tycoon,"
> God help the poor buffoon—and soon!

§ | *The Bells.* Here is the story of a term which was not created by an American author. Everyone remembers the word *tintinnabulation* in Poe's "The Bells." According to most English teachers it is a wonderfully onomatopoeic invention, having been coined to suit the tinkling notes of the poem. But according to Poe's biographer Hervey Allen, the word is not original with Poe at all: long before the birth of Christ musicians played bells called "tintinabula."

§ | *The Palindrome War.* Palindromes are words, like *civic*, which read the same backwards as they do forwards. They aren't difficult to find in English, especially short ones; but what is indeed difficult is writing a palindromic sentence such as the frequently reprinted *Rats live on no evil star.*

There was at one time a sort of war of palindromes between Roger Angell of the *New Yorker* and a Scots poet named Alastair Reid. The contest of course was to see who could compose the longest palindrome. Reid's blockbuster was *T. Eliot, top bard, notes putrid tang emanating. Is sad. I'd assign it a name: gnat-dirt upset on drab pot toilet.* The American, however, won hands down, even though his return barrage requires an explanation. One must allow that the following is a telegram sent by a survivor of World War Two presently confined in the psychiatric ward of a veteran's hospital. *Marge, let dam dogs in. Am on satire: vow I am Cain. Am on spot. Am a Jap sniper. Red, raw murder on G. I! Ignore drum. (Warder repins pajama tops.) No maniac, Ma! Iwo veritas: no man is God.—Mad Telegram.*

§ | *Edgar Rice Burroughs.* For his Venusian stories Burroughs invented an elaborate system of background information, a history, an etiquette, even an alphabet. The author actually published the alphabet with its English equivalents, and a number of the Burroughs fan clubs adopted it for their official use. It's reprinted here for benefit of those who were not among the original Burroughs bibliophiles:

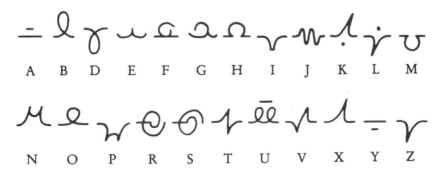

American Authors Born Outside the United States

Isaac Asimov	Russia	January 2, 1920
W. H. Auden	England	February 21, 1907
John James Audubon	Haiti	April 26, 1785
Saul Bellow	Canada	July 10, 1915
Frances Hodgson Burnett	England	November 24, 1849
Taylor Caldwell	England	September 7, 1900
Sadakichi Hartman	Japan	November 8, 1869
Lafcadio Hearn	Ionian Islands	June 27, 1850
John Hersey	Scotland	October 7, 1907
Helen MacInnes	Scotland	October 7, 1907
Claude McKay	Jamaica	September 15, 1890
Thomas Mann	Germany	June 6, 1875
Richard Mather	England	1596
Vladimir Nabokov	Russia	April 23, 1899
Thomas Paine	England	January 29, 1737
Ayn Rand	Russia	1905
Ole Rolvaag	Norway	April 22, 1876
George Santayana	Spain	December 16, 1863
Samuel Sewell	England	March 28, 1652
Trumbull Stickney	Switzerland	June 20, 1874
Edward Taylor	England	1645
A. E. Van Vogt	Canada	April 26, 1912
Michael Wigglesworth	England	October 18, 1631

Trivia But True

James Russell Lowell introduced Alfred, Lord Tennyson to Bull Durham tobacco.

Elias Boudinot's *The Star in the West* is the work responsible for the nineteenth century theory that the American Indians were the lost tribes of Israel.

Stephen Crane was the fourteenth child of a Methodist minister and married the madam of an English whorehouse.

William Carlos Williams delivered more than 2,000 babies.

The correct order of the Leatherstocking Series is *The Deerslayer, The Last of the Mohicans, The Pathfinder, The Pioneers,* and *The Prairie.* The published order was *The Pioneers, The Last of the Mohicans, The Prairie, The Pathfinder, The Deerslayer.*

There is a real creature called the bookworm—*anobium pertinax.*

Frank Norris worked for publishers Doubleday, Page, and Company around the turn of the century where he "discovered" both *Sister Carrie* and *Lord Jim.*

"O Little Town of Bethlehem" was a poem written by Phillips Books in the winter of 1865–66: it was sung as a hymn for the first time at Christmas, 1868.

The tallest American writers of any stature were Thomas Wolfe and Theodore Dreiser, both 6'6".

The highest short-term sales figure ever achieved by an American novelist was the 6,800,000 copies of Jacqueline Susann's *Valley of the Dolls* sold by Bantam during a six-month period in 1967.

Robert Frost is the only poet ever to win the Pulitzer Prize four times.

Robert Penn Warren is the only person ever to win Pulitzer Prizes in both fiction and poetry.

Only two Pulitzer Prize novels have also won Academy Awards for best motion picture, *Gone with the Wind* by Margaret Mitchell and *All the King's Men* by Robert Penn Warren.

Upton Sinclair ran for governor of California in 1934 and lost, but in the voting he attracted the highest number of votes ever given to a Democratic candidate up to that time.

Gore Vidal was another Democratic candidate. In 1960 he won the Democratic nomination for Congress in a New York District, but he achieved no record in losing.

In 1929 Stephen Vincent Benet became the first American since Longfellow to write a best selling poem: it was *John Brown's Body.*

Erskine Caldwell played professional football. He was also born in rural Georgia so far from a town, post office, or railroad crossing that his birthplace had no name.

Langston Hughes was the only Black war correspondent to cover the Spanish Civil War.

Jack Gasnick wrote two words in 1929 and thereby became the most successful advertising penman of all time. His Shakespearean slogan was "Think Mink," a sentiment which has been reproduced on more than 50,000,000 stickers, buttons, and ribbons since that time.

Sinclair Lewis holds the record for most simultaneous openings of a single play. During the evening of October 27, 1937, his *It Can't Happen Here* opened in twenty-one theatres in eighteen cities in fourteen states.

When Nathaniel Hawthorne composed his attack on the "terrible giant Transcendentalist" for his allegorical "Celestial Railroad," he was writing beneath the same window in the same room in the same house in which Ralph Waldo Emerson composed *Nature*, the first major document of the American Transcendental movement.

The printer kings of mass-market publishing are owners of the W. F. Hall Company who began manufacturing paperbacks in 1941. Now Hall does virtually all the printing for Bantam, Avon, New American Library, Grosset, Pyramid, Popular Library, Ballantine, and Universal. It also does magazines (*Playboy, Modern Screen, Oui, Ebony* to name a few), catalogues (Spiegel, Montgomery Ward), and even the S. & H. Green Stamp books. Hall's main plant is four blocks long, holds more than 100 presses, and turns 6,000 different titles into 350,000,000 books each year.

In 1904 Robert Sherwood gave up his position as the editor of *Children's Life* to devote himself to rewriting Dickens's *A Tale of Two Cities* insisting that he could improve upon the original. In 1936 he won a Pulitzer Prize for *Idiot's Delight*.

Thomas Hardy stole an entire chapter of Longstreet's *Georgia Scenes* to use in his *Trumpet Major*.

The fastest publication on record is that of *The Pope's Journey to the United States* written by fifty-one staffers of the *New York Times* and published by Bantam in October, 1965. The book was written and typeset in segments, the first of which reached the presses at 1:30 P.M. on October 4. Sixty-six and one-half hours later, at 8:00 A.M., October 7, completed copies of the book were being distributed for sale.

The United States Government is the largest publishing company in the world. A mere listing of its bibliography would fill several novel-length volumes. The Superintendent of Documents alone "superintends" the printing and distribution of some 220,000,000 items a year, enough for every man, woman, and child in the country to have a copy of—something. The government's list of new titles added yearly is edging toward 10,000.

When he was a student at Bowdoin, Nathaniel Hawthorne was fined twenty-five cents for "walking unnecessarily on the Sabbath."

The most successful collaborators in the history of American theatre are Howard Lindsay and Russel Crouse. In 1959 *Tall Story* became their twenty-fifth collaboration in twenty-five years of working together. Their *Life with Father* opened in 1939 featuring Lindsay and his wife in the title roles: they came back, so to speak, in June, 1947 to play the three thousand one hundred and eighty-third performance. And of course they also played in *Life with Mother* (1948).

One would have to be rather more scientific than this study pretends to be in order to determine the most prolific writer in American literature. There are few contenders for that title, but measuring their output is difficult. Cotton Mather published 444 separate works, but not all of these were full-length books. It is said that Increase Mather "was exceeded only by his son in productivity," which must mean that the Mathers were the most productive family in American letters. Burt L. Standish must be credited with 648 full-length novels, more than 200 of them dealing with a single hero, Frank Merriwell; but Standish (the pseudonym of Gilbert Patten) may have been helped along occasionally by his editors. Soap-opera writer Charles Andrews was producing 100,000 words a week in 1949 and may have gone as high as 100,000,000 words during his lifetime. But the most likely candidate for the publishing title is Edward L. Stratemeyer, whose literary production must be measured in whole series rather than in individual volumes.

Stratemeyer began writing short stories for magazines around 1884 but was more or less forced to found the Stratemeyer Syndicate in 1906. He finished one novel that Oliver Optic left behind when he died and edited about eighteen short stories which Horatio Alger left unfinished. At the same time he wrote dime novels under the names of Jim Bowie, Nat Woods, and Jim Daly as well as serials for women under the name of Julie Edwards. In 1894 he began a whole series of books with his novel *Richard Dare's Adventure:* it was called the "Bound to Win" series, then the "Dave Porter" series in 1905, the "Lakeport" series also in 1905, and the "Young Pioneer" series in 1912. In between these he wrote individual books using the pseudonyms of Captain Ralph Bonehill, Allen Chapman, Louis Charles, James A. Cooper, Ralph W. Hamilton, Chester K. Steele, E. Ward

Strayer, and others. He also founded but did not complete every volume of the "Old Glory" series in 1898, the "Pan-American" series in 1902, and the "Boy Hunters" series in 1904. Under the name of Arthur W. Winfield he founded the "Putnam Hall" series in 1905 and the "Rover Boys" series in 1899. The "Holly Library" series he started as Edna Winfield. By far his most popular creations were the Bobbsey Twins and Tom Swift, two series which still sell well today. By 1930 the Stratemeyer Syndicate had published more than 700 different books with Edward L. Stratemeyer having written or edited every one.

In 1951 William Burroughs killed his wife while trying to shoot a glass off her head.

Organizations, Schools, and Clubs

The Bread and Cheese Club.
James Fenimore Cooper
Henry Brevoort
William Dunlap
Charles Wiley
Gulian Verplanck
Fitz-Greene Halleck
James Kent
William Cullen Bryant
Samuel F. B. Morse

The Knickerbocker Group.
Washington Irving
William Cullen Bryant
James Kirke Paulding
Gulian Verplanck
Charles F. Hoffman
Fitz-Greene Halleck
Joseph Rodman Drake
Robert Charles Sands
Lydia M. Child
Nathaniel Parker Willis
Epes Sargent

The Connecticut Wits.
John Trumbull
Timothy Dwight
Joel Barlow
Lemuel Hopkins
David Humphreys
Richard Alsop
Theodore Dwight
E. H. Smith
Mason F. Cogswell

The Charleston School.
Hugh Swinton Legaré
William Gilmore Simms
Paul Hamilton Hayne
Henry Timrod
William John Grayson
S. H. Dickson

The Transcendental Club.
R. W. Emerson
Jones Very
H. D. Thoreau
William Ellery Channing

F. H. Hedge
Amos Bronson Alcott
J. F. Clarke
Theodore Parker
Margaret Fuller
George Ripley
Orestes Brownson
Elizabeth Peabody
Nathaniel Hawthorne
C. P. Cranch
Charles Follen
W. H. Channing
Convers Francis
Cyrus Bartol
Caleb Stetson

Muckraking Journalists.
Ida Tarbell
Lincoln Steffens
T. W. Lawson
R. S. Baker
S. S. McClure
Mark Sullivan
Samuel Hopkins Adams

Agrarians.
John Crowe Ransom

J. G. Fletcher
Robert Penn Warren
Allen Tate
Andrew Lytle
Donald Davidson
H. C. Nixon
Lyle Lanier
Frank Lawrence Owsley
John Donald Wade
Henry B. Kline
Stark Young

Fugitives.
Donald Davidson
Merrill Moore
John Crowe Ransom
Laura Riding
Allen Tate
Robert Penn Warren
Walter Clyde Curry
Stanley Johnson
Alex B. Stevenson
William Yandell Elliott
Ridley Wills
Edwin Mims
Sidney Hirsch

National, Nonprofit Literary Societies

African Studies Association
Brandeis University
Waltham, MA 02154

American Antiquarian
  Society
185 Salisbury
Worcester, MA 01609

American Society for Aesthetics
C. W. Post College
c/o Long Island University
Greenvale, NY 11548

American Studies Association
4025 Chestnut Street T7
University of Pennsylvania,
  PA 19104

Americana Twentieth
  Century Institute
c/o Post Office
Wasco, IL 60183

Authors Guild
234 W. 44th Street
New York, NY 10036

Authors League of America
234 W. 45th Street
New York, NY 10036

August Derleth Society
61 Tucomwas Drive
Uncasville, CT 06382

Burroughs Bibliophiles
6657 Locust
Kansas City, MO 64131

Children's Literature
  Association
English Department
Virginia Polytechnic
  Institute and State
  University
Blacksburg, VA 24061

Christopher Morley
  Knothole Association
Bryant Library
Paper Mill Road
Roslyn, NY 11756

Confederate Memorial
  Literary Society
The Museum of the
  Confederacy
1201 East Clay Street
Richmond, VA 23219

Edgar Allan Poe Society
c/o Alexander Rose
University of Baltimore
1430 N. Charles Street
Baltimore, MD 21201

Friends of ERB-Dom
Route 2, Box 119
Clinton, LA 70722

Grolier Club
47 East 60th Street
New York, NY 10022

Horatio Alger Society
4907 Allison Drive
Lansing, MI 48910

Institute for 21st Century
  Studies
c/o Prof. T. K. Cogswell
Department of English
Keystone College
La Plume, PA 18440

International Wizard of
  Oz Club
Box 95
Kinderhood, IL 62345

James Branch Cabell Society
665 Lotus Avenue
Oradell, NJ 07649

John Steinbeck Society
  of America
English Department
Ball State University
Muncie, IN 47306

Louisa May Alcott
  Memorial Association
P. O. Box 343
Concord, MA 01742

The Lunarians
1171 East 8th Street
Brooklyn, NY 11230

Mark Twain Home Board
208 Hill Street
Hannibal, MO 63401

Mark Twain Memorial
Nook Farm
351 Farmington Avenue
Hartford, CT 06105

Mark Twain Society
Math Department
Jersey City State College
2039 Kennedy Memorial
    Boulevard
Jersey City, NJ 07305

Marquandia Society
13342 Del Monte, 5-K
Seal Beach, CA 90740

Melville Society
Department of English
Glassboro State College
Glassboro, NJ 08028

Nathaniel Hawthorne
    Society
Department of English
North Texas State
    University
Denton, TX 76203

National Book Critics
    Circle
Box 6000, Radio City
    Station
New York, NY 10019

Philip Jose Farmer Society
710 W. Moss Avenue
Peoria, IL 61606

Poe Foundation
1914 E. Main Street
Richmond, VA 23223

PRAED Street Irregulars
P. O. Box 261
Culver City, CA 91105

R. W. Emerson Memorial
    Association
c/o J. M. Forbes & Co.
53 State Street, Room 903
Boston, MA 02109

Salmagundi Club
47 Fifth Avenue
New York, NY 10003

Science Fiction Research
    Association
c/o Arthur O. Lewis, Jr.
105 Sparks Building
Pennsylvania State
    University
State College, PA 16802

Sherwood Anderson Society
P. O. Box 51
University of Richmond
Richmond, VA 23173

Stowe-Day Foundation
77 Forest Street
Hartford, CT 06105

Theodore Roethke Memorial
    Foundation
11 W. Hannum Boulevard
University of Maine
Orono, ME 04473

Thoreau Society
State University College
Geneseo, NY 14454

Uncle Remus Museum
Eatonton, GA 31024

Vachel Lindsay Association
502 S. State Street
Springfield, IL 62704

Walt Whitman Birthplace
 Association
246 Walt Whitman Road
Huntington Station, NY
 11746

Willa Cather Pioneer
 Memorial and Educational
 Foundation
Red Cloud, NE 68970

William Faulkner Foundation
Dissolved

The Hall of Fame for Great Americans: Authors

George Bancroft
William Cullen Bryant
Samuel Langhorne Clemens
 (Mark Twain)
James Fenimore Cooper
Ralph Waldo Emerson
Nathaniel Hawthorne
Oliver Wendell Holmes
Washington Irving
Sidney Lanier

Henry Wadsworth Longfellow
James Russell Lowell
John Lothrop Motley
Thomas Paine
Francis Parkman
Edgar Allan Poe
Harriet Beecher Stowe
Henry David Thoreau
Walt Whitman
John Greenleaf Whittier

The American Academy and Institute of Arts and Letters: Literature

Léonie Adams
Edward Albee
Louis S. Auchincloss
James Baldwin
Djuna Barnes
John Barth
Donald Barthelme
Jacques Barzun
Saul Bellow
Elizabeth Bishop
Kay Boyle

John Malcolm Brinnin
Cleanth Brooks
Gwendolyn Brooks
Kenneth Burke
Erskine Caldwell
Hortense Calisher
Joseph Campbell
Truman Capote
Bruce Catton
Stuart Chase
John Cheever

Marchette Chute
John Ciardi
Eleanor Clark
Henry Steele Commager
Marc Connelly
Malcolm Cowley
James Gould Cozzens
Babette Deutsch
Peter De Vries
James Dickey
Will Durant
Richard Eberhart
Leon Edel
Ralph Ellison
Richard Ellmann
James T. Farrell
Francis Fergusson
Robert Fitzgerald
Janet Flanner
James Thomas Flexner
J. Kenneth Galbraith
Allen Ginsberg
Julian Green
Paul Eliot Green
Horace Gregory
Elizabeth Hardwick
Anthony Hecht
Joseph Heller
Lillian Hellman
John Hersey
Paul Horgan
Ada Louise Huxtable
Christopher Isherwood
Edgar Johnson
Alfred Kazin
George F. Kennan
Louis Kronenberger
Stanley Kunitz
Richmond Lattimore
Harry Levin

Dwight Macdonald
Archibald MacLeish
Norman Mailer
Bernard Malamud
Peter Matthiessen
William Maxwell
Mary McCarthy
Margaret Mead
William Meredith
James Merrill
W. S. Merwin
Arthur Miller
Henry Miller
Joseph Mitchell
Wright Morris
Howard Moss
Lewis Mumford
Robert Nathan
Howard Nemerov
Joyce Carol Oates
Walker Percy
S. J. Perelman
Katherine Anne Porter
J. F. Powers
Kenneth Rexroth
Philip Roth
Muriel Rukeyser
Harrison E. Salisbury
William Saroyan
Meyer Schapiro
Arthur Schlesinger, Jr.
Karl Shapiro
Isaac Bashevis Singer
William Jay Smith
W. D. Snodgrass
Jean Stafford
Francis Steegmuller
Wallace Stegner
William Styron
May Swenson

Allen Tate
Peter Taylor
Barbara W. Tuchman
John Updike
Kurt Vonnegut, Jr.
Austin Warren
Robert Penn Warren

Eudora Welty
Glenway Wescott
Elwyn Brooks White
Richard Wilbur
Tennessee Williams
C. Vann Woodward
James A. Wright

The American Academy of Arts and Sciences: Literature

Edward Franklin Albee
William Alfred
Isaac Asimov
John Simmons Barth
Saul Bellow
Elizabeth Bishop
Marie Borroff
Joseph Alexander Brodsky
Kenneth Duva Burke
Chiang Yee
John Ciardi
James Lafayette Dickey, III
Richard Ghormley Eberhart
Walter Dumaux Edmonds
Ralph Waldo Ellison
Robert Stuart Fitzgerald
Albert Joseph Guerard
Jorge Guillen
John Hawkes
Anthony Evan Hecht
Lillian Hellman
John Hollander
Paul Horgan
Alfred A. Knopf
James Laughlin
Mary McCarthy

David Thompson Watson McCord
Norman Mailer
Bernard Malamud
Robert Joseph Manning
Wright Morris
Howard Nemerov
Iris Origo
Walker Percy
Philip Roth
Harrison Evans Salisbury
Mary Sarton
Karl Jay Shapiro
Isaac Bashevis Singer
Wallace Earle Stegner
William Clark Styron, Jr.
Peter Hillsman Taylor
Diana Trilling
John Hoyer Updike
Kurt Vonnegut, Jr.
Robert Penn Warren
Edward Augustus Weeks
Eudora Welty
Elwyn Brooks White
Theodore Harold White
Edward Reed Whittemore
Richard Purdy Wilbur

Calendar of
Birth Dates

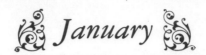

January

1 J. D. Salinger, 1919 Paul Hamilton Hayne, 1830	**2** Philip Freneau, 1752 Isaac Asimov, 1920	**3** Thomas Robinson Hazard, 1797 John Gould Fletcher, 1886	**4** Max Eastman, 1883
5	**6** Wright Morris, 1910 Carl Sandburg, 1878	**7**	**8**
9	**10** Robinson Jeffers, 1887	**11** Bernard DeVoto, 1897 Bayard Taylor, 1825	**12** Jack London, 1876
13 Horatio Alger, 1834	**14** John Dos Passos, 1896	**15**	**16**
17 Charles Brockden Brown, 1771 Benjamin Franklin, 1706	**18** Daniel Webster, 1782	**19** Edgar Allan Poe, 1809	**20** N. P. Willis, 1806
21	**22** (Lord) Timothy Dexter, 1747	**23**	**24** Edith Wharton, 1862 Mary Noailles Murfree, 1850
25	**26**	**27**	**28**
29 Thomas Paine, 1737	**30**	**31** Zane Grey, 1875 Norman Mailer, 1923 John O'Hara, 1905	

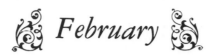

1 Langston Hughes, 1902 S. J. Perelman, 1904	**2** Delia Bacon, 1811 William Rose Benet, 1886	**3** Sidney Lanier, 1842 James A. Michener, 1907 Gertrude Stein, 1874 Horace Greeley, 1811	**4**
5 Father Ryan, 1838 Dwight Moody, 1837	**6**	**7** Sinclair Lewis, 1885	**8** Kate Chopin, 1851
9 George Ade, 1866 Amy Lowell, 1874 William Bartram, 1739	**10**	**11**	**12** Cotton Mather, 1663
13	**14** George Jean Nathan, 1882	**15** Rufus Griswold, 1815 Joseph Herge-sheimer, 1880	**16** Henry Adams, 1838
17 Dorothy Fisher Canfield, 1879	**18**	**19** Carson McCullers, 1917 William Dunlap, 1766	**20**
21 W. H. Auden, 1907 Brander Matthews, 1852	**22** James Russell Lowell, 1819 Edna St. Vincent Millay, 1892	**23** W. E. B. Dubois, 1868	**24** August Derleth, 1909
25 Frank G. Slaughter, 1908	**26**	**27** James T. Farrell, 1904 Henry Wadsworth Longfellow, 1807 John Steinbeck, 1902	**28** Ben Hecht, 1893 George Lyman Kittredge, 1860
29			

 March

1 Ralph Ellison, 1914 William Dean Howells, 1837 Robert Lowell, 1917 Richard Wilbur, 1921	**2**	**3**	**4**
5 Frank Norris, 1870	**6** Ring Lardner, 1885	**7**	**8**
9	**10**	**11**	**12** Edward Albee, 1928 Jack Kerouac, 1922
13	**14** Joel Barlow, 1754	**15**	**16**
17 Paul Green, 1894	**18** John Updike, 1932	**19** Frances Gray Patton, 1906 Philip Roth, 1933	**20** Charles William Eliot, 1834 George Washington Harris, 1814 Ned Buntline, 1823
21	**22**	**23** John Bartram, 1699	**24**
25	**26** Edward Bellamy, 1850 Robert Frost, 1874 Tennessee Williams, 1914	**27**	**28** William Byrd, 1674 Samuel Sewell, 1652
29 Frank Leslie, 1821	**30**	**31**	

April

1	**2**	**3** Edward Everett Hale, 1822 Washington Irving, 1783	**4** Robert Sherwood, 1896
Richard Eberhart, 1904 Frank Stockton, 1834 Booker T. Washington, 1856 **5**	**6**	**7** William Ellery Channing, 1780 Walter Winchell, 1897	**8**
9	**10** Clare Boothe Luce, 1903 Lew Wallace, 1827	**11**	**12**
John Burroughs, 1837 Thomas Jefferson, 1743 Eudora Welty, 1909 John Trumbull, 1750 **13**	**14** James Branch Cabell, 1879	**15** Henry James, Jr., 1843	**16**
17 William Gilmore Simms, 1806 Thornton Wilder, 1897	**18** Richard Harding Davis, 1864	**19** Sarah Kemble Knight, 1666	**20**
21 Josh Billings, 1818	**22** Ellen Glasgow, 1874 Ole Rolvaag, 1876	Vladimir **23** Nabokov, 1899 Thomas Nelson Page, 1853 Edwin Markham, 1852	**24** Robert Penn Warren, 1905
25 John Berry, 1915	**26** Bernard Malamud, 1914 A. E. Van Vogt, 1912 Artemus Ward, 1834	**27**	**28**
29	**30** John Crowe Ransom, 1888		

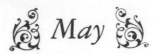 May

1	**2**	**3** William Inge, 1913	**4** Horace Mann, 1796
5 Paul Eldridge, 1888 Christopher Morley, 1890	**6** Randall Jarrell, 1914 Harry Golden, 1902	**7** Archibald MacLeish, 1892	**8** Edmund Wilson, 1895
9	**10**	**11**	**12** Philip Wylie, 1902
13	**14** Timothy Dwight, 1752	**15** Katherine Anne Porter, 1890 Frank L. Baum, 1856	**16** Elizabeth Palmer Peabody, 1804
17	**18**	**19**	**20**
21	**22**	**23** Margaret Fuller, 1810	**24**
25 Ralph Waldo Emerson, 1802 Theodore Roethke, 1908	**26**	**27** John Cheever, 1912 Dashiell Hammett, 1894 Julia Ward Howe, 1819 Herman Wouk, 1915	**28**
29 Max Brand, 1892	**30**	**31** John William DeForest, 1826 Walt Whitman, 1819	

1	**2**	**3** Allen Ginsberg, 1926 Henry James, Sr., 1811	**4**
5 Sylvanus Cobb, 1821	**6** Thomas Mann, 1875	**7** Gwendolyn Brooks, 1917	**8**
9 S. N. Behrman, 1893 Johnson Jones Hooper, 1815	**10**	**11** William Styron, 1925	**12**
13	**14** John Bartlett, 1820 Harriet Beecher Stowe, 1811	**15**	**16**
17 John Hersey, 1914	**18**	**19**	**20** Lillian Hellman, 1905 Trumbull Stickney, 1874
21 Mary McCarthy, 1912 Increase Mather, 1639	**22** Julian Hawthorne, 1846	**23**	**24** Ambrose Bierce, 1842 John Ciardi, 1916 Norman Cousins, 1912
25	**26** Pearl Buck, 1892	**27** Paul Laurence Dunbar, 1872 John Golden, 1874 Lafcadio Hearn, 1850	**28**
29	**30**		

1	*2* Richard Henry Stoddard, 1825	*3*	Stephen Foster, 1826 Nathaniel Haw- thorne, 1804 Lionel Trilling, 1905 *4*
5	*6*	*7*	*8* Shirley Ann Grau, 1929 Fitz-Greene Halleck, 1790
9 Samuel Eliot Morison, 1887	Saul Bellow, 1915 *10* Albert Bigelow Paine, 1861 Finley Peter Dunne, 1867	*11* John Quincy Adams, 1767 E. B. White, 1899	*12* Henry David Thoreau, 1817
13	*14* Owen Wister, 1860	*15* Clement Clark Moore, 1779	*16* Mary Baker Eddy, 1821 Kathleen Norris, 1880
17	*18* Clifford Odets, 1906 Royall Tyler, 1757	*19*	*20* Augustin Daly, 1838
21 Ernest Hemingway, 1899 Hart Crane, 1899	*22* Stephen Vincent Benet, 1898 Emma Lazarus, 1849	*23* Raymond Chandler, 1888 Sylvester Judd, 1813	*24*
25	*26*	*27*	*28*
29 Booth Tarkington, 1865 Don Marquis, 1878	*30* Thorstein Veblen, 1857	*31*	

1 Richard Henry Dana, Jr., 1815 Herman Melville, 1819 Francis S. Key, 1779	**2** Irving Babbitt, 1865 James Baldwin, 1924	**3**	**4**
5 Conrad Aiken, 1889	**6**	**7**	**8** Jesse Stuart, 1907 Sara Teasdale, 1884
9	**10**	**11**	**12** Flannery O'Connor, 1925
13	**14**	**15**	**16**
17	**18** Donald Davidson, 1893	**19** James Gould Cozzens, 1903 Harold Frederic, 1856 Ogden Nash, 1902	**20** H P Lovecraft, 1890
21	**22** Ray Bradbury, 1920 Dorothy Parker, 1893 James Kirke Paulding, 1778	**23** Edgar Lee Masters, 1868	**24** Malcolm Cowley, 1898 Theodore Parker, 1810
25 Bret Harte, 1836 Bill Nye, 1850 Waldo Frank, 1889	**26** John James Audubon, 1785	**27** Theodore Dreiser, 1871	**28** Jones Very, 1813
29 Oliver Wendell Holmes, Sr., 1809	**30** John Gunther, 1901	**31** William Saroyan, 1908	

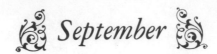

September

1 Edgar Rice Burroughs, 1875	**2** Lucretia Peabody Hale, 1820 Eugene Field, 1850 Cleveland Amory, 1917	**3** Sarah Orne Jewett, 1849	**4** Hamlin Garland, 1860 Richard Wright, 1908
5	**6**	**7** Taylor Caldwell, 1900 Elinor Wylie, 1885	**8** Joaquin Miller, 1837
9 Granville Hicks, 1901	**10** Hilda Doolittle, 1886	**11** O. Henry, 1862 Merrill Moore, 1903	**12** H. L. Mencken, 1880 Charles Dudley Warner, 1829
13 Sherwood Anderson, 1876	**14**	**15** James Fenimore Cooper, 1789 Claude McKay, 1890	**16** Orestes Brownson, 1803 Francis Parkman, 1823
17 William Carlos Williams, 1883	**18**	**19**	**20** Petroleum V. Nasby, 1833 Maxwell Perkins, 1884 Upton Sinclair, 1878
21	**22** Augustus Baldwin Longstreet, 1790	**23** William Holmes McGuffey, 1800	**24** F. Scott Fitzgerald, 1896 Richard Henry Wilde, 1789
25 William Faulkner, 1897	**26** T. S. Eliot, 1888	**27**	**28** Elmer Rice, 1892
29	**30** Truman Capote, 1924		

1 Edward Coote Pinkney, 1802	**2**	**3** Gore Vidal, 1925 Thomas Wolfe, 1900 George Bancroft, 1800	**4** Damon Runyon, 1884
5 Jonathan Edwards, 1703	**6** Caroline Gordon, 1895	**7** Helen MacInnes, 1907 James Whitcomb Riley, 1849	**8**
9 Edward Bok, 1863	**10**	**11** Stark Young, 1881	**12** George Washington Cable, 1844
13 Conrad Richter, 1890	**14** e. e. cummings, 1894	**15** Helen Hunt Jackson, 1830 Robert Edwin Lee, 1918	**16** Eugene O'Neill, 1888 Noah Webster, 1758
17 Arthur Miller, 1915 George L. Duyckinck, 1823	**18** Thomas Holley Chivers, 1809 Michael Wiggles- worth, 1631	**19** Lewis Mumford, 1895 John Adams, 1735	**20**
21	**22**	**23**	**24** Denise Levertov, 1923
25 John Pendleton Kennedy, 1795	**26**	**27** Whitelaw Reid, 1837	**28** Cornelius Mathews, 1817
29 Bill Mauldin, 1921	**30** Zoë Akins, 1886 Ezra Pound, 1885 Gertrude Atherton, 1857	**31**	

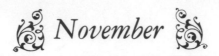

1 Stephen Crane, 1871	**2** Daniel Boone, 1734	**3** William Cullen Bryant, 1794 Ignatius Donnelly, 1831	**4**
5	**6** James Jones, 1921	**7**	**8** Sadakichi Hartman, 1869 John Dickinson, 1732
9	**10** John Marquand, 1893 Vachel Lindsay, 1879 Karl Shapiro, 1913 Mabel Loomis Todd, 1856	**11**	**12**
13	**14** Constance Rourke, 1885	**15** Richard Henry Dana, Sr., 1787 Marianne Moore, 1887	**16** George S. Kaufman, 1889
17	**18**	**19** Allen Tate, 1899	**20**
21	**22**	**23** Evert A. Duyckinck, 1816	**24** Frances Burnett, 1849
25	**26**	**27**	**28** Brooks Atkinson, 1894
29 Amos Bronson Alcott, 1799 Louisa May Alcott, 1832	**30** Mark Twain, 1835		

December

1	2	3	4
Julia A. Moore, 1847			
5	**6** Joyce Kilmer, 1886	**7** Willa Cather, 1876	James Thurber, 1894 Delmore Schwartz, 1913 Hervey Allen, 1889 Henry Timrod, 1828 **8**
9 Joel Chandler Harris, 1848	Emily Dickinson, 1830 Edward Eggleston, 1837 **10**	**11**	**12** Frederic Henry Hedge, 1805
13	**14** Shirley Jackson, 1919	**15** Maxwell Anderson, 1888	**16** George Santayana, 1863 Margaret Mead, 1901
17 Erskine Caldwell, 1903 John Greenleaf Whittier, 1807	**18**	**19**	**20**
21	**22** Thomas Wentworth Higginson, 1823 E. A. Robinson, 1869 Kenneth Rexroth, 1905	**23** Harriet Monroe, 1860	**24**
25	**26** Henry Miller, 1891 Jean Toomer, 1894	**27** Hinton Rowan Helper, 1829	**28**
29	**30**	**31**	

Names

American Writers Who Have Changed Their Names

William Falkner to William Faulkner
Nathaniel Hathorne to Nathaniel Hawthorne
Leroi Jones to Imamu Amiri Baraka
Jean-Louis Kerouac to Jack Kerouac
William Sidney Porter to O. Henry
David Henry Thoreau to Henry David Thoreau
Thomas Lanier Williams to Tennessee Williams
Malcolm Little to Malcolm X

Initialed Names

Frank L. Baum   Frank Lyman Baum
S. N. Behrman   Samuel Nathaniel Behrman
e. e. cummings   Edward Estlin Cummings
H. D.   Hilda Doolittle
W. E. B. DuBois   William Edward Burghardt DuBois
T. S. Eliot   Thomas Stearns Eliot
Edward S. Ellis   Edward Sylvester Ellis
F. Scott Fitzgerald   Francis Scott Key Fitzgerald
E. Z. C. Judson   Edward Zane Carroll Judson (Ned Buntline)
H. L. Mencken   Henry Louis Mencken

S. J. Perelman   Sidney Joseph Perelman
E. A. Robinson   Edwin Arlington Robinson
J. D. Salinger   Jerome David Salinger
W. D. Snodgrass   William DeWitt Snodgrass
E. D. E. N. Southworth   Emma Dorothy Eliza Nevitte Southworth
Ann S. Stephens   Ann Sophia Stephens
A. E. Van Vogt   Alfred Elton Van Vogt
Booker T. Washington   Booker Taliaferro Washington
N. P. Willis   Nathaniel Parker Willis

Sobriquets

Samuel Adams   The American Cato
Amos Bronson Alcott   The Concord Seer; The American Pestalozzi
Louisa May Alcott   The Children's Friend
Horatio Alger   Holy Horatio
American Dictionary of the English Language   Dr. Webster's Old Curiosity Shop
Sherwood Anderson   The D. H. Lawrence of American Literature
Sarah Wentworth Appleton   The American Sappho
Artillery of Time (Chard Smith)   The Northern *Gone with the Wind*
William Bradford   The Father of American History
Boston   The Hub of the Universe (First used satirically in Holmes's *Autocrat*)
Ambrose Bierce   Bitter Bierce; The Devil's Lexicographer
Anne Bradstreet   The Tenth Muse
Max Brand   The King of the Pulp Writers
William Cullen Bryant   The American Wordsworth; The Father of American Song
William Byrd   The American Pepys
Truman Capote   The Tiny Terror
Bennett Cerf   The Buzz Bomb of Publisher's Row
Raymond Chandler   The Poet of Violence
Thomas Holley Chivers   The Lost Poet
McDonald Clark   The Mad Poet
Samuel L. Clemens   The Lincoln of Our Literature; The People's Author; The Wild Humorist of the Pacific Slopes
James Fenimore Cooper   The American Hesiod; The American Scott; Effingham Cooper (after one of his own characters)
David Crockett   The Munchausen of the West

Edward Estlin Cummings   Lower Case Cummings

Joseph Dennie   The American Addison

Emily Dickinson   The Belle of Amherst; The Recluse of Amherst

Ignatius Donnelly   The Apostle of Protest

Thomas Dowse   The Literary Leather Dresser (a leather dresser of Cambridge, Massachusetts who gave a large sum to Harvard; in return the school gave him an LL.D., which Edward Everett translated as "literary leather dresser")

Jonathan Edwards   The Artist of Damnation

Ralph Waldo Emerson   The Sage of Concord; The American Montaigne; The Columbus of Modern Thought

William Faulkner   Count No 'count (by the townspeople of Oxford, Mississippi); The American Balzac

Eugene Field   The Gay Poet; The Poet of Childhood

F. Scott Fitzgerald   The Spokesman for the Jazz Age; The Father of the Jazz Age; The Last Laocoon

Benjamin Franklin   The American Socrates; The Liberator of the World

Erle Stanley Gardner   The Fiction Factory

Hamlin Garland   The Ibsen of the West

Ellen Glasgow   The Only Socialist in Richmond

Henry Grady   The Spokesman for the New South

Joel Chandler Harris   Uncle Remus

William Hope Harvey   Coin Harvey

Paul Hamilton Hayne   The Longfellow of the South; The Poet Laureate of the South

Nathaniel Hawthorne   The Genius of Romance; The Hermit of Salem

Ernest Hemingway   The Spokesman for the Lost Generation; The Monarch of American Arts; Papa Hemingway

Oliver Wendell Holmes   The Autocrat

William Dean Howells   The Dean of American Letters; The Father of Realism

Langston Hughes   The Laureate of Harlem

Washington Irving   The Father of American Literature

Thomas Jefferson   The Sage of Monticello

Rudyard Kipling   America's Unofficial Poet Laureate

Sidney Lanier   The Poet of the Marshes; The Sunrise Poet; The Sir Galahad of American Literature

Murray Leinster   The Dean of Science Fiction Writers

Jack London   The Prince of the Oyster Pirates
Henry Wadsworth Longfellow   America's Poet Laureate
Amy Lowell   The Unacknowledged Head of Literary America; the Hippopoetess
James Russell Lowell   The Best Read Man of the Century
Richard Henry Lee   The American Cicero
Sinclair Lewis   The Bad Boy of the National Letters
John Pendleton Kennedy   The Gentleman from Baltimore
Herman Melville   The Man Who Lived Among the Cannibals
H. L. Mencken   The Sage of Baltimore; The Ringmaster
Edna St. Vincent Millay   The American Female Byron
Julia Moore   The Sweet Singer of Michigan
Marianne Moore   The First Lady of American Poetry
Merrill Moore   The Psychiatrist-Poet
New York   The City of Splendid Exile (by William Dean Howells); Gotham (by Washington Irving)
The New York Times   The Great Gray Lady
Walter Hines Page   The Friendly Critic of the South
Frances Gray Patten   The Jane Austen of North Carolina
Edgar Allan Poe   The Father of the Short Story; The Father of the Detective Story
Ezra Pound   The Perpetual Adolescent of American Poetry
James Ryder Randall   The Laureate of the War Between the States
Sampson Reid   The Transcendental Druggist
James Whitcomb Riley   The Children's Poet; The Hoosier Poet
Damon Runyon   The Prose Laureate of the Semi-Literate Masses
Lu Sarens   The American Jules Verne
William Gilmore Simms   The James Fenimore Cooper of the South
Booth Tarkington   The Gentleman from Indianapolis
Richard W. Thompson   The Ancient Mariner of the Wabash
Henry David Thoreau   The Sage of Walden Pond; The Concord Rebel; The Poet Naturalist
Henry Timrod   The Poet Laureate of the Confederacy
Uncle Tom's Cabin   The *Iliad* of the Blacks
Noah Webster   The Schoolmaster to America
Edith Wharton   The *Grande Dame* of American Letters
Phillis Wheatley   The Black Sappho
Walt Whitman   The Good Gray Poet; The Solitary Singer
John Greenleaf Whittier   The Fighting Quaker; The Poet Laureate of New England; The American Burns
Michael Wigglesworth   The Doggerel Dante

Pseudonyms

Conrad Aiken   Samuel Jeake, Jr.

John Adams   Novanglus

William Taylor Adams   Oliver Optic

Louisa May Alcott   Flora Fairfield; A. M. Barnard

Mrs. Isabella Alden   Pansy

Horatio Alger   Caroline F. Preston; Arthur Lee Putnam; Julian Starr

Mrs. Elizabeth Allen   Florence Percy

Isaac Asimov   Paul French

Frank L. Baum   Floyd Akens; L. Frank Baum; Edith Van Dyne

Elizabeth Bogart   Adelaide

Maria Gowen Brooks   Maria dell'Occidente (given to her by Robert
Southey who called her "the most impassioned and imaginative of
all poetesses."

Charles F. Browne   Artemus Ward

William Cullen Bryant   Francis Herbert

George Washington Cable   Drop Shot

C. Augusta Cheney   Caroline F. Preston (also used by her brother,
Horatio Alger)

Samuel L. Clemens   Mark Twain; Carl Byng; Thomas Jefferson
Snodgrass; G. Ragsdale McClintock

Captain Roland F. Coffin   Nemo

James L. Cole   Adrian

John Esten Cook   C. Effington

James Fenimore Cooper   Cornelius Littlepage; Anabel Penfeather;
Jane Morgan

Susan Fenimore Cooper   A Lady

Stephen Crane   Johnston Smith

Frederic Dannay   Ellery Queen

Bernard DeVoto   John August

Mary Abigail Dodge   Gail Hamilton

Hilda Doolittle   H. D.

Thomas F. Donnelly   Bookworm

Edward S. Ellis   Captain Bruin Adams; Captain J. F. C. Adams;
James Fenimore Cooper Adams; Boynton Belknap, M. D.; J. G.
Bethune; Captain Latham C. Carleton; Frank Faulkner; Col. H. R.
Gordon; Oscar A. Gwynne; Oswald A. Gwynne; Captain R. M.
Hawthorne; Lt. Ned Hunter; Lt. R. H. Jayne; Charles E. LaSalle;
Seward D. Lisle; Captain H. R. Millbank; Billex Muller; Geoffrey
Randolph; Rollo Robins; Seelin Robins; Emerson Rodman; E. S.

St. Mox—A U. S. Detective; Egbert S. Thomas; Captain Wheeler

Frederick Faust   John Frederick; David Manning; Hugh Owen; Nicholas Silver; George Owen Baxter; George Challis; Peter Dawson; Martin Dexter; Evin Evans; Max Brand

Julia Constance Fletcher   George Fleming (wrote *Kismet*)

Benjamin Franklin   Silence Dogood; Father Abraham; Richard Saunders; Poor Richard

Major General John Charles Frémont   Pathfinder

Fugitives   For the first three issues of *The Fugitive* the major writers used the following pen names:

John Crowe Ransom   Roger Prim

Donald Davidson   Robin Gallivant

Allen Tate   Henry Feathertop

Robert Penn Warren didn't have one because he didn't join the group until 1923.

Erle Stanley Gardner   A. A. Fair; Grant Holiday; Robert Parr; Carleton Kendrake; Charles J. Kenny; Charles M. Green; Charles M. Stanton; Arthur Mann Sellers; Les Tilbray; Dane Rigley; Kyle Corning

Theodore Geisel   Dr. Seuss

Samuel Griswold Goodrich   Peter Parley

Rufus Griswold   Ludwig

William McCrillis Griswold   Arthur Venner

Edward Everett Hale   Col. Ingram

Harland P. Halsey   Old Sleuth

Alexander Hamilton   Publius

Samuel Dashiell Hammett   Peter Collinson

Mrs. Alice Haven   Cousin Alice; Alice E. Lee

Henry William Herbert   Frank Forrester

Josiah Gilbert Holland   Timothy Titcomb

John Treat Irving   John Quod (brother of Washington Irving)

Washington Irving   Launcelot Langstaff; Fray Antonio Agapida; Geoffrey Crayon, Gent.; Evergreen; Jonathan Oldstyle

William Irving   Launcelot Langstaff; Pindar Cockloft (brother of Washington Irving)

Helen Hunt Jackson   H. H.

Sarah Orne Jewett   Alice Eliot

E. Z. C. Judson   Ned Buntline

Mrs. Emily Judson   Fanny Forrester

John Pendleton Kennedy   Mark Littleton; Solomon Secondthought

Allen Stewart Konigsberg   Woody Allen

Louis D. L'Amour   Tex Burns

Thomas C. Latto   Aiken Dunn

Manfred B. Lee   Ellery Queen

Estelle Anna Lewis   Stella

Mrs. Sara J. Lippincott   Grace Greenwood

David Ross Locke   Petroleum V. Nasby

Henry Wadsworth Longfellow   Joshua Coffin

Grace V. Lord   Virginia Champlin

Mrs. H. M. Lothrop   Margaret Sidney

James Russell Lowell   Hosea Biglow

John Lowell   Boston Rebel

Cotton Mather   An American; A Christian; A Christian in a Cold Season Sitting Before It; One of the Ministers in Boston; One of the Ministers in the North Part of Boston

Increase Mather   Philadelphus

H. L. Mencken   James P. Radcliffe, Ph.D.; Harriet Morgan; William Fink; George Weems Peregoy

Edna St. Vincent Millay   Nancy Boyd

Cincinnatus Heine Miller   Joaquin Miller

Donald Grant Mitchell   Ik Marvel

Mary Noailles Murfree   Charles Egbert Craddock

E. W. Nye   Bill Nye

Dorothy Parker   Squidge; Helene Rousseau

Sara P. Willis Parton   Fanny Fern

Gilbert Patton   Burt L. Standish

James Kirke Paulding   Launcelot Langstaff

George W. Peck   Cantell A. Bigly

Sylvia Plath   Victoria Lucas

William Sydney Porter   O. Henry

Janet Reback   Taylor Caldwell

Whitelaw Reid   Agate

James Whitcomb Riley   Benj. F. Johnson of Boone

Benjamin P. Schillaber   Mrs. Partington

Laura C. Searing   Howard Glydon

Henry W. Shaw   Josh Billings

Benjamin Henry Francis Shepard   Francis Grierson

William Gilmore Simms   Frank Cooper

Upton Sinclair   Clark Fitch; Ensign Clark Fitch, U. S. N.; Lt. Frederick Garrison

Charles Henry Smith   Bill Arp
Harriet Mulford Stone   Margaret Sidney
Harriet Beecher Stowe   Christopher Crowfield
Mrs. Emma D. E. Southworth   E.D.E.N.
Edward L. Stratemeyer   Ralph Bonehill; Allen Chapman; Louis
   Charles; James A. Cooper; Ralph W. Hamilton; Chester K. Steele;
   E. Ward Strayer; Arthur W. Winfield; Edna Winfield
David Hunter Strother   Porte Crayon
Henry Timrod   Aglaus
Mortimer Thomson   Doesticks
Unknown   B. Traven
Susan Warner   Elizabeth Wetherell
Noah Webster   Candor
Nathan Wallenstein Weinstein   NathanaelWest
Daniel Wise   Francis Forrester
Willard Huntington Wright   S. S. Van Dine
William Wright   Dan DeQuille
Berd H. Young   Simon Suggs

Collective Pseudonyms

Victor Appleton	Tom Swift series
	Movie Boys series
	Don Sturdy series
Victor Appleton II	Tom Swift, Jr. series
Allen Chapman	Radio Boys series
	The Darwell Chums series
	The "Railroad" series (e.g., *Ralph of the Roundhouse*—1906)
Franklin W. Dixon	The Hardy Boys series
	Ted Scott Flying Stories series
Alice B. Emerson	Betty Gordon series
	Ruth Fielding series
James Cody Ferris	The X Bar X Boys series
Alice Dale Hardy	The Riddle Club series
Laura Lee Hope	The Bobbsey Twin series
	The Blythe Girls series
	Bunny Brown series
	Make Believe Stories series
	Outdoor Girls series
	Six Little Bunkers series

Clinton W. Locke	Perry Pierce Mystery series
Eugene Martin	Sky Flyers series
Fenworth Moore	Jerry Ford Wonder Stories series
Margaret Penrose	Motor Girls series
	Dorothy Dale series
Nat Ridley, Jr.	Nat Ridley Detective Stories series
Roy Rockwood	Great Marvel series
	Dave Fearless series
	The Bomba Books series
Ann Sheldon	Linda Craig series
Alan Stone	Tolliver series
Frank V. Webster	Books for Boys series
Ramy Allison White	Sunny Boy series
Clarence Young	Motor Boys series
	Jack Ranger series
	Racer Boys series

§ | *Types of Pseudonyms.* The word *pseudonym* is a general bibliographical term having extended meaning. In fact, any word, symbol, or borrowed name is sufficient to make a work pseudonymous (rather than anonymous) if it appears on the title page in place of an author's true name. Here's a list of more particular kinds of pseudonyms:

Adulterism: a name which has been physically altered or adulterated, usually by a slight spelling change or shift in capitalization, although a more unusual example would be the use of *Henry David Thoreau* rather than the author's given name of *David Henry Thoreau.*

Allonym: a false proper name. Here the work is published under the name of a real person who did not write the work itself, a common practice in the McCarthy era.

Alphabetism: used by a number of authors as A B C, X Y Z, or some variation.

Anagram: this is an arbitrary mixing of the author's name, perhaps in a non-sensical way, such as *Tilly V. Asiaph* for *Sylvia Plath.*

Ananym: the real name written backwards, as in Ralph Waldo *Nosreme.*

Apoconym: a name minus one or more initial letters.

(Apocryphal): really not a pseudonym, but refers instead to a work whose authorship is uncertain or doubtful.

Aristonym: a title of nobility used as a proper name.

Ascetonym: the name of a saint used as a proper name: Edna St. Vincent Millay would not be an example since that is the writer's given name.

Asterism: any asterisks or stars used in any fashion along with or in place of a writer's name or any part of a writer's name.

(Autonym): the opposite of a pseudonym, an author's real name.

Boustrophedon: same as an *ananym.*

Cryptonym: in practice the same as an anagram, but in theory a cryptonym is a more deliberate scrambling of letters in an effort to hide authorship.

Demonym: a quality or description used as a name, such as the great number of writers who have signed themselves merely *An Amateur* or *A Booklover.*

Enigmatic Pseudonym: a combination of parts of names or initials to form another kind of pseudonym: for instance *Radatat* would have been an enigmatic-pseudonym for John Crowe *Ransom,* Donald *Davidson,* and Allen *Tate.*

Geonym: a location used as a name, implied in John Adams's use of *Novanglus.*

Hagionym: same as *ascetonym.*

Hieronym: a sacred name used on the title page.

Initialism: only the initials of the writer, such as *Hilda Doolittle's H. D.*

Pharmaconym: a substance instead of a name, e.g., *Agate* for *Whitelaw Reid.*

Phraseonym: as the word implies: Cotton Mather once signed himself *A Christian In a Cold Season Sitting Before It.*

Phrenonym: a quality taken for a proper name as when *John Pendleton Kennedy* issued himself as *Solomon Secondthought.*

Polynym: several authors listed as the single writer of a work.

Prenonym: any name taking the place of an author's family name.

Pseudandry: occurs when a woman signs a man's name.

Pseudoinitialism: false initials.

Pseudojyn: occurs when a man signs a woman's name.

Pseudo-titlonym: any false quality or title, as *Col. Ingram* for *Edward Everett Hale* or *Dr. Seuss* for *Theodore Geisel.*

Scenonym: an author's stage name.

Sideronym: a celestial or astronomical name, used by *Estelle Anna Lewis* with *Stella.*

Stigmonym: the use of dots instead of letters to print a "name."

Syncopism: a name lacking several letters, usually indicated by blanks.

Telonism: the last letters of a writer's name used to stand for the whole, such as *L. T.* for Nathanael West.

Titlonym: a quality of title taken as a real name: a number of early American writers, for instance, signed themselves *A Minister.*

Translationym: the literal translation of an author's proper name.

§ | *Names Behind the Titles.* American literature contains a number of popular or historically significant titles whose authors have been buried by the years or simply overshadowed by the works themselves. Here's a list of well known works whose creators are considerably less well known:

"There Was a Little Girl (Who Had a Little Curl)"	Henry Wadsworth Longfellow
The Book of Mormon	Joseph Smith
West Side Story	Arthur Laurents
Ben-Hur	Lew Wallace
"America"	Samuel F. Smith
Madame Butterfly	David Belasco and J. L. Long (originally a short story)
"Men Seldom Make Passes. . . ."	Dorothy Parker
"Mary Had a Little Lamb"	Sarah Josepha Hale
Ten Nights in a Bar-Room	T. S. Arthur
The Great White Way (source of Broadway's nickname)	Albert Bigelow Paine
The Wonderful Wizard of Oz	L. Frank Baum
"The Man Without a Country"	Edward Everett Hale
The "Tom Swift" Books	Victor Appleton (collective pseudonym)
Mutiny on the Bounty	Charles B. Nordhoff and James N. Hall
Anthony Adverse	Hervey Allen
Hans Brinker and His Silver Skates	Mary Mapes Dodge
Rebecca of Sunnybrook Farm	Kate Douglas Wiggin
"The Night Before Christmas" (actual title "A Visit from St. Nicholas")	Clement C. Moore
Good Morning, Miss Dove	Frances Gray Patten
"The Children's Hour"	Henry Wadsworth Longfellow (also a play by Lillian Hellman)
"Dangerous Dan McGrew" (actual title "The Shooting of Dan McGrew")	Robert W. Service

Peg O'My Heart	J. Hartley Manners
"Sweet Adeline"	Richard Gerard (originally a poem: music added by Harry W. Armstrong)
"I think that I shall never see A poem lovely as a tree"	Joyce Kilmer

§ | *All in the Family*. Cotton Mather was the son of Increase Mather who married his own stepsister Maria Cotton who was the daughter of John Cotton who had previously died, thus allowing Increase's father Richard Mather to marry John Cotton's widow.

Jonathan Edwards was Aaron Burr's grandfather.

Owen Wister (*The Virginian*) was the grandson of Fanny Kemble.

Katherine Anne Porter was the great great great granddaughter of Daniel Boone.

James Woodrow, uncle of Woodrow Wilson, taught Sidney Lanier (at Oglethorpe University), who was an ancestor of Thomas Lanier Williams, better known as Tennessee Williams.

Gertrude Atherton was a great grandniece of Benjamin Franklin.

Amos Bronson Alcott was the father of Louisa May Alcott.

Nathanael West's sister Laura was married to S. J. Perelman.

Popular novelist Kathleen Norris was the wife of Charles G. Norris, who was the brother of Frank Norris.

Constance Fenimore Woolson was a grandniece of James Fenimore Cooper.

Henry Wadsworth Longfellow was a distant ancestor of Ezra Pound.

F. Scott Fitzgerald was descended from and named after Francis Scott Key.

One of T. S. Eliot's ancestors was a juror at the Salem witch trials.

Elinor Wylie was the wife of William Rose Benét (who won a Pulitzer Prize for *The Dust Which Is God* in 1942) and who was Stephen Vincent Benét's brother.

William Sydney Porter was Katherine Anne Porter's father's second cousin.

John Marquand's mother was Margaret Fuller's niece.

The children in "The Children's Hour" were Longfellow's own: "grave" Alice, "laughing" Allegra, and "golden-haired" Edith. Edith became the wife of Richard Henry Dana.

Colonel William Faulkner, the prototype of John Sartoris in *Sartoris,* was an author himself as well as the great grandfather of William Faulkner. The colonel wrote *The White Rose of Memphis* which sold more than 160,000 copies.

Gilbert Imlay (*The Emigrants*, 1787) returned from America to London where he became the lover of Mary Wollstonecraft and the father of her daughter Fanny before Mary married William Godwin.

Anecdotes

§ | *Mark Twain.* Perhaps the most famous single name in all of American literature is Mark Twain, the pseudonym of Samuel L. Clemens. But before the name belonged to Clemens, it belonged to Captain Isaiah Sellers, who in the 1820s and '30s published notes about the Mississippi in the New Orleans *Picayune.* According to his reminiscences in *Life on the Mississippi* Clemens frequently heard the other steamboat pilots mocking the captain's literary pretentions, and the novice author himself followed suit with a parody he published in the New Orleans *True Delta.* Clemens recalled that,

> Colonel Sellers did me the honor to profoundly detest me from that day forth. When I say he did me the honor, I am not using empty words. It was a very real honor to be in the thoughts of so great a man as Captain Sellers, and I had wit enough to appreciate it and be proud of it. It was distinction to be loved by such a man; but it was a much greater distinction to be hated by him, because he loved scores of people, but he didn't sit up nights to hate anybody but me.
>
> He never printed another paragraph while he lived, and he never again signed "Mark Twain" to anything. At the time that the telegraph brought the news of his death, I was on the Pacific coast. I was a fresh new journalist, and needed a *nom de guerre*; so I confiscated the ancient mariner's discarded one, and have done my best to make it remain what it was in his hands—a sign and symbol and warrant that whatever is found in its company may be gambled on as being the petrified truth; how I have succeeded, it would not be modest in me to say.

§ | *William Faulkner.* There are several accounts of the *u* Faulkner added to his last name. The two most likely are that Faulkner himself made the change in 1918 on joining the Canadian Air Force and, second, that a careless typesetter immortalized the misspelling. According to the latter story, a misprint on the title page of Faulkner's first book escaped the proofreaders. When asked about the error, Faulkner supposedly replied, "Either way suits me."

§ | *Harlan Page Halsey.* The word *sleuth* means, literally, a bloodhound although almost no one uses it to mean that anymore. Harlan P. Halsey was the first man to use it in its modern sense of *detective* by giving the name to one of his characters, Old Sleuth. It became finally a sobriquet for Halsey himself who allowed no one else to publish the name: he had in fact copyrighted it and once insisted that his publisher Frank Toussey obtain an injunction against another author about to use *sleuth* as we use it today.

§ | *Jack London.* It wasn't until some years after he was born that the boy Jack took the surname London. He was born the illegitimate son of Flora Wellman and "Professor" W. H. Chaney, finally assuming the family name of his mother's husband when she married John London, a widower with eleven children of his own. At fifteen Jack London was on his own as an oyster pirate; at twenty-one he became part of the gold rush to the Klondike; in 1900 at age twenty-four he established himself as a writer with "An Odyssey of the North"; and at age forty he was dead, a possible suicide. In sixteen years he had written fifty books.

§ | *Charlotte M. Brame.* Bertha M. Clay was one of the most popular and prolific writers working during the reign of the Street and Smith publishing firm in the nineteenth century. She began as the popular British novelist Charlotte M. Brame, but Francis Smith in effect bought her for his American audiences by doubling her yearly income. Smith also transposed her initials to B. M. C. and then transliterated those into Bertha M. Clay. When her English lords and ladies found a market in this country, she buried Charlotte M. Brame forever. When the first Bertha died, her daughter assumed the name and continued with the writing; then later other men and women became Bertha M. Clay: it took some fifteen or sixteen writers in all to keep up with the demand for her stories.

§ | *Edwin Arlington Robinson.* When Edward and Mary Robinson gave birth to their third son in 1869, they gave him everything but a name. For a time no one worried; but when the anonymous infant reached six months, relatives in South Harpswell, Maine, suggested that something be done. The parents were agreeable but had no particular names in mind. The solution came from a summer visitor to South Harpswell who mentioned drawing names from a hat. That they did, and out came the slip marked *Edwin*. Instead of a second drawing, though, Mary Robinson honored the summer guest by choosing for her baby the name of the woman's home town, Arlington, Massachusetts.

§ | *Scotty Fitzgerald.* In October 1921 Zelda and Scott Fitzgerald became the parents of a baby girl. Although the child was always known as Scotty, her full name was Frances Scott Key Fitzgerald. She was in fact one of the few female infants ever named after their fathers.

§ | *Poe.* The actress mother of Edgar Allan Poe opened the season of 1809 playing Cordelia in *King Lear*. She determined fairly early that if the baby she carried were a girl, it would be named after Shakespeare's heroine. Unfortunately, "Cordelia" was a boy; and although the father, David Poe, acted in the same play, his role was that of the bastard villain Edmund. The proud parents reached a compromise by naming the baby Edgar, after Edmund's legitimate brother.

§ | *Maurice Thompson.* Sometimes an author does not have a right to or control over his own name: that's what Maurice Thompson learned in a lawsuit that he lost shortly after becoming famous. Thompson was a not-very-important pulp writer of the late 1800s who manufactured Indian stories by the pound under various pseudonyms. He turned a corner in 1900 by producing a phenomenally successful novel called *Alice of Old Vincennes*; and it seemed that he had escaped his past. Soon, however, publisher Francis Smith located one of the old stories and published it under Thompson's real name. The author saw a potential danger to his new career and sued; but the court ruled that a publisher may always use a writer's real name unless specifically forbidden to do so by a contract, a legal principle that still holds today.

§ | *Edgar Rice Burroughs.* Burroughs's classic science fiction novel *Dejah Thoris, Princess of Mars* was first published in 1912 with six installments of *All-Story* magazine. In this first version it appeared as *Under the Moons of Mars* and is considered today quite a collector's find. One of the reasons for the value is that for the only time in his life Burroughs used a pen name,

Normal Bean. But apparently an anonymous typesetter thought that he was correcting an error in spelling when he changed the pseudonym to "Norman" Bean. And that's how it appeared in the credits.

§ | *Frank Leslie*. One of the biggest money-makers of the nineteenth century was a weekly publication called *Frank Leslie's Illustrated Newspaper*, a sensation-mongering collection of news stories, fiction, and lurid engravings that survived until 1922. Who was Frank Leslie? The answer is—nobody. It was just a name used by Henry Carter to sign engravings done for the *London Illustrated News*. When Carter immigrated to America, he founded a newspaper on this pseudonym and subsequently found himself at the head of a publishing empire. Soon *Frank Leslie* was a valuable literary property, and the astute newspaperman sought to protect the investment by a method other than copyrighting. Finally Henry Carter found his solution: by a special act of the New York legislature he simply became Frank Leslie, casting off his former identity forever.

§ | *Samuel L. Clemens*. In 1866 Clemens was still several years away from the fame that would make Mark Twain a familiar name in every household. To be sure, he had a reputation in the West already; but to be anything at all he had to establish himself in the East. He made his first effort with "Forty-three Days in an Open Boat," an article which was accepted for the December 1866 issue of *Harper's New Monthly Magazine*. Here at last was the national recognition on which he could build a literary career. The dreams crumbled, however, as the young author scanned the lines for his name: he found it at last, indexed as Mark Swain.

§ | *William Vaughan Moody*. When Moody taught English at the University of Chicago in the late 1890s and early 1900s, he had a reputation among the students of being stern, formal, and reserved. They referred to him as The Man in the Iron Mask.

§ | *The Dreisers*. The brothers Theodore and Paul Dreiser grew up in a family of strict, conservative German Catholics. Paul became famous as a songwriter, producing such hits as "My Gal Sal" and "On the Banks of the Wabash"; but he did not keep the family name. He changed to Paul Dresser because, according to some versions, he did not want to be associated with the pornography of his brother's books.

§ | *Smith's Magazine*. Ormond Smith wanted an "average" magazine that would appeal to "the John Smiths of America," so he founded one in 1905 that became a moderately successful middle-brow review of theatre, art, fiction, and poetry for the ordinary man of average income in mid-America. He named it *Smith's*, not after himself but in honor of the John Smiths he idealized. For his first editor he chose Theodore Dreiser.

§ | *Frederick Douglass*. In 1838 a slave then known simply as Frederick took the name of Douglass after the fugitive chieftain in Scott's *The Lady of the Lake*. In the same year he was bought by the Society of Friends in order to arrange his freedom.

§ | *William Wells Brown*. Brown was the first black man in America to write a novel or a play. He was born a slave although his mother may have been Daniel Boone's daughter. A first attempt to escape resulted in capture and punishment with his mother, who had accompanied him, being sold "down the river." Brown tried again, however, and this time succeeded with the help of a Quaker. So grateful was the slave that he adopted the man's name, Wells Brown.

§ | *James Branch Cabell*. James Branch Cabell was Branch Cabell off and on. In order to set off the *Biography of Manual* from the rest of his works, the author dropped his first name. He liked the new identity well enough to publish *Their Lives and Letters*, *The Nightmare Has Triplets*, and *Heirs and Assigns* (all three of which were themselves trilogies) as Branch Cabell. By 1946, though, he saw the public was not making the distinctions he was trying to create by using his double identity; so with his next book, *There Were Two Pirates*, he became again the tripartite James Branch Cabell.

§ | *Henry Patterson*. The United States Library of Congress had its own ideas about names, and British author Harry Patterson had his. For some sixteen years he was listed wrongly as "Henry" Patterson and then finally asked in 1979 that the Library of Congress correct its files. Stein & Day, his American publishers, obligingly wrote to Washington requesting changes—and got immediate results. Patterson's name was officially changed to "Jack Higgins."

Now, lest one jump to conclusions, it must be pointed out that the writer himself was not really outraged because "Jack Higgins" is one of the pseudonyms under which he'd written seventeen books (among them *The*

Eagle Has Landed published by Holt, Rinehart, and Winston). Stein & Day, on the other hand, didn't want the author listed by a name he'd used when publishing with their competitors. Why couldn't the librarians make the simple change from "Henry" to "Harry"? It couldn't be done, said Chief of the Office for Descriptive Cataloging Ben Tucker, because a 1967 regulation required that an author's name be the one used predominantly in his works. The publishers protested, at which the librarians hinted that Stein & Day might be dropped from the library's cataloging program altogether, after which "Henry Patterson" became even more officially "Jack Higgins." "It's the bureaucratic mind gone mad," fumed partner Sol Stein.

Collectors' Items

§ | *Introduction*. What makes a rare book rare, and why are some volumes more collectable than others? Curiously, these are rather difficult questions to answer, even for the experts. First editions are not always the most valuable ones. Popularity of an author is no safe guide to the worth of his individual volumes. And as for expensive bindings—well, everyone knows what you can't judge a book by. Although one would think that scarcity might be the best indicator of value, there are many extremely rare books in much less demand than more numerous editions. In 1794, for instance, there was printed in Boston an anonymous novel entitled *The History of Pulchera*, or *Constancy Rewarded: An American Novel*. There exists only one known copy of this work bearing the 1794 date, and it would indeed be a worthy addition to any collector's library; but as for its intrinsic worth, it does not compare well to some works by Poe, Melville, or even Faulkner. Usually there is some specific circumstance that makes a volume a true collector's item, hence the importance of knowing the stories *behind* the books. While the only known copy of an autographed first edition written by an important author and bound in gold-stamped full morocco may be the most expensive book in town, it may not be the most prized or the most interesting. In this chapter are examples of books, some extremely rare, some cheap and readily available, which have become collectable rather than marketable.

§ | *The Bay Psalm Book*. Only one copy of the first book printed in America has ever been put up for public sale. Cornelius Vanderbilt bought it in 1878 for $1,200. This same *Bay Psalm Book* went on auction again January 28, 1947, at the Parke-Bernet Galleries in New York. The new price was $151,000, the highest ever paid for an American printed volume at that time. The money was donated to a hospital. The book went to Yale.

§ | *Tamerlane*. It is called the Black Tulip of American publishing, Poe's *Tamerlane*, and it is as rare and as exotic and as sought after as anything that will ever come on the market. The last copy to be auctioned went for $125,000—in the era before inflation; and should that buyer turn seller tomorrow, he could literally name his own price. *Tamerlane* is not, as some authorities have written, the most expensive American collectors' item ever published, but it is in a sense the most valuable because it comes bound in its own legend and lore.

Tamerlane by "A Bostonian" was printed, rather badly, in 1827 by a young man named Calvin F. S. Thomas. He was eighteen years old at the time and a near contemporary of the poet himself. Nothing further is known about him. The book is actually little more than a pamphlet and sold for very small amounts during a very short time. Some scholars argue that it never went on sale at all, distribution being limited to a few review copies mailed to important readers. Poe, though, implies otherwise in a note attached to the 1829 edition published in Baltimore; and he creates at the same time one of the mysteries surrounding the first edition:

> The poem was printed for publication in Boston, in the year 1827, but suppressed through circumstances of a private nature.

Whatever the circumstances, suppression was effective. By 1925 there were four known copies of *Tamerlane*. One had been bought by the British Museum in 1867 for a single shilling. A clerk named Richard Lichtenstein found the second *Tamerlane* a few years later at a sidewalk bookstall in Boston: he paid fifteen cents. The third copy surfaced in Richmond, went through two collectors, and was sold in November 1900 for $2050. And the fourth sold in 1914 at an undisclosed amount: it came from a woman in Boston who told the purchaser P. K. Foley it was a pity they had not met two years earlier, before "I had that bonfire of old books on my lawn. . . ."

While another rare book might have its value damaged with the discovery of new volumes, that has not proved to be the case with Poe's charmed book. In 1925 Vincent Starrett published in the *Saturday Evening Post* an article entitled "Have You a Tamerlane in Your Attic?" A *Post* subscriber named Mrs. Ada Dodd (of Worcester, Massachusetts) read the article, marched up to her attic, and brought down as near perfect a copy of *Tamerlane* as has ever been located. She sold it a year later for something over $18,000. This was the fifth known copy of the book. Still others of the volume have surfaced since 1925, each one bringing its own story and a higher price than its predecessors.

Have you a *Tamerlane* in your attic?

§ | *Robert Frost.* Scarcity does count for something, especially if one owns the single existing copy of Robert Frost's first book of poetry. The volume is called *Twilight*, published at Lawrence, Massachusetts, in 1894. A job printer did two copies for Frost, and one was later destroyed.

§ | *Pilgrim's Progress.* It's a commonplace of social history that every pioneer family had its copy of the Bible and John Bunyan's *Pilgrim's Progress*. That may not be more than a slight exaggeration. In 1681 appeared the first American edition of this Puritan gospel, after which it became an immediate and powerful bestseller for some two hundred years. In all, there were more than 120 American editions of *The Pilgrim's Progress*, enough for a collector to specialize in this one book. Some have. Yes, the 1678 English edition is rather costly; but then, as now, the American editions went for much less. The original purchase price for many of these was 10¢.

§ | *Dime Novels.* Beadle & Adams, the "fiction factory" which published dime novels by the railroad flatcar, published at its height as many as forty new novels a week. From 1861 to 1900 the publishers of this most popular form of literature turned out 1,000,000,000 volumes, although many of the titles are very scarce today because the pulp paper on which they were printed simply disintegrated in a relatively short time. As early as the 1920s the little books were already collectors' items. For a set of 200 dime novels the Huntington Library in 1922 paid $15,000, a tiny fraction of their current value.

§ | *The Heathen Chinee.* Time has not improved the reputation of Bret Harte, a name on every lip when his ballad of the "Heathen Chinee" was taking the country by storm during the Gilded Age. Time has, though, increased the value of his poem, with all early editions bringing much more than their original cost. The very first edition is something unusual and well worth collecting: it is a packet of nine lithographed cards, the poem by Harte and the illustrations by Joseph Hull. They were published in Chicago in 1870.

§ | *The Wicked Primer*. In an attic somewhere may be a copy of the so-called *Wicked Primer*, a special, and therefore extremely valuable, edition of the famous *New England Primer*. There is no known copy of this work, but experts know that it did exist at one time. The book is "wicked" because of the unfortunate juxtaposition of certain poetry and pictures. Here's what happened.

Around 1750 the Reverend Thomas Prince of Boston revised some of the couplets in the alphabet section of the text, his feeling being that the earlier verses were too secular. So for the lines "The cat doth play/And after, slay" he substituted this:

> Christ crucified
> For sinners died.

The new lines were to appear, of course, with a new woodcut, in this case a picture of Jesus on the cross. When the new edition went to press, however, someone apparently misunderstood the instructions and printed the old pictures beside the new poems. Thus "Christ crucified . . ." appeared with the woodcut of a cat tormenting its prey. This, and other examples of sacrilege, earned the book its sobriquet.

While bibliographers and the major auction houses continue their search for the *Wicked Primer*, interested parties might content themselves with a sort of collateral collector's item. For considerably less than the book itself might bring, one can have a copy of the *Boston Gazette* for September 24, 1759, in which "A child's instructor" publishes his letter complaining about Thomas Prince's luckless revision.

§ | *The Wicked Wife*. In 1935 a woman named Louise Perkins, in a fit of enthused housecleaning, discarded a number of outdated editions taking up space in her home. She paid a book dealer five dollars to haul away the boxes and barrels thus filled.

Now, it might be worth mentioning at this point that in those days before feminine assertiveness Louise Perkins was also known as Mrs. Maxwell Perkins, wife of the famous Scribners editor. The books she had thrown away belonged principally to Max, many of them inscribed by the likes of Scott Fitzgerald, Thomas Wolfe, and John Galsworthy.

By sheerest accident a rare book expert and friend of Mr. Perkins named David Randall discovered the volumes at a used book stand on New York's Second Avenue. Immediately Randall surmised enough of the truth to know that he must recover the books. He set about his bargaining with the patience and skill and knowledge developed over years in the book trade. At first the dealer wanted $500 for the lot, but Randall kept at his man and at last reversed a potential disaster for the Depression-weary sum of twenty-five dollars.

§ | *Fanshawe.* Just as bestsellers can be "engineered," so can collectors' items, the difference being one of intent. Nathaniel Hawthorne, for example, intended to destroy every copy of his *Fanshawe,* a less than successful first novel based on some of his undergraduate experiences. Although the author's first enthusiasms caused him to publish the book at his own expense in 1828, he grew ashamed of the work and tried to suppress it throughout the rest of his life. Apparently Hawthorne succeeded better at suppressing than at writing since *Fanshawe* is now one of the most difficult works in American literature to collect, and one of the most expensive. Horatio Bridge, the author's close friend, had to destroy his personal copy and was forbidden to mention the title in Hawthorne's presence. For a long time Mrs. Hawthorne knew absolutely nothing about the book: when someone showed her a copy of *Fanshawe* shortly after her husband's death, she insisted that Hawthorne had never written a book by that title.

§ | *The Phrenology Edition.* The first edition of *Leaves of Grass* is beyond the means of most amateur collectors; but the second edition is not, and it is in a sense more valuable because of its unusual publishers. Sometime during 1849 Whitman began consulting Phrenologists Fowler and Wells at their "Phrenological Cabinet" in New York City. Lorenzo Fowler carefully charted the bumps and depressions on the poet's head, offering at last this evaluation:

> Leading traits of character appear to be Friendship, Sympathy, Sublimity, and Self-Esteem, and markedly among his combinations the dangerous faults of Indolence, a tendency to the pleasure of voluptuousness and alimentiveness and a certain reckless swing of animal will, too unmindful, probably, of the conviction of others.

—the second half of which exactly matched what critics said on reviewing the 1855 edition of *Leaves of Grass*. Few book dealers stocked this "voluptuous" text, happily published by Whitman himself, although Fowler and Wells offered it in their bookstore on Broadway. The forward-looking phrenologists themselves brought out the second edition of the work in 1856. It's a collector's item now, but only for those who know the "publishers" for what they were.

§ | *Walt Whitman and Henry David Thoreau.* An association copy is usually a book which has been owned by someone meaningful to the author's life. Melville's own copy of *The Scarlet Letter*, for example, would be worth considerably more than an ordinary first edition of Hawthorne's novel. But Melville and Hawthorne were friends. What about association copies linking famous adversaries?

About the best one could do in American literature would be to own the copies of *A Week on the Concord and Merrimack Rivers* and *Leaves of Grass* exchanged by Thoreau and Whitman. Although the two were not enemies in the conventional sense of the word, one might say they had a healthy disrespect for one another. Whitman insisted that the Concord philosopher nursed "a very aggravated case of superciliousness" while Thoreau grumbled of Whitman's poetry, "He does not celebrate love at all. It is as if the beasts spoke." Still, they came together on November 10, 1856, and traded volumes. Whitman wrote, "H.D. Thoreau from Walt Whitman" in the book he gave to Thoreau, and the latter filled in some missing lines in *A Week* and gave it to Whitman. Each, in addition, managed to utter a few polite sentiments about the other.

§ | *N. C. Wyeth and Edgar Rice Burroughs.* For some collectors "literary appreciation" has more to do with projecting future book values than with a love of literature. They might see illustrations or inscriptions in a text as features which could dramatically increase a book's worth in the future. So when a particularly collectable author is somehow linked to a particularly collectable illustrator, someone stands to reap a bonanza. Of course one of the most valuable association items one can find would be the original painting or drawing from which a work is illustrated: it would be analogous to owning the manuscript of that work.

Edgar Rice Burroughs must have had thoughts similar to these in 1913 when he set out to buy N. C. Wyeth's illustration for one of his novels. It was the dramatic cover of that June's *New Story* magazine which interested the writer. Burroughs did, after all, already own the manuscript of *The Return of Tarzan*, and he saw Wyeth's drawing as a valuable "companion piece." Accordingly, he wrote to editor A. L. Sessions of *New Story* inquiring about the illustration. Through various mediators came Wyeth's reply—$100 for the original. It was in fact a stiff price for 1913. Burroughs thought it was outrageous. He replied through channels, "I want to thank you for the trouble you have taken relative to the cover design by Mr. Wyeth. I am afraid, however, that Mr. Wyeth wants it worse than I do, so I shall be generous and let him keep it."

§ | *The American Alice.* Usually the first foreign printing of a book is much less valuable than the domestic first edition (*Moby-Dick* is a grand exception), but from time to time there occur enough quirks and complications in getting an "import" published to pique the interest of a collector. In the case of *Alice in Wonderland* there are complications aplenty. Here's a condensed history of the book.

In 1865 Macmillan's of London prepared to print the first edition, but initial press runs revealed engravings so poor that the publishers and author agreed to start again with a whole new set of illustrations. The next run proved to be satisfactory: it was completed in December, 1865 but actually dated 1866 because it would not go on sale until the next year. Of the original, inferior edition many copies went to the children's wards of various London hospitals; but a great batch fell into the hands of William Worthen Appleton who brought them back to America, substituted a title page from his own firm, dated the copies 1866 (to match the English edition), and put them on sale.

Obviously what this means is that the "legitimate" first edition of *Alice in Wonderland* was published in the United States, not in England.

There is another irony however. Although the American edition might seem to be the more valuable of the two, and is in fact a true collector's item, time has thinned the English texts down to a few extremely rare copies. Thus, the "second" edition of *Alice* is the far more valuable one.

§ | *Carl Sandburg.* After he wrote his own poems, Carl Sandburg set his own type, rolled his own press, and bound his own book. He did this for his first collection of poetry entitled *In Reckless Ecstasy* (1904) while he was attending Lombard College in Galesburg, Illinois. Sandburg's instructor was Professor Philip Green Wright who allowed the poet to use the Gordon press located in Wright's basement. Together they printed fifty copies of fifty pages each, bound these in cardboard, and tied them with ribbon. Today the little books would sell for around $700.

§ | *The Declaration of Independence.* Sometimes it's not the attic. Sometimes it's the cellar. In 1968 a Philadelphia book dealer rummaged through his basement materials long enough to turn up the last printed copy of the Declaration of Independence, now the only one in private hands. The following year a gentleman from Texas paid for this document the highest price ever given for a single broadsheet: $404,000.

§ | *The Other Autocrat.* In November, 1857 the *Atlantic Monthly* began its serialization of Oliver Wendell Holmes's *Autocrat of the Breakfast-Table.* Nothing unusual here, except that the first line seemed a peculiar one simply to be ignored by the readers; it said this: "I was just going to say, when I was interrupted. . . ." Since the rest of the piece made perfectly good sense, most people assumed that this startling "introduction" was a part of the fiction. It was not. The author had indeed been interrupted.

This Holmesian hiatus extended back to February, 1832 and into a different periodical, the *New England Magazine.* It was then and there that Holmes had published the first installments of his *Autocrat of the Breakfast Table* (note the different title). Twenty-five years later he "continued" the series in the *Atlantic Monthly.* When the book version of the *Autocrat* appeared, Holmes did not include the two essays he wrote originally for the *New England Magazine.* "They will not be reprinted here," he said, "nor, as I hope, anywhere." They were of course reprinted at other times, but not in the first book edition. They became in a sense Holmes's "Other Autocrat," a collector's item overlooked in the common rush for books.

§ | *The Other Milton.* In his day Frank Stockton was one of the most famous writers in America even though his fame rested on a single tale, "The Lady or the Tiger?" Before he became famous though he created—one can't properly say *wrote*—a collector's item which is still waiting for discovery and is to be had no doubt for a very small sum. The problem is that the few Stockton biographers have all neglected a full explanation of one interesting adolescent episode.

Sometime between 1848 and 1852 Frank and his brother John submitted some poems for publication in a Baltimore religious paper. When their work was rejected, they decided that the tasteless editor could not appreciate good poetry when he saw it. To prove the point Frank copied some lines of Milton's *Paradise Regained* and mailed these to the same editor—who gratefully accepted them for publication. So there is now apparently, somewhere, waiting to be found, a truly American edition of *Paradise Regained*—by Frank Stockton.

§ | *E. A. Robinson.* A collector should never make careless assumptions about what is truly rare in American literature. One of the rarest volumes ever published, for instance, would be an *unautographed* copy of E. A. Robinson's *The Torrent and the Night Before.* Here's why.

In 1896 Robinson himself paid fifty-two dollars to have his collection of forty-four poems printed by the Riverside Press: he was almost completely unknown at the time, and no publishing company was willing to risk its capital and reputation trying to market these grim verses. For his money Robinson received 312 paperback copies of *The Torrent and the Night Before.* Since he wanted to earn fame rather than fortune, the poet immediately began mailing review copies to newspapers, magazines, and important literary figures. As his pile of books dwindled, Robinson autographed some of them and then sent these to his friends and relatives.

Of course most of the potential reviewers merely tossed their unwanted books into the garbage while the cousins and aunts and grandmothers and uncles kept their inscribed copies. Such callousness by the one group and such care by the other insured that the overwhelming majority of books surviving from the original printing would be autographed ones. In fact, there has been only one known unautographed copy offered for sale by a public broker, and that book brought a handsome price.

§ | *Philip Wylie.* Wylie's *The Paradise Crater* is now something of a collector's item; but when the book first began circulating in 1945, it scared the pants off the F.B.I. This science fiction novella is about a World War II which is still being fought in 1965. The plot has a Nazi group in Wyoming attempting to conquer the rest of the United States with a fantastic new weapon, an atom bomb made of enriched uranium. The problem was that in 1945 no one but a tiny group of scientists was supposed to know about the atomic bomb, yet here was a fellow ready to publish a book about one.

When Wylie's agent submitted the story to *Blue Book*, publishers passed the manuscript on to Washington, where American counterespionage specialists nearly panicked. The intelligence community had Wylie put under house arrest in Westbury, Connecticut, and released four months later (while the book lingered under lock and key). Then Donald

Kennicott finally brought out the story in the October, 1945 issue of *Blue Book*. One can still buy copies for only a few dollars.

§ | *Sample Prices*. Although rare books are generally an excellent investment, one might be surprised at the relatively low cost of most American first editions. Actually the number of American books which could sell for $10,000 or more is very small: Hawthorne's *Fanshawe*, Whitman's *Leaves of Grass*, Cooper's *Last of the Mohicans*, Poe's *Al Aaraaf* and *The Raven*, Emerson's *Letter to the Second Church,* and Longfellow's 1865—67 translation of Dante would be the majority. In the hundred-thousand-dollar range would be the *Bay Psalm Book*, Poe's *Tamerlane* (perhaps the *Murders in the Rue Morgue*), Audubon's *Birds of America*—few others. What follows is not a comprehensive price guide but rather a sampler showing relative market values of some famous American authors.

James Agee
    Let Us Now Praise Famous Men. Boston, 1941. $125
    A Death in the Family. N.Y., (1957). $75
Conrad Aiken
    Earth Triumphant. N.Y., 1914. $150
    The Jig of Forslin. Boston, 1916. $100—150
Louisa May Alcott
    Little Women. Boston, 1869. $45
Hervey Allen
    Anthony Adverse. N.Y., 1933. $50
John H. Alexander
    Mosby's Men. N.Y., 1907. $60
Horatio Alger
    Adrift in the City. Philadelphia. n.d., $30
    Ragged Dick. Boston, 1868. (12 known copies). $700
Sherwood Anderson
    Winesburg, Ohio. N.Y., 1919. $125
    The Triumph of the Egg. N.Y., 1921. $100
    A Story Teller's Story. N.Y., 1924. $60
    Dark Laughter. N.Y., 1925. $30
John James Audubon
    Birds of America. London, 1828—38. $300,000—500,000
Stephen Vincent Benét
    John Brown's Body. N.Y., 1928. $25—30

Johnny Pye & the Fool Killer. Weston, 1938.
(Limited Edition). $100
They Burned the Books. N.Y., 1942. $20

Ambrose Bierce
Tales of Soldiers & Civilians. San Francisco, 1891. $225
Shapes of Clay. San Francisco, 1903. $175
Letters. N.Y., 1922. $75
Battle Sketches. London, 1930. $100

William Cullen Bryant
The Embargo. Boston, 1809. $700
Poems. Cambridge, 1821. $1,000 – 1,500
The Fountain & Other Poems. N.Y., 1842. $150
Hymns. N.Y., 1864. $75

Frances H. Burnett
Little Lord Fauntleroy. N.Y., 1886. $175

Edgar Rice Burroughs
Jungle Tales of Tarzan. Chicago, 1919. $90
Tarzan the Terrible. Chicago, 1921. $60
The Chessmen of Mars. Chicago, 1922. $70

James Branch Cabell
The High Place. N.Y., 1923. $30
Something About Eve. N.Y., 1927. $30
The Cream of the Jest. N.Y., 1927. $40

George Washington Cable
Old Creole Days. N.Y., 1877. $20

Erskine Caldwell
God's Little Acre. N.Y., 1933. $90

Willa Cather
The Song of the Lark. Boston, 1915. $25
Death Comes to the Archbishop. N.Y., 1929. $400
Lucy Greyheart. N.Y., 1935. $25

Samuel L. Clemens
The Celebrated Jumping Frog of Calaveras County and Other Sketches.
N.Y., 1867. $800 – 2,000
The Innocents Abroad. Hartford, 1869. $75 – 150
The Adventures of Tom Sawyer. Hartford, 1876. $700 – 2,000
The Adventures of Huckleberry Finn. N.Y., 1885. $1,000 – 3,000
A Connecticut Yankee in King Arthur's Court. N.Y., 1889. $325

James Fenimore Cooper
The Spy. London, 1822. $400

The Last of the Mohicans. Philadelphia, 1826. $10,000
The Prairie. London, 1827. $150–200
The Deerslayer. Philadelphia, 1841. $100–175

Stephen Crane
The Red Badge of Courage. N.Y., 1895. $400

Emily Dickinson
Poems. Boston, 1890. $450
Poems: Second Series. Boston, 1891. $150

Walt Disney
The Adventures of Mickey Mouse, Book I. Philadelphia, 1931. $500

Mary Mapes Dodge
Hans Brinker or the Silver Skates. N.Y., 1874. $60

John Dos Passos
Three Soldiers. N.Y., 1921. $50
Manhattan Transfer. N.Y., 1925. $25

Theodore Dreiser
Sister Carrie. N.Y., 1900. $700
Jennie Gerhardt. N.Y., 1911. $25
An American Tragedy. N.Y., 1925. $225

T. S. Eliot
Ash Wednesday. London, 1930. $25
Four Quartets. N.Y., 1943. $1,500

William Faulkner
Mosquitoes. N.Y., 1927. $1,500–2,000
Sartoris. N.Y., 1929. $700
The Sound and the Fury. N.Y., 1929. $1,000
Sanctuary. N.Y., 1931. $1,000–1,500
Light in August. N.Y., 1932. $150
Knight's Gambit. N.Y., 1949. $700
Requiem for a Nun. N.Y., 1951. $75

Eugene Field
Little Willie. n.p., n.d., $30

F. Scott Fitzgerald
This Side of Paradise. N.Y., 1920. $400
Flappers & Philosophers. N.Y., 1920. $200
Tales of the Jazz Age. N.Y., 1922. $300
The Great Gatsby. N.Y., 1925. $150

Robert Frost
A Boy's Will. N.Y., 1915. $200

North of Boston. N.Y., 1917 (not a first edition). $150

West Running Brook. N.Y., 1928 (signed). $200

Zane Grey

The Last of the Plainsmen. Toronto, (1908). $50

Joel Chandler Harris

Uncle Remus, His Songs and Sayings. N.Y., 1881. $400

Bret Harte

The Heathen Chinee. Chicago, 1870. $150

Nathaniel Hawthorne

Twice Told Tales. Boston, 1837. $500–700

The Scarlet Letter. Boston, 1850. $225

The House of the Seven Gables. Boston, 1851. $100

Tanglewood Tales. Boston, 1853. $150

Lafcadio Hearn

Stray Leaves from Strange Literature. Boston, 1884. $200

Ernest Hemingway

The Sun Also Rises. N.Y., 1926. $600

The Green Hills of Africa. N.Y., 1935. $100

For Whom the Bell Tolls. N.Y., 1940. $150

The Old Man and the Sea. N.Y., 1952. $60

Oliver Wendell Holmes

The Autocrat of the Breakfast Table. Boston, 1858. $150

W. Hubbard

A Narrative of the Troubles with the Indians in New England. Boston,
    1677. $25,000–40,000

Washington Irving

The Sketch Book of Geoffrey Crayon. N.Y., 1822. $75

A History of New York. Philadelphia, 1838. $75

Henry James

The American. Boston, 1877. $150

Daisy Miller. London, 1880. $25

Portrait of a Lady. Boston, 1882. $400

What Maisie Knew. Chicago & N.Y., 1897. $150–200

Robinson Jeffers

Californians. N.Y., 1916. $300–400

Sidney Lanier

The Boy's King Arthur. N.Y., 1880. $55

Sinclair Lewis

Babbitt. N.Y., 1922. $400

    Elmer Gantry. N.Y., 1927. $50
    Dodsworth. N.Y., 1929. $40
    It Can't Happen Here. N.Y., 1935. $25
Vachel Lindsay
    Collected Poems. N.Y., 1923. $25
Jack London
    The Call of the Wild. N.Y., 1903. $40
    The Sea Wolf. N.Y., 1904. $400
    White Fang. N.Y., 1906. $25
Henry Wadsworth Longfellow
    Hyperion. N.Y., 1837. $150
    The Song of Hiawatha. Boston, 1855. $100
    The Courtship of Miles Standish. Boston, 1858. $75
Archibald MacLeish
    Einstein. Paris, 1929. $150
    Frescoes for Mr. Rockefeller's City. N.Y., 1933. $30
Edgar Lee Masters
    Spoon River Anthology. N.Y., 1915. $200
    Poems of People. N.Y., 1936. $40
Herman Melville
    Typee. N.Y., 1846. $500−2,000
    Redburn: His First Voyage. London, 1849. $2,000
    The Whale. London, 1851. $20,000−40,000
    Moby-Dick: or, the Whale. N.Y., 1851. $2,000−6,000
    Israel Potter. N.Y., 1855. $150
H. L. Mencken
    Prejudices. N.Y., 1922. $35
    Happy Days. N.Y., 1940. $25
Edna St. Vincent Millay
    The Lyric Year. N.Y., 1912. $70
    Three Plays. N.Y., 1926. $20
Henry Miller
    Tropic of Cancer. N.Y., 1940. $60−90
    Plexus. Paris, 1953. $70
Margaret Mitchell
    Gone with the Wind. N.Y., 1936. $150−300
Clement C. Moore
    A Visit from St. Nicholas. N.Y., 1837. $200

John O'Hara
> *Butterfield 8.* N.Y., 1935. $100
> *Pal Joey.* N.Y., 1940. $60

Eugene O'Neill
> *The Emperor Jones.* N.Y., 1921. $200
> *The Hairy Ape.* N.Y., 1922. $70
> *Mourning Becomes Electra.* N.Y., 1931. $45

Thomas Nelson Page
> *The Little Confederates.* N.Y., 1888. $70

Edgar Allan Poe
> *Tamerlane & Other Poems.* Boston, 1827. $125,000—200,000
> *Al Aaraaf, Tamerlane & Minor Poems.* Baltimore, 1829.
> $15,000—50,000
> *Poems.* N.Y., 1831. $8,000—15,000
> *The Raven & Other Poems.* N.Y., 1845. $10,000
> *Tales.* N.Y., 1845. $5,000—7,000

William Sydney Porter
> *Cabbages and Kings.* N.Y., 1904. $175
> *The Four Million.* N.Y., 1906. $75
> *The Gift of the Magi.* London, 1939. $100

Ezra Pound
> *Personae.* London, 1909. $250
> *Cantos.* London, 1940. $40

William Saroyan
> *The Daring Young Man on the Flying Trapeze and Other Stories.*
>   N.Y., 1934. $100
> *My Name is Adam.* N.Y., 1940. $20

Upton Sinclair
> *The Jungle.* N.Y., 1906. $30
> *The Metropolis.* N.Y., 1908. $25
> *Samuel the Seeker.* N.Y., 1910. $25
> *Roman Holiday.* N.Y., 1931. $25

Burt L. Standish
> *Frank Merriwell's Tact.* N.Y., 1910. $20

Gertrude Stein
> *Three Lives.* N.Y., 1909. $800—1,200
> *The Making of Americans.* N.Y., 1926. (One of five). $7,500
> *How to Write.* Paris, 1931. (Limited to 1,000). $100

The Autobiography of Alice B. Toklas. N.Y., 1933. $100
Four Saints in Three Acts. N.Y., 1934. $150
Lectures in America. N.Y., 1935. $300

John Steinbeck
Tortilla Flat. N.Y., 1935, $200
In Dubious Battle. N.Y., 1936. $150
The Red Pony. N.Y., 1937. (Limited to 699). $175
Of Mice and Men. N.Y., 1937. $100
The Grapes of Wrath. N.Y., 1939. $150
The Grapes of Wrath. London, 1939. $40
The Grapes of Wrath. N.Y., 1940. (Limited Editions Club). $200

Harriet Beecher Stowe
Uncle Tom's Cabin. Boston, 1852. $15,000—25,000
Men of Our Times. Hartford, 1868. $25
The American Woman's Home. N.Y., 1869. $15

Henry David Thoreau
Walden. Boston, 1854. $600
Excursions. Boston, 1863. $200
Letters to Various Persons. Boston, 1864. $200
Cape Cod. Boston, 1865. $45

John Greenleaf Whittier
Poems. Philadelphia, 1838. $40

Thornton Wilder
The Cabala. N.Y., 1926. $200
The Bridge of San Luis Rey. N.Y., 1927. $100
The Ides of March. N.Y., 1948. $80

Tennessee Williams
The Glass Menagerie. N.Y., 1945. $125
A Streetcar Named Desire. Norfolk, 1947. $150
The Roman Spring of Mrs. Stone. N.Y., 1950. (Limited to 500, signed). $200
Cat on a Hot Tin Roof. (N.Y., 1955). $50

Thomas Wolfe
Look Homeward, Angel. N.Y., 1929. $500—700
Of Time and the River. N.Y., 1935. $100
From Death to Morning. N.Y., 1935. $100
You Can't Go Home Again. N.Y., 1940. $70
The Hills Beyond. N.Y., 1941. $100

Sample Autograph Prices

William Cullen Bryant: Under $75 for letters
Samuel L. Clemens: $1,000
James Fenimore Cooper: $500 for letters; manuscripts $10,000 up
Stephen Crane: $500
R. W. Emerson: $300 for letters: $2,000 up for essays
F. Scott Fitzgerald: $500
Robert Frost: $400
Bret Harte: $100
Nathaniel Hawthorne: $1,500 for letters; various government
    documents $200 up
Washington Irving: $700−900
Henry James: $100
Sinclair Lewis: $200
Jack London: $500−700
Henry Wadsworth Longfellow: $50−100
Herman Melville: $2,000−4,000
Eugene O'Neill: $500−700
Edgar A. Poe: $2,000−14,000
James Whitcomb Riley: $40
Harriet Beecher Stowe: $70
Booth Tarkington: $200
Henry D. Thoreau: $1,000−2,000
Walt Whitman: $1,000−2,000
John Greenleaf Whittier: $50
William Carlos Williams: $200
Thomas Wolfe: $500−1,000

Short Glossary of Collector's Terms

Acting Edition: The complete text of a play as it was performed on stage
    including all stage business.
Ad Interim Copyright: Temporary copyright protection for a foreign book
    being marketed in the U.S.
Added Title Page: A complement to the main title page appearing either
    before or after the main title page and giving a translation of the title,
    the series in which the work is published, or other such general
    information.

Advance Reading Copy: A copy of a text released before actual publication, usually for reviewers.

Alternative Title: A subtitle beginning with *or*.

Americana: Anything printed in America, about America, or by Americans.

—ana: Suffix. A descriptive term for material about a subject, as above.

Apograph: An original manuscript of a work.

Association Copy: A book which has special or significant connection to the author or other famous person. A book is not an association copy simply because it has been autographed.

Autograph: Any manuscript in the author's own hand.

Back: (Backbone, Backstrip). The back edges of a book ready for covering.

Bands: Cords onto which gatherings of a book are sewn, frequently seen as ridges across the back of finely bound books.

Bead: Headband.

Black Letter: Gothic type, not the same as *Boldface*, q.v.

Blackface (Type): Type that is broader than ordinary type, also called *Boldface*.

Blind Stamping: An impression stamped, not tooled, on the covers of a book (without coloration).

Buckram: A coarse, filled, cotton-based cloth used for binding books.

Calf: Calfskin used for binding.

Cancel: Any section of a book which has been physically substituted for what was originally printed for the book.

Chapbook: Cheap, paperback publications of the seventeenth and eighteenth centuries featuring ballads, legends, etc.

Colophon: A block of information usually including title, author, printer-publisher, place of printing, and date, which appears at the end of a text. Frequently there appears also the printed symbol of the publisher or printer although the symbol alone is not a colophon.

Copyright: The exclusive rights to print and sell a work.

Cut (Edges): The three "free" edges of a book which have been trimmed, usually by machine. See *Uncut, Unopened*.

Deluxe Edition: Often a limited edition of a work, supposedly bound with fine materials and craftsmanship.

Deckle (Edge): The rough edges of handmade paper, although "feathered" edges can also be produced by machine.

Dodger: A flyer or handbill.

Dummy: A block used to replace a book on a shelf, or a mock-up of a book, pamphlet, etc., to serve as a model.

Dust Cover: A wrapper, plain or ornamental, folded over the cover of a book; often a valuable collector's item itself. Also called *Dust Jacket, Book Jacket, Dust Wrapper, Jacket Cover, Jacket,* or *Wrapper.*

Edition: Every impression of a work printed from the same setting of type. Note that the same edition of a work may be printed over a number of years.

Elephant Folio: An oversized *Folio,* q.v. (ca. fourteen by twenty-three inches.)

End Paper: Leaves used by the binder at the front and the back of a book to line the inside cover. Also free leaves, which have not been printed, at the front and back of a book.

Errata: Lists of errors in a text with corrections tipped in or laid in.

Exact Size: The measured size of a book as opposed to its size letter or named size.

Extra Binding: Fine ornamental binding.

Facsimile: An exact reproduction of a text.

False First Edition: A publisher may term his own first printing of a text a first edition even if it has been previously published: such is a false first edition.

Folio: A book printed on papers which have been folded once, hence two leaves of four pages. Also a size notation of a book which has been printed as a folio, usually refers to a book over thirty centimeters high.

Foxing: A rusty discoloration of a book's pages occurring in spots or faint patches, caused over time by fungus or chemical impurities in the paper. Foxing may actually increase the value of a book.

Frontispiece: An illustration appearing before the title page.

Galley: A trial printing of a text before it is set into final pages.

Gathering: All the leaves of a single *Signature,* q.v.

Grangerized: A text which has been enhanced with additional pages, frequently hand-painted or finely engraved illustrations, bound into the book itself.

Half Leather: Refers to the leather back and corners of a book's binding.

Half Title: A page preceding the title page bearing a short title of the book or the series in which the book is being published.

Holograph: A manuscript completely written in the author's hand.

Impression: Copies of a book printed at the same time from the same setting of type.

Issue: An identifiable subgroup of an edition characterized by slight textual variants from all other issues. The first edition, first issue of a book is frequently the most valuable.

Juvenilia: An author's youthful works.

Legend: A caption beneath an illustration.

Limited Edition: A small, numbered edition of a work frequently done on fine papers in extra binding.

List: The price of a work as advertised by the publisher.

Manuscript: Any holographic work or typewritten copy of a work not yet printed.

Marbled Paper: Paper which has been dipped into swirling dyes, frequently used for end papers or binding the sides of half leather books.

Miniature: Any picture done by hand for an illuminated text, not necessarily "small."

Mint: Indicating a book is in the condition it was when it came from the publisher.

Morocco: A covering made from goatskin or sheep's leather textured to look like goatskin.

Mottled Calf: Calf colored by dabbing the leather with sponges or cloth dipped in dye.

Octavo: A book printed on papers which have been folded to make eight leaves. Also the size notation of a book which has been printed as an octavo, between twenty and twenty-five centimeters.

Offprint: An impression of part of a larger work issued separately.

Out of Print: Signifies that the publisher no longer stocks a book.

Page: One side of a leaf.

Palimpsest: A text which has been written or printed over an earlier, erased text.

Parchment: An animal skin (goat, sheep,) treated with oils and used for writing or binding.

Period Printing: A type of facsimile printing in which no particular book has been used as a model but rather an attempt has been made to reproduce the print style of a certain era.

Pirated Edition: An illegal edition, publishers of which have ignored copyright convention.

Preface: An author's note on the scope and object of a book, preceding the text, as opposed to an introduction, which defines the subject of a work.

Presentation Copy: An inscribed copy of a book presented by the author or by the publisher.

Princeps (Edition): A first edition.

Private Press: A publisher which offers books to a limited group of buyers, as opposed to a trade press.

Privately Printed: Not for public sale or issued for limited distribution.

Proof: A first impression to be examined for correction of the type.

Publication Date: The day on which a work is actually offered for sale by a publisher, as opposed to a copyright date which can be much earlier.

Pulp: Coarse paper of wood and vegetable fibre. Also a cheap magazine printed on pulp paper.

Quarter Leather: Refers to leather back only of a hand-bound book.

Quarto: A book printed on papers folded to make four leaves. Also the size notation of a book which has been printed as a quarto, between twenty-five and thirty centimeters.

Rag: Paper made at least in part from rags, generally superior to pulp papers.

Recto: The right-hand page of a book or folded manuscript (generally odd numbered).

Reprint: A new printing from original type, sometimes issued as a cheap edition by a publisher different from the original one.

Revised Edition: A new, corrected edition of a work, sometimes with added material.

Roman à Clef: A novel which disguises real people as fictional characters.

Signature: One or more folded sheets arranged in order of proper reading sequence. A gathering of such sheets. Also a number, symbol, or letter at the bottom of the first page of such a gathering.

Slipcase: A box which covers and protects a book while it is on the shelf.

Spine: The back cover of a book protecting the bound edge of pages.

Tail: The lower part of a page.

Title Edition: An edition which differs from all other editions only by a variant of the title page, often a date change.

Tooling: Impressions and decorations on a book's covers made with heated metal dies.

Trade Book: A book published for the general public.

Transcript: Any copy, often typewritten, of a manuscript.

Unauthorized: Signifies a text issued without the consent of the author or, more loosely, without the consent of the subject of the book.

Uncut: The ragged edges of an opened book which have not been trimmed smooth by machine. A book may be "opened" and still uncut.

Unopened: The folded closed edges of a book that have not been slit open to allow reading the pages.

Verso: The left-hand page of a book or folded manuscript (generally even numbered).

Watermark: A translucent symbol or letter manufactured into a sheet of paper.

Wormed: A text which has been bored by bookworms.

Yellowback: A cheap, sensational novel, so named for the earlier habit of binding such books in coarse yellow covers.

Bestsellers

§ | *Introduction.* Calculation of the single best-selling book by an American author is impossible because of a lack of reliable records. But in contemporary times one could point to Benjamin Spock's *Common Sense Book of Baby and Child Care:* since its first publication in 1946 this book has averaged selling about a million copies a year, every year. On a purely percentage basis the all-time bestseller would probably be Michael Wigglesworth's *The Day of Doom*, an epic poem concerning a Puritan account of the Last Judgment. Although only a fragment of the first edition survives, scholars judge that as many as one person in twenty owned a copy of this book by the end of 1663, a year after its first issue. Within that year *The Day of Doom* sold more copies in America *and* England than Milton's *Paradise Lost* in twice the time.

Harry Thurston Peck was the first American attempting to identify best-selling books on a regular and official basis. His method involved a crude polling of book sales in several large northeastern cities and publication of the "six bestsellers" monthly in *The Bookman*, a literary and trade magazine that he began in 1895. Since 1912 *Publisher's Weekly* has kept a running account of best-selling books in the United States and remains today the best single source of data on popular reading. Alice Payne Hackett's *Eighty Years of Best Sellers, 1895–1975* and James D. Hart's *The Popular Book* supply additional information beyond mere listings.

Contrary to what some assume, American reading tastes have always been varied; and even candidates for the all-time bestseller have had little in common except high sales. Some titles, like the Bible, seem permanently on the bestseller list. Some, such as Webster's *Bluebacked Speller*, have long seasons of popularity from which they eventually fade. And a few writers, like Upton Sinclair, seem to achieve fame by a combination of perseverance and accident. Five publishers refused *The Jungle* before he decided to publish it himself, and then the novel became an immediate bestseller. Nevertheless, popular fiction in this country has always depended to some degree on sensationalism, character stereotyping, emphasis on individuals, and action as opposed to contemplation. In 1791, for instance, Susan Rowson took such a route in producing what may have been America's first formulaic bestseller, *Charlotte Temple*. This is a novel featuring a schoolgirl who elopes to America with a British officer: she dies in childbirth, but the baby lives on to become the heroine of a sequel, *Charlotte's Daughter* (1828). Sound familiar?

In reality there was only one book produced in the eighteenth century that deserves consideration as the best-selling title of American literary history. When Noah Webster published an *American Spelling Book, Containing the Rudiments of the English Language for the United States* in 1783, he had no idea that the book would sell at all. In truth, publishers had refused his book because it seemed presumptuous: who in the world cared about an *American* language? The answer of course is that quite a few people cared. Colonists who had asserted political independence in the previous decade were no longer inclined to accept anything, even the rudiments of language, as being legitimate simply because it came from across the sea. The book that eventually became known as the *Blue-backed Speller* chronicled the development of a uniquely American idiom and because of that sold well for more than a hundred years. Before it went out of print, the "colonists" had bought between 75 and 100 million copies.

Here is a list of other titles that were selling particularly well in this country during the eighteenth and early nineteenth centuries:

The Holy Bible   King James Version
The Pilgrim's Progress   John Bunyan
Plays   William Shakespeare
Poems   Robert Burns
Gulliver's Travels   Jonathan Swift
Autobiography   Benjamin Franklin
Robinson Crusoe   Daniel Defoe
The Vicar of Wakefield   Oliver Goldsmith
Mother Goose
Aesop's Fables

The Sketch Book of Geoffrey Crayon, Gent.   Washington Irving (Thomas
Paine's *Common Sense* sold rapidly, 120,000 copies in three months;
but it did not have a very long life)

It was not until the nineteenth century that American authors really
began to assert themselves in the American market. But even at mid-
century certain British books, most notably those by Scott and Dickens,
could outsell the productions of native Americans. If it can be said that any
one author put an end to the English domination of American bestseller-
dom, of course one would argue that it was Harriet Beecher Stowe. In 1853,
one year after the publication of *Uncle Tom's Cabin*, Mrs. Stowe had sold two
and a half million copies worldwide.

More subtle was the influence of three books whose authors are
virtually unknown today. Almost nowhere will one find them on lists of
early bestsellers, yet each one remained popular longer than *Uncle Tom's
Cabin*, which went out of print some thirty years after publication. None of
these authors was a writer by profession. None of them had reason to expect
success through publishing. And all of them were forgotten before their own
books went out of print.

§ | *Mason Locke Weems.* Weems, the youngest of nineteen children, was
born in 1759. Later he was ordained an Episcopal priest, but he had no
pastorate for most of his life. Although he worked at various trades,
including bookselling, he enjoyed no success and gave no indication that
success was to come. Nevertheless, he insisted that his idea for a biography
of George Washington would catch the public eye. For Weems there was a
sort of macabre good fortune in the fact that Washington had but six
months to live when publisher Mathew Carey reluctantly agreed to accept
the manuscript. When it appeared in 1800, the complete title read, *The Life
of Washington the Great, Enriched With a Number of Very Curious Anecdotes,
Perfectly in Character, and Equally Honorable to Himself, and Exemplary to His
Young Countrymen.* "Enriched" was the right word, for much of the material
in the book came directly from Weems' own imagination. The famous
cherry tree legend, for instance, got its start in this biography; but myth-
making exactly matched the public taste, and the book sold in staggering
numbers at an unheard of price of fifty cents. By 1962 Parson Weems was
unknown, but his legendary book had gone through eighty-three editions.

§ | *General Henry M. Robert.* Having distinguished himself as a cadet at
West Point and in a career as a military engineer, General Robert attacked a
different sort of problem when he took assignment at the military garrison

in San Francisco in 1867. The chaos of the city's public assemblies impressed him so much that he wrote a set of rules and procedures designed to govern meetings. Not surprisingly, commercial publishers saw no need for a *Pocket Manual of Rules of Order for Deliberative Assemblies*, so Robert decided to publish the text himself. The first edition of 1876 sold out immediately, and the original 176 pages increased considerably in subsequent editions. Even though the general himself sank into anonymity, over the years clergymen, professionals, and executives insured that Robert's *Rules of Order* never went out of print. Today its sales have to be numbered in the millions.

§ | *Fannie Farmer.* It is difficult now to imagine the stir created in 1896 when Little, Brown & Company of Boston published a cookbook. The publishers themselves were originally so unsure of sales that they kept the first edition to a skimpy 3,000 copies: that's why it's a collector's item today. Fannie Farmer's *Boston Cooking-School Cook Book* was much more than a list of recipes however: the author included whole menus, explained how to set a table, and instructed cooks on building a fire with any of a half dozen different fuels. What is obvious in retrospect is that Miss Farmer tapped an audience publishers had previously ignored. She mixed etiquette tips and cooking instructions carefully enough to capture the precise tastes of the 1890s, and many subsequent decades, probably because she wrote for the "average" family of six rather than for professional cooks. In any case, the book had gone through eleven editions and countless printings by 1965 and along the way had opened a whole new area of publishing. Calorie conscious moderns would do well, however, to stick with Betty Crocker: a typical Fannie Farmer breakfast might consist of beef *and* sausage *and* bacon, eggs, potatoes, bread, cream, coffee, cheese, and pie or strawberry shortcake.

Throughout the nineteenth century, as one might suspect, it was likely to be authors of fiction who achieved highest book sales in the United States. What follows is a select listing of what were in all probability yearly bestsellers of the 1800s:

1815	Walter Scott	*Waverley*
1818	Walter Scott	*Rob Roy*
1820	Walter Scott	*Ivanhoe*
1821	James Fenimore Cooper	*The Spy*
1822	James Fenimore Cooper	*The Pilot*
1823	James Fenimore Cooper	*The Pioneers*
1826	James Fenimore Cooper	*The Last of the Mohicans*
1827	James Fenimore Cooper	*The Prairie*

1832	Jane Austen	*Pride and Prejudice*
1832	Johann R. Wyss	*Swiss Family Robinson*
1834	Victor Hugo	*The Hunchback of Notre-Dame*
1837	Robert Montgomery Bird	*Nick of the Woods*
1837	Charles Dickens	*Pickwick Papers*
1838	Charles Dickens	*Oliver Twist*
1840	James Fenimore Cooper	*The Pathfinder*
1841	James Fenimore Cooper	*The Deerslayer*
1841	Charles Dickens	*The Old Curiosity Shop*
1844	Alexandre Dumas	*The Three Musketeers*
1845	Alexandre Dumas	*The Count of Monte Cristo*
1848	Charlotte Bronte	*Jane Eyre*
1848	Emily Bronte	*Wuthering Heights*
1848	William M. Thackeray	*Vanity Fair*
1850	Charles Dickens	*David Copperfield*
1850	Nathaniel Hawthorne	*The Scarlet Letter*
1851	Nathaniel Hawthorne	*The House of the Seven Gables*
1851	Herman Melville	*Moby-Dick*
1852	Charles Dickens	*Bleak House*
1852	Harriet Beecher Stowe	*Uncle Tom's Cabin*
1855	T. S. Arthur	*Ten Nights in a Bar-Room*
1859	Charles Dickens	*A Tale of Two Cities*
1861	Charles Dickens	*Great Expectations*
1861	George Eliot	*Silas Marner*
1863	Mrs. E. D. E. N. Southworth	*The Fatal Marriage*
1865	Mary Mapes Dodge	*Hans Brinker and His Silver Skates*
1866	Lewis Carroll	*Alice's Adventures in Wonderland*
1867	Horatio Alger	*Ragged Dick*
1868	Louisa May Alcott	*Little Women*
1869	Mark Twain	*Innocents Abroad*
1871	Edward Eggleston	*The Hoosier School-Master*
1873	Jules Verne	*Around the World in Eighty Days*
1876	Mark Twain	*The Adventures of Tom Sawyer*
1880	Margaret Sidney	*Five Little Peppers and How They Grew*
1880	Lew Wallace	*Ben-Hur*
1881	Gustave Flaubert	*Madame Bovary*
1884	Johanna Spyri	*Heidi*
1885	Robert Louis Stevenson	*Treasure Island*

1886	Frances H. Burnett	*Little Lord Fauntleroy*
1886	Leo Tolstoy	*War and Peace*
1888	Edward Bellamy	*Looking Backward*
1890	Sir Arthur Conan Doyle	*A Study in Scarlet*
1890	Anna Sewell	*Black Beauty*
1893	Robert Louis Stevenson	*Dr. Jekyll and Mr. Hyde*

What follows is the OFFICIAL listing of yearly best-selling books in the United States beginning in 1895 with compilations from *The Bookman* and in 1912 from *Publisher's Weekly*:

1895	Ian Maclaren	*Beside the Bonnie Brier Bush*
1896	F. Hopkinson Smith	*Tom Grogan*
1897	Henryk Sienkiewicz	*Quo Vadis*
1898	F. Hopkinson Smith	*Caleb West*
1899	Edward Noyes Westcott	*David Harum*
1900	Mary Johnston	*To Have and to Hold*
1901	Winston Churchill	*The Crisis*
1902	Owen Wister	*The Virginian*
1903	Mrs. Humphry Ward	*Lady Rose's Daughter*
1904	Winston Churchill	*The Crossing*
1905	Mrs. Humphry Ward	*The Marriage of William Ashe*
1906	Winston Churchill	*Coniston*
1907	Frances Little	*The Lady of the Decoration*
1908	Winston Churchill	*Mr. Crewe's Career*
1909	Basil King	*The Inner Shrine*
1910	Florence Barclay	*The Rosary*
1911	Jeffrey Farnol	*The Broad Highway*
1912	Gene Stratton Porter	*The Harvester* fiction
	Mary Antin	*The Promised Land* nonfiction
1913	Winston Churchill	*The Inside of the Cup* fiction
	Gerald Stanley Lee	*Crowds* nonfiction
1914	Harold Bell Wright	*The Eyes of the World* fiction
1915	Booth Tarkington	*The Turmoil* fiction
1916	Booth Tarkington	*Seventeen* fiction
1917	H. G. Wells	*Mr. Britling Sees It Through* fiction
	Robert W. Service	*Rhymes of a Red Cross Man* nonfiction
1918	Zane Grey	*The U. P. Trail* fiction
	Robert W. Service	*Rhymes of a Red Cross Man* nonfiction

1919	V. Blasco Ibanez	*The Four Horsemen of the Apocalypse* fiction
	Henry Adams	*The Education of Henry Adams* nonfiction
1920	Zane Grey	*The Man of the Forest* fiction
	Philip Gibbs	*Now It Can Be Told* nonfiction
1921	Sinclair Lewis	*Main Street* fiction
	H. G. Wells	*The Outline of History* nonfiction
1922	A.S.M. Hutchinson	*If Winter Comes* fiction
	H. G. Wells	*The Outline of History* nonfiction
1923	Gertrude Atherton	*Black Oxen* fiction
	Emily Post	*Etiquette* nonfiction
1924	Edna Ferber	*So Big* fiction
	Lulu Hunt Peters	*Diet and Health* nonfiction
1925	A. Hamilton Gibbs	*Soundings* fiction
	Lulu Hunt Peters	*Diet and Health* nonfiction
1926	John Erskine	*The Private Life of Helen of Troy*
	Bruce Barton	*The Man Nobody Knows* nonfiction
1927	Sinclair Lewis	*Elmer Gantry* fiction
	Will Durant	*The Story of Philosophy* nonfiction
1928	Thornton Wilder	*The Bridge of San Luis Rey* fiction
	Andre Maurois	*Disraeli* nonfiction
1929	Erich Maria Remarque	*All Quiet on the Western Front* fiction
	Ernest Dimnet	*The Art of Thinking* nonfiction
1930	Edna Ferber	*Cimarron* fiction
	Axel Munthe	*The Story of San Michele* nonfiction
1931	Pearl S. Buck	*The Good Earth* fiction
	Grand Duchess Marie	*Education of a Princess* nonfiction
1932	Pearl S. Buck	*The Good Earth* fiction
	James Truslow Adams	*The Epic of America* nonfiction
1933	Hervey Allen	*Anthony Adverse* fiction
	Walter B. Pitkin	*Life Begins at Forty* nonfiction
1934	Hervey Allen	*Anthony Adverse* fiction
	Alexander Woollcott	*While Rome Burns* nonfiction
1935	Lloyd C. Douglas	*Green Light* fiction
	Anne Morrow Lindbergh	*North to the Orient* nonfiction
1936	Margaret Mitchell	*Gone with the Wind* fiction
	Alexis Carrel	*Man the Unknown* nonfiction

1937	Margaret Mitchell	*Gone with the Wind* fiction
	Dale Carnegie	*How to Win Friends and Influence People* nonfiction
1938	Marjorie Kinnan Rawlings	*The Yearling* fiction
	Lin Yutang	*The Importance of Living* nonfiction
1939	John Steinbeck	*The Grapes of Wrath* fiction
	Pierre van Paassen	*Days of Our Years* nonfiction
1940	Richard Llewellyn	*How Green Was My Valley* fiction
	Osa Johnson	*I Married Adventure* nonfiction
1941	A. J. Cronin	*The Keys of the Kingdom* fiction
	William L. Shirer	*Berlin Diary* nonfiction
1942	Franz Werfel	*The Song of Bernadette* fiction
	Marion Hargrove	*See Here, Private Hargrove* nonfiction
1943	Lloyd C. Douglas	*The Robe* fiction
	John Roy Carlson	*Under Cover* nonfiction
1944	Lillian Smith	*Strange Fruit* fiction
	Bob Hope	*I Never Left Home* nonfiction
1945	Kathleen Winsor	*Forever Amber* fiction
	Ernie Pyle	*Brave Men* nonfiction
1946	Daphne du Maurier	*The King's General* fiction
	Betty MacDonald	*The Egg and I* nonfiction
1947	Russell Janney	*The Miracle of the Bells* fiction
	Joshua L. Liebman	*Peace of Mind* nonfiction
1948	Lloyd C. Douglas	*The Big Fisherman* fiction
	Dwight D. Eisenhower	*Crusade in Europe* nonfiction
1949	Mika Waltari	*The Egyptian* fiction
	Clare Barnes	*White Collar Zoo* nonfiction
1950	Henry Morton Robinson	*The Cardinal* fiction
		Betty Crocker's Picture Cook Book nonfiction
1951	James Jones	*From Here to Eternity* fiction
	Gayelord Hauser	*Look Younger, Live Longer* nonfiction
1952	Thomas B. Costain	*The Silver Chalice* fiction
		The Holy Bible: Revised Standard Version nonfiction

1953	Lloyd C. Douglas	*The Robe* fiction
		The Holy Bible:
		Revised Standard
		Version nonfiction
1954	Morton Thompson	*Not as a Stranger* fiction
		The Holy Bible
		Revised Standard
		Version nonfiction
1955	Herman Wouk	*Marjorie Morningstar* fiction
	Anne Morrow Lindbergh	*Gift from the Sea* nonfiction
1956	William Brinkley	*Don't Go Near the Water* fiction
	Dan Dale Alexander	*Arthritis and Common Sense*
		nonfiction
1957	James Gould Cozzens	*By Love Possessed* fiction
	Art Linkletter	*Kids Say the Darndest Things*
		nonfiction
1958	Boris Pasternak	*Doctor Zhivago* fiction
	Art Linkletter	*Kids Say the Darndest Things*
		nonfiction
1959	Leon Uris	*Exodus* fiction
	Pat Boone	*'Twixt Twelve and Twenty*
		nonfiction
1960	Allen Drury	*Advise and Consent* fiction
	D. C. Jarvis	*Folk Medicine* nonfiction
1961	Irving Stone	*The Agony and the Ecstasy* fiction
		The New English Bible:
		The New Testament
1962	Katherine Anne Porter	*Ship of Fools* fiction
	Herman Teller	*Calories Don't Count* nonfiction
1963	Morris L. West	*The Shoes of the Fisherman* fiction
	Charles M. Schulz	*Happiness Is a Warm Puppy*
		nonfiction
1964	John Le Carre	*The Spy Who Came in from the Cold*
		fiction
	American Heritage	*Four Days* nonfiction
	and UPI	
1965	James A. Michener	*The Source* fiction
	Dan Greenburg	*How to Be a Jewish Mother*
		nonfiction
1966	Jacqueline Susann	*Valley of the Dolls* fiction
	Norman F. Dacey	*How to Avoid Probate* nonfiction

1967	Elia Kazan	*The Arrangement* fiction
	William Manchester	*Death of a President* nonfiction
1968	Arthur Hailey	*Airport* fiction
		Better Homes and Gardens New Cook Book nonfiction
1969	Philip Roth	*Portnoy's Complaint* fiction
		American Heritage Dictionary of the English Language nonfiction
1970	Erich Segal	*Love Story* fiction
	David Reuben	*Everything You Always Wanted to Know About Sex But Were Afraid to Ask* nonfiction
1971	Arthur Hailey	*Wheels* fiction
	Lyle Stuart	*The Sensuous Man* nonfiction
1972	Richard Bach	*Jonathan Livingston Seagull* fiction
		The Living Bible nonfiction
1973	Richard Bach	*Jonathan Livingston Seagull* fiction
		The Living Bible nonfiction
1974	James A. Michener	*Centennial* fiction
	Marabel Morgan	*The Total Woman* nonfiction
1975	E. L. Doctorow	*Ragtime* fiction
	Billy Graham	*Angels: God's Secret Agents* nonfiction

§ | *Cotton Mather.* There is no question that Cotton Mather believed in witchcraft and no question that the rest of Massachusetts Bay did also in the late seventeenth century. One might even say that he did no more than later writers would do when he seized on an idea already current and published a book which became a powerful and immediate influence on the times. The subject was timely to be sure, and in calculating the number of books distributed in relation to the total population one sees that it must have been an overpowering bestseller. Still, this one book did more than any other thing to destroy the influence of the Mathers and to end their golden reign in the Massachusetts colony.

The title was *Wonders of the Invisible World*, published in 1693. Its success came in great measure from the hysteria generated during the Salem witch trials of the previous year when twenty witches had been hanged. It is ironic in retrospect that Mather was one of those urging moderation in 1692: he was against "spectral" evidence and did not favor hanging. Nevertheless he wrote his book on witchcraft and became allied in the public mind with the vigorous prosecution, persecution it would be later, of those accused in various compacts with the devil. When the trials ended, and the panic subsided, there came a general revulsion for the whole sorry fiasco. Of course the most visible target was the book which remained in the public mind, the one seeming to advocate the earlier tragic blunders.

In 1700 a Boston merchant named Robert Calef published *More Wonders of the Invisible World*, which was principally a vicious attack on Cotton Mather and others "responsible" for the witchcraft trials. By way of reply Increase Mather had Calef's book burned publicly in Harvard Yard, but it did no good. Enemies of the Mathers were gathering, and in every quarter they brandished Cotton Mather's "guilty" book. Slowly the Mathers lost influence, first with Increase ousted from the presidency of Harvard and finally with a general realignment of the entire state legislature. As for Cotton Mather himself, having been condemned for writing one bestseller, he did in fact turn immediately to writing another, producing at last in 1702 his greatest work, *The Magnalia Christi Americana*.

§ | *Benjamin Franklin.* A very popular seller in the Colonies during Franklin's day, though it would never quite challenge the sales figures for *Gone with the Wind*, was a sweet little book by James Janeway entitled *A Token for Children*, whose more specific subtitle was *Being an Exact Account of the Conversion, Holy and Exemplary Lives, and Joyful Deaths of Several Young Children*. It was a successful book because Americans of the eighteenth century literally doted on elegies and literature of the deathbed. There were exceptions of course, one of them being Benjamin Franklin, who grew so disgusted with the genre that he composed a formula for writing a bestselling elegy. It is reprinted here for the benefit of young poets, preachers, and professional mourners:

> For the subject of your Elegy, Take one of your Neighbors who has lately departed this Life; it is no great matter of what Age the Party dy'd, but it will be best if he went away suddenly, being *Kill'd, Drown'd* or *Frose to Death*.
>
> Having chose the Person, take all his Virtues, Excellencies, &c. If he had not enough, you may borrow some to make up a sufficient Quantity. To these add his last Words, dying Expressions, &c. if they are to be had; mix all these together, and be sure you strain them well. Then season all with a Handful or two of Melancholy Expressions, such as, *Dreadful, Deadly, cruel cold Death,*

unhappy Fate, weeping Eyes, &c. . . . let them ferment for the space of a Fortnight, and by that Time they will be incorporated into a Body, which take out, and having prepared a sufficient Quantity of double Rhimes, such as *Power, Flower; Quiver, Shiver; Grieve us, Leave us; Tell you, Excel you; Expeditions, Physicians; Fatigue him, Intrigue him;* &c. you must spread all upon Paper, and if you can Procure a scrap of Latin to put at the End, it will garnish it mightily; then having affixed your Name at the Bottom, with a *Moestus Composuit*, you will have an Excellent Elegy.

§ | *Henry Wadsworth Longfellow.* Although he was to become in his time the best-selling poet in the English language, the joy of first publication turned bitter for Longfellow when his "Battle of Lovell's Pond" got sneering condemnation from its only reviewer. As he did later in some of his more successful works, Longfellow attempted in this first effort to retell a local legend in verse form. The manuscript went first to the Portland *Argus* and then to the rival *Gazette* where it appeared on November 17, 1820. The poet was identified only as "Henry." Although "Lovell's Pond" still appears in anthologies of American literature from time to time, it attracted almost no attention when it first appeared in print, with one exception. On the very evening of his triumph Longfellow visited the home of a friend where he heard the father, a Judge Mellen, refer to "that piece in the paper" as being "remarkably stiff" and clearly "borrowed from some other source." Resolved never to be a poet, Longfellow stumbled home and cried himself to sleep, a bitter initiation for the thirteen-year-old author.

§ | *James Fenimore Cooper.* America's first great novelist began his career more or less by accident. He was thirty years old at the time and not the least inclined toward literature as a profession. According to the now famous anecdote, Cooper waded through a few pages of a bestseller recently imported from England and then hurled it aside claiming that even he could write a better book than that—which is exactly what his family challenged him to do. With his pride at stake now, Cooper set about writing the novel *Precaution.* Part of the manuscript he mailed to his friend John Jay in Bedford, New York, where a female guest of the Jays insisted that she had read *Precaution* before and that it had been written by a woman. Mercifully, Cooper did not hear of this charge, and the reaction of other readers seemed so favorable that the book was finally published on August 25, 1820.

The first telling of this anecdote was by Susan Fenimore Cooper in 1861 when she produced reminiscences called *Pages and Pictures.* For more than a hundred years since that time trivia experts and literary historians have been trying to guess the identity of the novel which so annoyed Cooper and which launched the career of one of America's best-selling authors. No one is certain yet. In 1940, though, Professor George E. Hastings of the University of Arkansas made a long and grave study of this weighty problem and published his results in "How Cooper Became a Novelist" in *American Literature*. He concludes that the phantom English novel was none other than Jane Austen's *Persuasion* (1818). An interesting conjecture for the modern reader is that if Professor Hastings is correct in making his lengthy catalog of parallels between *Persuasion* and *Precaution*, then the anonymous guest of John Jay may not have been a crackpot after all; and we must *then* be thankful that the fledgling novelist sought inspiration from other areas in *The Spy* (1821), *The Pioneers* (1823), and *The Pilot* (1824). It was these latter that established him as the first American writer to produce best-selling novels.

§ | *Maria Monk*. The most shocking exposé of the nineteenth century is not shocking at all today: it isn't even remembered. It had nothing to do with Tammany Hall or corruption in the Grant administrations, and it had little to do with the truth either. It did represent, on the other hand, the first major attempt to engineer a book into bestsellerdom and became the first real proof that mere truth doesn't pay as well as believability. The provocative title of this document was *The Awful Disclosures of Maria Monk, as Exhibited in a Narrative of Her Suffering During a Residence of Five Years as a Novice, and Two Years as a Black Nun, in the Hotel Dieu Nunnery at Montreal*. It appeared in 1836.

In many ways this year was an ideal one for the publication of such a book: anti-Catholic sentiment was at a high point in this country, and potential readers still remembered the mobbing of a Charlestown, Massachusetts, convent which had occurred in 1834 after stories of obscenity and perversion had aroused the people throughout the region. Miss Monk (an unlikely name if there ever was one) at last offered detailed confirmation that licentiousness was a way of life in Catholic convents, or at least at the nunnery in Montreal. She described underground passages linking the sleeping quarters of nuns and priests; she implied that the holy sisters regularly murdered the infants resulting from conjugal visits; and she recounted her own escape, while pregnant herself, to the Magdalen Society in New York. In short, the book was a gothic novel passed off as fact.

Certainly the *Awful Disclosures* would not have sold as well as they did had it not been for a sort of prepublication campaign begun by the *Protestant Vindicator* of New York City. Today we would say that this newspaper leaked portions of the book, implying that a trickle of information reached the public before full disclosure of facts. In truth, the *Vindicator* made long and shrill accusations full of vitriol and grotesque imaginings. When the Montreal papers got wind of this tactic, they collected evidence indicating that Maria Monk had never been in a convent in her life and that she was mentally unbalanced. New York Protestants countered with their own battery of affidavits "proving" the original charges and establishing the author as a woman of good character and sound mind.

At the very height of the controversy, publishers Howe and Bates released *The Awful Disclosures of Maria Monk*, and the book sold in fantastic numbers. Some of the reprintings even contained maps of the secret passages mentioned in the text. For a time both enemies and supporters of the writer bought copies of her book to use as evidence of one kind or another in a religious war of words that approached hysteria. Throughout 1836 wild charges from both sides fed the publicity which fed on itself, and prominent figures were forced into taking sides on the issue (at one point, for instance, James Fenimore Cooper worried that his friend Samuel F. B. Morse was about to marry Miss Monk).

At last a committee made up of both Protestants and Catholics visited the Hotel Dieu, made careful measurements and searches for any secret passages, and concluded that the book was a fantasy and Miss Maria Monk an imposter. Many people held fast to their prejudices, though, and supported the author when she published *Further Disclosures by Maria Monk Concerning the Hotel Dieu Nunnery at Montreal*. Although interest in the two books gradually faded, ugly rumors continued, and other rumblings grew louder when the publishers and financial backers fell to quarrelling over profits. Miss Monk insisted that these "Protestant Jesuits" were conspiring to steal her own share of the loot and "escaped" again, this time to Philadelphia where she started a new and short-lived controversy in saying that she had been kidnapped by six Catholic priests. Now, however, few people wanted to believe her tales of conspiracy; and soon Maria Monk disappeared entirely from the public eye although her books continued to sell for a few years. She died finally in 1849, penniless and friendless, an inmate of what came to be known as Welfare Island.

§ | *Joseph A. Adams.* Although the Bible has always been a bestseller in the United States, one particular edition of the Bible published in 1844 made fortunes for its producers and revolutionized the way books were illustrated. When Harper and Brothers decided to bring out the *Harper's Illuminated and New Pictorial Bible*, the firm hired Joseph A. Adams to make wood engravings of John G. Chapman's illustrations. Adams was a peculiar man, unknown outside of publishing circles even though four years earlier he had invented an experimental technique now known as electrotyping. Once more, this time with the new family Bible, Adams decided to experiment. The publishers watched in horror as Adams shut down their printing operation after every impression, cutting and building by hand on each overlay. For weeks Adams scraped and doodled, and the idle presses became an expensive concern.

At last Adams granted an initial press run which the Harper brothers themselves supervised. Concern changed to amazement when the presses began throwing the most technically perfect, and indeed beautiful, engravings ever produced in America. So successful was Adams's procedure that the publishers ordered a Boston inventor to design a new press for turning out what quickly became known as the Adams Bible. The first of fifty-four numbers in editions of 50,000 printings went on sale in 1844. Then, since the Adams Bible was still selling well in 1846, Harper and Brothers published a special edition of 25,000 volumes in hand-tooled, gold-embossed, gilt-edged, full morocco. It too sold briskly, at a handsome price; and Joseph A. Adams became the first engraver in literary history to retire on his profits from a single book. The formerly worried publishers built themselves a new office and manufacturing complex.

§ | *The British in America. The Americans in Britain.* There is a strong conviction that throughout the nineteenth century unscrupulous American publishers exploited the important British authors by reprinting their works in cheap editions without paying copyright fees. Dickens, particularly, suffered at the hands of the pirates, as these publishers were called; and it was he and Arnold and others who, partly in retaliation, helped to foster the idea of English writers being one of the few sources of culture in a backward country which was, nevertheless, discriminating enough to ignore its native writers. Now, to be sure, pirates did thrive during the 1800s, and best-selling authors suffered mightily; but they suffered on both sides of the Atlantic, not just in this country.

The truth of the matter, and a fact never mentioned in histories of British literature, is that English editions of pirated American works frequently outsold books by the British immortals. Peter Parley and Louisa May Alcott, for instance, outsold *in England* any writers of their day. In pirated editions Longfellow outstripped Tennyson. Even Dickens's *David Copperfield* had to bow to Susan B. Warner's *Wide, Wide World.*

Nor was this a case of formulaic fiction by Americans displacing high-minded literature by the English. Indeed, the worst offender in this vein seems to have been British, a student of Walter Scott named G. P. R. James, and noted for such works as *The Robber, The Smuggler,* and *The Gentlemen of the Old School.* No one knows the exact number of titles by James, but between 1829 and 1860 he dominated the market for novels (frequently turning out seven books a year). This is an impressive record without a doubt but slightly tarnished by the fact that Mr. James relied heavily on paradigm: at least seventeen of his books, for example, open as the last rays of a summer sun strike (a) solitary figure(s) on horseback galloping through a forested landscape.

Once when James asked an American reporter if his works were read in America, the reply came, "Your *work,* I presume you mean, why, my dear Sir, it is published once a month regularly by one of our great publishers and always with a new title."

As for our convictions regarding bestsellers of the nineteenth century, let us merely say in the future that there was a strong foreign influence in both England and America—and then let us resolve to examine our prejudices.

§ | *Huckleberry Finn.* Samuel L. Clemens had been publishing books for nearly twenty years by the time he completed *The Adventures of Huckleberry Finn,* and he had every reason to think that he knew his business. He understood, for instance, that a well-written book had little chance of becoming a bestseller without an effective marketing strategy. He remembered too how unscrupulous Canadian publishers had pirated the text of *Tom Sawyer* in 1876 and preempted legitimate sales in America and abroad with cut-rate editions of the book. So Clemens spent the summer and fall of 1884 planning his latest sales tactics in an atmosphere that causes one to think only of military metaphors. He was absolutely determined to conquer the odds, the opposition, and the public's sales resistance in one great campaign.

Huck was to be sold by the author's own publishing company run by his nephew Charles L. Webster. Part of their plan involved keeping the book off the market until Webster had received advance orders for 40,000 copies, the theory being that high initial sales would create a good press for the book which would in turn encourage more sales. That was the theory. The reality was a nightmare. One can imagine something of the reaction when in December, 1884, Mark Twain came across an Estes and Lauriat catalogue advertising *The Adventures of Huckleberry Finn,* "now ready," for $2.25. This was a full two months before the authorized edition was to have gone on sale for $2.75.

Young Charley Webster was merely dumbfounded, but Twain's outrage grew into an almost insane fury. Over the objections of his wife Livy, he sued. The case went to the United States Circuit Court in Boston, with Judge Le Baron Colt presiding. The judgment came on February 10, 1885; and it was against the plaintiff. Now it was Mark Twain who was dumbfounded, for a time completely without words. At last he did make a public statement regarding the judge who, according to Clemens, allowed his adversary,

> to sell property which does not belong to him but to me—property which he has not bought and I have not sold. Under this same ruling I am now advertising the judge's homestead for sale; and if I make as good a sum out of it as I expect I shall go on and sell the rest of his property.

As for *Huckleberry Finn*, it did eventually make money for Clemens, but over years, not months.

§ | *Zane Grey.* Some writers have to be rationed rather than censored. That was the case with Zane Grey, a New York dentist so down on his luck that he had to publish his first novel with private funds. The luck changed in 1906, however, when he brought out *The Spirit of the Border;* for a time publishers took his books as fast as he could turn them out, which was at an incredible rate. In fact, after 1917 Zane Grey was never *off* of the bestseller lists until 1925, a record equalled by no other American author. Then by the late 1920s this writer of western romances had become such a valuable literary property that his publishers were releasing only one of his books a year. The result of this is that when Zane Grey died in 1939 he left behind a stockpile of manuscripts that lasted well into the fifties. His total sales were substantially over twenty million copies even at that early date, and his prudent publishers continued to ration for some time to come.

§ | *Emily Post.* In 1901 Emily Price Post divorced her husband. Subsequently she wrote *Etiquette,* a book which has gone through one hundred printings to date. No one seems to worry about these things.

§ | *Ben-Hur.* Lew Wallace's tale of the Christ probably is not the best-selling novel in American publishing history, but its great popularity did give it a unique distinction. This is the only book in the history of world literature to come out in separate editions issued by Sears, Roebuck and the Pope.

§ | *Anthony Adverse.* Hervey Allen's novel did not appear in print, as advertised, on March 17, 1933. Then it didn't appear the following month either and that fact made editors at Farrar and Rinehart more than a little apprehensive. Here was a gigantic book (more than 1,200 pages) written by an unknown author and scheduled to be sold at a very high price (three Depression-cherished dollars). If *Anthony Adverse* were to become even a modest success, clearly it would have to overcome some handicaps, not the least of which was belying its own advertising in, of all things, *Publishers' Weekly*. The seventeenth of March indeed!

While there are still some who believe that bestsellers are "manufactured" by cynical ad-men, publishers have always known that to achieve high sales a book must stand, as it were, without crutches. Consequently, even today book advertising is notoriously low-keyed and old-fashioned compared to most Madison Avenue shenanigans; in the 1930s it was downright naive. For instance, the editors of *Anthony Adverse* still had in April, 1933, a childish faith that their book would sell if only they could get it before the reading public. The best advertising they felt would be the book itself, and in a way they were more right than they knew.

The first hint of success came when judges for the Book of the Month Club made *Anthony* their featured selection for July after having passed over it the previous month. At about the same time advance orders from bookstores increased as the owners and reviewers began reading their prepublication copies. All told, the first promotions of the book yielded a respectable, but not really remarkable, advance sale of 15,000 copies. The total spent on advertising had been a paltry $5,000.

On publication day another singular event did not take place. Nowhere could one find gaudy, full-page ads bruiting *Anthony Adverse* as the novel of the decade and Hervey Allen as the author of the century. On the contrary, early advertising for the novel was as conservative as a dose of the old-time religion—and as blindly inspired. In holding to their original policy the publishers bought very small ads in a number of newspapers rather than having expensive work done in only a few places. Such caution proved to be a brilliant strategy because it got the book to a relatively few readers over a relatively wide area: after these few had become enthused, they advertised the book by word of mouth. Within a week after publication *Anthony* was selling at a crisp 2,000 copies a day. By September, 1933, the novel was in a position to illustrate a paradox which has since become a cliché in the publishing industry, namely that heavy advertising only helps a book that is already selling well. "The ten best books of the year," said the giant new ads, "are the 1,200 pages of *Anthony Adverse*"—a catchy enough line, but hardly what one would call ingenious advertising.

Nevertheless, the book had been on sale only half a year when in December it topped 275,000 copies. It was not until 1934 that the publishers agreed to any kind of innovation, but what they did try was remarkably clever, or else remarkably lucky: company artists designed a dozen new dust jackets featuring different scenes from the novel and in effect making the novel itself seem brand new. Sales soared. During the filming of the book Warner Brothers sponsored various contests, and the bosses at Farrar and Rinehart at last okayed the other gimmicks, stunts, and monkey-shines so carefully eschewed earlier. Now everything they did increased orders. Unlike most other bestsellers, *Anthony Adverse* enjoyed something of a second heyday in 1934 and then again in 1935 and 1936 and 1937. Even by 1939, after nearly a million copies were distributed, sales were still respectable. And for Hervey Allen it was a very good year.

§ | *Margaret Mitchell.* Editor Harold Strong Latham of the Macmillan Company toured the South in 1935 scouting for promising new authors. In Atlanta he encountered Margaret Mitchell Marsh, an unassuming woman with a very unpromising stack of pages that turned out to be yet another Civil War novel. The manuscript, some of it nine years old, was crumbling and burdened with sloppy corrections in pencil; it had no title; and it even lacked a first chapter. Latham reluctantly crammed the mess into a suitcase and left by train for his next appointment in New Orleans. When he arrived at his hotel, a telegram greeted him: "SEND MANUSCRIPT BACK. I'VE CHANGED MY MIND." But so had Latham. As he read from page to tattered page, his excitement grew; and he was not about to surrender what was to become the literary find of the century. The book was published, with its hastily contrived title and opening chapter, in 1936. The woman who hoped to earn as much as a thousand dollars received in July, 1936, a check for $10,500; and then one for $43,500; and then one for $99,700; and so on and so forth. When David O. Selznick bought the movie rights for *Gone with the Wind*, he offered the highest price for any first novel up to that time, $50,000. Then in 1974 the NBC corporation paid a cool five million for a single broadcast of Margaret Mitchell's work.

§ | *The Oz Books.* Very rarely an author achieves a sort of bestsellerdom over a period of time and by virtue of his many titles rather than through the sales record of any single book. That's the case with L. Frank Baum, whose immensely popular *Wonderful Wizard of Oz* never quite became a bestseller. The sequel to *Oz* enjoyed something of the same popularity but never quite became a bestseller either, and neither did the next sequel or the next one or the next one or the next one, and so on through some forty titles.

The Oz books were so popular, in fact, that they outlived their author. New writers were publishing new Oz books more than fifty years after the first adventures of Dorothy and Toto came on the market. As a whole, the Oz phenomenon now is considered one of the most successful sales stories in American literature. Here's an alphabetical listing of the separate titles, by author.

>L. Frank Baum (died 1919)
>>*Dorothy and the Wizard of Oz*— 1908
>>*The Emerald City of Oz*— 1910
>>*Glinda of Oz*— 1920
>>*Jack Pumpkinhead and the Sawhorse of Oz*— 1939
>>*The Land of Oz*— 1904
>>*The Laughing Dragon of Oz*— 1934
>>*Little Dorothy and Toto of Oz*— 1943
>>*Little Wizard Stories of Oz*— 1914
>>*The Lost Princess of Oz*— 1917
>>*The Magic of Oz*— 1919
>>*The Marvelous Land of Oz*— 1904
>>*The New Wizard of Oz*— 1903
>>*Ozma and the Little Wizard*— 1932
>>*Ozma of Oz*— 1907
>>*The Patchwork Girl of Oz*— 1913
>>*Rinkitink in Oz*— 1916
>>*The Road to Oz*— 1909
>>*The Royal Book of Oz*— 1921
>>*The Scarecrow of Oz*— 1915
>>*Tik-Tok of Oz*— 1914
>>*The Tin Woodman of Oz*— 1918
>>*The Wonderful Wizard of Oz*— 1900
>Ruth Plumly Thompson
>>*Captain Salt in Oz*— 1936
>>*The Cowardly Lion of Oz*— 1923
>>*The Giant Horse of Oz*— 1928
>>*The Gnome King of Oz*— 1927

Grampa in Oz — 1924
Handy Mandy in Oz — 1937
The Hungry Tiger of Oz — 1926
Jack Pumpkinhead of Oz — 1929
Kabumpo in Oz — 1922
The Lost King of Oz — 1925
Ojo in Oz — 1933
Ozoplaning with the Wizard of Oz — 1939
Pirates in Oz — 1931
The Purple Prince of Oz — 1932
The Silver Princess in Oz — 1938
Speedy in Oz — 1934
The Wishing Horse of Oz — 1935
The Yellow Knight of Oz — 1930

Rachel Cosgrove
The Hidden Valley of Oz — 1951

Jack Snow
The Magical Mimics in Oz — 1946
The Shaggy Man of Oz — 1949

John R. Neill
Lucky Bucky in Oz — 1942
The Scalawagons of Oz — 1941
The Wonder City of Oz — 1940

§ | *Ernie Pyle.* By all odds Ernest Taylor Pyle should not have produced a best-selling book; he was a journalist from Indiana whose writings never lost their smalltown flavor. He should have remained in the Midwest, but he didn't. He went to Washington and became managing editor of the *Daily News*. Dissatisfied with the job he was doing, Ernie Pyle fired himself and took to the road as a travelling correspondent for Scripps-Howard. He wrote about everyday people and ordinary events, and he even developed something of a following before World War II changed the direction of his travels and the tenor of his reports.

His first book came out of that great change: he called it *Ernie Pyle in England*, a compilation of notes on the London blitz. There was still that folksy something about the writing which annoyed the British and embarrassed some Americans. The book didn't sell well; and Pyle continued his roving, next to North Africa in the awful winter of 1942. Here in Tunisia his career made another turn, based on his writing about everyday people in extraordinary events. Ernie Pyle travelled with the common G.I.'s; he ate with them; he joked with them; he cringed under fire with them; and he wrote about them. He wrote about them just as a smalltown reporter would write: he mentioned the homesickness, the hardships, and the reactions to a strange land. Ernie Pyle remembered the common soldier's first name and a little something about his hometown too. In return the G.I.'s themselves, and later their families back in America, took Ernie Pyle to heart as no reading audience had done since the time of Mark Twain.

Henry Holt & Company published Pyle's *Here Is Your War* in 1943, then reprinted it four times within six months. Then Pocket Books brought out a paperback version in August, 1944. Then United Artists used the book as the foundation of *The Story of G.I. Joe*. Then the World Publishing Company brought out a book version of the movie version of the book (which sold over 350,000 copies in fewer than thirty days). In 1944 also Book of the Month Club featured Pyle's next title, *Brave Men*, as its December selection and thereby contributed to one of the strangest paradoxes in modern publishing history: this new book was so successful that the publishers had to release their rights to it for a time in order to keep *Brave Men* in print.

When editors saw that advanced orders alone totalled half a million copies, they designed a special two-columned page for the book. Their aim, simply, was to save paper, because the government was keeping a sharp eye on natural resources in 1944−45. Of course, the worst possible thing happened—or maybe the best possible thing: *Brave Men* outsold all other books in 1945. And Henry Holt & Company ran out of paper. Holt surrendered the book to Grosset & Dunlap who also ran out of paper and who in turn surrendered it to the World Publishing Company. When the government released the new paper rations in January, 1946, Holt resumed publication of the golden book; but time had run out for Ernie Pyle himself.

While his book was selling so well at home, the writer had continued to travel with his beloved G.I.'s arriving finally in the Pacific Theatre at the height of the Japanese resistance to new advances by the Allies. He was killed in action on Ie Shima, and the common soldiers wrote his epitaph:

> At this spot the 77th Infantry Division lost a buddy—
> Ernie Pyle, 25 April, 1945.

§ | *Nathanael West and Dashiell Hammett.* Sometimes bestsellers are born of unusual collaborations. There was one during 1927 in the case of what may be the most popular detective novel ever written in America, and it involved an exchange of rooms rather than ideas. In that pre-Depression year Nathanael West used the influence of his rich uncle to secure a night job at the Kenmore Hall Hotel on East 23rd Street in New York. There he felt free to read and to write during the long hours after midnight or to grumble away the evenings with other not yet famous writers such as S. J. Perelman.

Dashiell Hammett, on the other hand, had no steady income in 1927 and spent tension-fraught nights trying to complete a novel being serialized in *Black Mask*. It was a good plot, the author sensed; but pressures from another direction hampered his writing: the impatient manager of his hotel threatened to have Hammett evicted for nonpayment of rent.

To the rescue came Quentin Reynolds, a mutual friend of the two writers and a schemer of the first order. Reynolds telephoned West explaining matters and then putting forth his own plot. He suggested registering Hammett at the Kenmore under a pseudonym and that West then stall the day manager until Hammett completed his book at which point the author would run like hell and West would pretend to have been suckered by a con artist. West hesitated long enough to make Reynolds nervous and then answered, "How do you like 'T. Victrola Blueberry'?" In short, the plan worked, and Hammett finished his novel—*The Maltese Falcon*.

Losers

Pulitzer Prize Losers

1919   The same year that *The Magnificent Ambersons* wins a Pulitzer Prize. *My Antonia* loses.

1920   There's no Pulitzer for fiction this year; and *Winesburg, Ohio* loses.

1921   When *The Age of Innocence* wins a Pulitzer Prize, *This Side of Paradise* and *Main Street* lose.

1922   *Alice Adams* wins. *Three Soldiers* loses.

1923   *Icebound* wins in drama while *The Hairy Ape* loses.

1924   As *Hell-Bent for Heaven* wins a Pulitzer Prize in drama *No! No! Nanette* loses.

1925   *They Knew What They Wanted* wins a Pulitzer Prize in drama the same year that *Desire Under the Elms* loses.

1926   When *Arrowsmith* takes a Pulitzer Prize, *The Great Gatsby*, *Dark Laughter*, *An American Tragedy*, *The Professor's House*, and *Manhattan Transfer* lose.

1927   Before *Early Autumn* wins a Pulitzer Prize, *The Sun Also Rises* loses.

1928   It's a hard decision when *The Bridge of San Luis Rey* wins a Pulitzer Prize and *Death Comes for the Archbishop* loses.

1929   And hard too when *Street Scene* wins in drama and *Strange Interlude* loses.

1930   The same year that *Laughing Boy* wins a Pulitzer Prize *Sartoris;*

The Sound and the Fury; Look Homeward, Angel; and *A Farewell to Arms* lose.

1931   The same year that *Years of Grace* wins a Pulitzer Prize *As I Lay Dying* loses.

1932   The same year that *Of Thee I Sing* wins a Pulitzer Prize in drama *Mourning Becomes Electra* loses.

1933   The same year that *The Store* wins a Pulitzer Prize *Light in August* and *Tobacco Road* lose.

1934   Although *Lamb in His Bosom* wins this year, *Anthony Adverse* loses.

1935   When *Now in November* wins a Pulitzer *Tender Is the Night* and *Appointment in Samarra* lose.

1936   Before *Honey in the Horn* wins a Pulitzer Prize, *Studs Lonigan, Tortilla Flat*, and *Of Time and the River* lose.

1937   When *Gone with the Wind* wins nobody else stands a chance.

1938   The same year that *The Late George Apley* wins a Pulitzer Prize *Of Mice and Men* loses.

1939   As *Abe Lincoln in Illinois* wins a Pulitzer Prize in drama, *Our Town* loses.

1940   It's a good year when *The Grapes of Wrath* wins a Pulitzer Prize although *The Web & The Rock, The Day of the Locust*, and *Adventures of a Young Man* lose.

1941   Even though no prize is awarded for fiction, losers are *Native Son, You Can't Go Home Again*, and *For Whom the Bell Tolls*.

1942   No Pulitzer for drama this year as *Watch on the Rhine* is sandbagged.

1943   When *Dragons Teeth* wins, *The Robe* and *The Moon is Down* (*novel version*) lose.

1944   The same year that *Journey in the Dark* wins a Pulitzer Prize *A Tree Grows in Brooklyn* and *The Human Comedy* lose.

1945   Thankfully *A Bell for Adano* wins and *Forever Amber* loses.

1946   But as *State of the Union* wins a Pulitzer Prize in drama, *The Glass Menagerie* loses.

1947   No Pulitzer is given in drama, and *The Iceman Cometh* loses.

1948   When *Streetcar Named Desire* is nominated in drama nobody else even tries.

1949   The same year that *Guard of Honor* wins a Pulitzer Prize the Supreme Court by a deadlocked vote of 4—4 upholds obscenity charges against Edmund Wilson's *Memoirs of Hecate County*. This is the very first Supreme Court test of a specific book judged against a state obscenity law, and Wilson is a sore loser.

1950   A toss-up for the judges: *South Pacific* wins a Pulitzer Prize in drama; *Death of a Salesman* loses.

1951   No Pulitzer is given in drama this year, and *Member of the Wedding* withers.

1952   The same year that *The Shrike* wins a Pulitzer Prize in drama *Requiem for a Nun* (in play form), *Darkness at Noon, The Rose Tattoo, I Am a Camera*, and *The King and I* lose.

1953   *The Old Man and the Sea* wins. *Invisible Man* loses.

1954   They give no prize in fiction and *The Adventures of Augie March* loses.

1955   The same year that *A Fable* wins a Pulitzer Prize *The Ponder Heart* loses.

1956   When *The Diary of Anne Frank* wins a Pulitzer Prize in drama, *A View from the Bridge* and *Inherit the Wind* lose.

1957   Thankfully the judges award no prize in fiction so *Peyton Place* can lose.

1958   The same year that *A Death in the Family* wins a Pulitzer Prize *The Town* loses. Also in 1958 the play of *Look Homeward, Angel* wins a Pulitzer Prize in drama having lost as a novel.

1959   The same year that *The Travels of Jamie McPheeters* wins *Breakfast at Tiffany's* and *Lolita* lose.

1960   *Advise and Consent* wins a Pulitzer Prize; *Henderson the Rain King* and *The Mansion* lose.

1961   The same year that *To Kill a Mockingbird* wins a Pulitzer Prize *The Child Buyer* loses.

1962   The same year that *The Edge of Sadness* wins a Pulitzer Prize *Tropic of Cancer* loses.

1963   The same year that *The Reivers* wins a Pulitzer Prize *Ship of Fools* loses.

1964   The same year that both fiction and drama are ignored *The Group* and the revision of *Strange Interlude* lose.

1965   When *The Keepers of the House* wins a Pulitzer, *Herzog* loses.

1966   Although Katherine Anne Porter wins with *The Collected Stories of Katherine Anne Porter, Everything That Rises Must Converge, An American Dream*, and *The Source* lose.

1967   The same year that *The Fixer* wins a Pulitzer Prize *The Crying of Lot 49* loses.

1968   They award no Pulitzer in drama, and Edward Albee, Thornton Wilder, and Arthur Miller all have plays that lose.

1969   The same year that *The Great White Hope* wins a Pulitzer Prize
        in drama *Plaza Suite* loses.

1970   The same year that the *Collected Stories* of Jean Stafford wins a
        Pulitzer Prize *The Godfather, Slaughterhouse Five*, and *Port-
        noy's Complaint* lose.

1971   While judges give no Pulitzer this year, losers in fiction are
        Losing Battles, QBVII, and *Mr. Sammler's Planet*.

1972   The same year that *Angle of Repose* wins a Pulitzer Prize *Rabbit
        Redux* loses.

1973   The same year that *The Optimist's Daughter* wins a Pulitzer Prize
        The Sunlight Dialogues loses.

1974   Again no prize in fiction, and *Gravity's Rainbow* loses.

1975   The same year that *The Killer Angels* wins a Pulitzer Prize *Some-
        thing Happened* and *Centennial* lose.

1976   The same year that *Humbolt's Gift* wins a Pulitzer *The Surface of
        Earth* loses.

§ | *Worst Sellers*. There are probably lots of students who assume that any
book which has made it into an English class is bound to have been a dud in
its own day. In truth, that's not the case. A number of the so-called classic
authors were very popular: Irving, Cooper, Emerson, Longfellow, Holmes,
Lowell, and Clemens come to mind immediately. Although his major
writings were ill appreciated until the twentieth century, Melville's sea
stories were money-makers, and poor Poe himself cultivated a wide
readership in certain magazines. Even Walt Whitman managed to sell a
rather ponderous and expensive sixth edition of *Leaves of Grass* in 1876.

Still, there have been notable failures among the great and near-great.
Here's a sampling:

In 1892 Stephen Crane borrowed $700 to print *Maggie: A Girl of the
Streets*. He sold it under the name of Johnston Smith and disposed of exactly
100 copies. The rest of this first edition he burned in the winter to heat his
Bowery apartment.

Henry David Thoreau actually lost money by publishing *A Week on the
Concord and Merrimack Rivers*. His royalties were fifteen dollars, but he had to
pay $290 for the remaindered copies. In his journal he recorded the
following on October 27, 1853:

> For a year or two past, my *publisher*, falsely so called, has been writing from
> time to time to ask what disposition should be made of the copies of *A Week on
> the Concord and Merrimack Rivers* still on hand, and at last suggesting that he
> has use for the room they occupied in his cellar. So I had them all sent to me

here, and they arrived to-day by express, filling the man's wagon,—706 copies out of an edition of 1000 which I bought of Munroe four years ago and have ever since been paying for, and have not quite paid for yet. The wares are sent to me at last, and I have an opportunity to examine my purchase. They are something more substantial than fame, as my back knows, which has borne them up two flights of stairs to a place similar to which they trace their origin. Of the remaining two hundred and ninety and odd, seventy-five were given away, the rest sold. I have now a library of nearly nine hundred volumes, over seven hundred of which I wrote myself.

Ralph Waldo Emerson admired the first edition of *Leaves of Grass*, but he was one of the few. Whittier threw his copy into the fire. Reviewers called it "Transcendental bombast," and clergymen declared it obscene. Whitman solved part of the problem by writing favorable reviews himself under various pseudonyms, but the total number of sales never went over 1,500. What is remarkable, though, is that the book increased in popularity as the poet added to it and brought out subsequent editions. Although he was always controversial, by the time Whitman died in 1892 he was well known in literary circles and much loved by many readers.

Emily Dickinson wrote more than 1,700 poems. In her lifetime she published seven.

In 1900 *Sister Carrie* sold 456 copies, and the Doubleday company quickly withdrew it from publication because of the moral indignation it fired. Seven years later the book was reprinted and marked as "a work of genius."

Lynn Riggs wrote *Green Grow the Lilacs* in 1931—and nobody cared. But with a little tinkering here and a little tuning there a writing team named Rogers and Hammerstein transformed this loser into a musical called *Oklahoma*. It won a Pulitzer Prize in 1943.

Edgar Allan Poe's *Tales of the Grotesque and Arabesque* sold well, after he died.

Ernest Hemingway felt that his first book, *In Our Time*, would establish his reputation; and it did, as a loser. In 1925 he sold 500 copies. The result was that he switched to novel writing. In 1926 he published *The Sun Also Rises*. It didn't set the world on fire either.

In his first five years as a professional writer Booth Tarkington earned $22.50.

Robert Frost sold his first poem at age fourteen and then practically nothing for another fourteen years. American editors rejected his poetry with such clockwork regularity that Frost sold his New Hampshire farm in 1912 and moved to England. There he published two books, *A Boy's Will* (1913) and *North of Boston* (1914), both of which received handsome reviews. He returned to America in 1915 to find himself one of the most famous poets in the country.

In two years Sherwood Anderson sold fewer than 5,000 copies of *Winesburg, Ohio*. In a like period of time Jean Toomer's *Cane* sold about one tenth of *Winesburg's* number, yet by the 1960s critics were telling him that he had started something called the Harlem Renaissance.

Hart Crane's *White Buildings* had a critical introduction by Allen Tate, a jacket blurb by Eugene O'Neill, and at least some chance for success. All told, publishers Boni and Liveright managed to unload 499 copies: 121 went free to reviewers; two-hundred-odd were remaindered; a few actually sold. By the time Crane committed suicide in 1932 he owed his publishers $210.

§ | *Maxwell Bodenheim*. Although he did write an extraordinarily popular novel, Maxwell Bodenheim himself grew more notorious than famous. The book, entitled *Replenishing Jessica*, concerned a girl for whom "the simple feat of keeping her legs crossed was a structural impossibility." One might guess enough about the content to understand why Bodenheim and publisher Horace Liveright were hauled into court in 1926 to answer charges of obscenity. Nevertheless, a sympathetic judge dismissed the case; sales of the book skyrocketed; and the author settled comfortably into his role as Greenwich Village roué. Why, then, would one include Maxwell Bodenheim in a chapter of losers?

The answer, without the usual disquisition on truth being stranger than fiction, is that Bodenheim allowed too many Jessicas into his own life. The trouble started in 1928, first in the form of Gladys Loeb, a bright-eyed youngster from the Bronx. Her pretext for seeing the author was some poetry she had dedicated to him; but as soon as Bodenheim tired of her favors, he dismissed the poems as mere garbage. Gladys marched straight home, stuck her head in the oven, and flipped on the gas. Her landlady found Gladys in time to save her life but not in time to quell rumors. Thus, Bodenheim became a sort of American Byron, at least in reputation.

It was, no doubt, this very reputation which prompted twenty-two-year-old Virginia Drew to write Bodenheim requesting "advice" on her efforts at creative writing. He took in the second girl and soon discarded her too, whereupon Virginia threw herself into the East River and drowned. Immediately the New York newspapers ran exposés of bohemian life in

Greenwich Village, with most giving considerable space to the writer who had "enmeshed himself in a case as bizarre as any of his own books." Both the police and the general public wanted more information; but Bodenheim had skipped town, as it happened, at exactly the wrong moment. The police did catch up with their man not long after reporters had discovered him in the company of, believe it or not, Gladys Loeb—who had to be talked out of committing suicide by her father.

Back in the village another woman, one Bodenheim knew but had not seen in some time, contemplated doing away with herself. Her name was Aimee Cortez. No sooner had the cops released Bodenheim for lack of criminal charges, than someone turned up the body of Miss Cortez, who had asphyxiated herself while clutching to her breast a photograph of the infamous author. But most incredible of all is the fact that the King of Bohemia (as the newspapers now styled him) refused to change his lifestyle in any way. There were to be two more Jessicas.

By the summer of 1928 Bodenheim was well into another affair, one with a teenager named Dorothy Dear. The tragedy this time involved a subway accident which occurred at Times Square on an afternoon in August when Dorothy was riding to meet Bodenheim. In the collision Dorothy's body was mangled almost beyond recognition, her poetry and love letters scattered throughout the wreckage. Bodenheim appeared to be genuinely shaken by the news of her death and insisted long afterward that he had really been in love. After the accident he degenerated quickly.

Although he was still around in the 1950s, he had written little and had long outlived any success he had once known. He seemed self-destructive. Having no money and few friends, he merely drifted about the city begging drinks and occasionally being arrested for sleeping in the subway. Then sometime before the fall of 1953 he married a Ruth Fagin, who was to be the last woman to die for him.

On February 6, 1954, Ruth and Max went to the apartment of Harold Weinberg, a dishwasher and former mental patient who offered the two whiskey and a warm place for the night. Ruth hesitated at first, but Max insisted he knew exactly what he was doing. At the apartment the writer settled down with a book by Rachel Carson; the host settled down with Ruth. When Weinberg made sexual advances, Bodenheim lunged toward the pair screaming. Just as if he had expected the attack, Weinberg raised a pistol and calmly shot the husband, after which he stabbed the hysterical Ruth until she no longer moved. Once more Bodenheim made it into newspapers, most of the articles referring to him only as a former author. But some of the reporters who knew of his past went further: they interpreted Bodenheim's desperate lunge as the last act in a prolonged suicide.

§ | *Horace Liveright and Harry Kemp*. Some people are born to lose, and then there are a few who really have to work at it. Such a one was Horace Liveright, partner in the firm of Boni & Liveright in the 1920s and a man for all seasons up to about 1930. He took extravagant chances with some of the titles he published; and when a book succeeded, he threw extravagant parties. One result, to nobody's surprise but Horace's, was a cash-flow problem: the flow in was steady enough, but the flow out was a riptide. To make matters worse, Horace was a sucker for good stories—not the kind written for literary magazines, but the kind told by con artists. That's how he got involved with Harry Kemp.

In 1920 Kemp approached Liveright for the first time. His plot began with a wife named Dreamy who had tuberculosis; she was dying, sobbed Kemp, and needed the comfort of a sanitarium for her last months. The cupboard being bare, he thought Horace might advance him a few hundred dollars on a book of poems, which incidentally hadn't been written yet because Kemp had been so depressed lately. As soon as Dreamy passed to her reward though, he would finish the manuscript and deliver it post haste to Boni & Liveright. And, oh yes, he was sure the book would be a money-maker. For this tale alone Kemp made more money than for any of his earlier literary enterprises: Liveright gave him $1,200 for a "novel," knowing that the company treasurer would never approve that amount of money for poetry. A year later Kemp showed up again, this time with even worse news: Dreamy was still alive. Could Horace spare a few hundred more? Well, Horace was touched, so to speak, and renewed the contract for another $1,200 after which Honest Harry disappeared into the night presumably to cure his depression and write poems.

Another year passed; and with it came two, by now, unexpected events. Dreamy died, or else somehow removed from the scene, and Harry Kemp proved to be an honest man after all: the author presented his benefactor with a hefty manuscript which turned out to be the auto-biographical novel that Horace had predicted in the first place. While the publisher himself seemed gratified, it would be more accurate to say that his colleagues were astounded: no one but Horace Liveright had expected a book from the venture. The work was published immediately as *Tramping on Life* and astonished the trade insiders once again by actually making money, just as Kemp had foretold. It made money, that is to say, for everyone except Liveright. In the weeks following publication the author took to comfortable living, and the publisher took to overspending his advertising budget: on what could have been a quick profit of $10,000 the company barely managed to recover costs. But by then the firm was well into Horace's next project. He was nevertheless more than just a soft touch: he was indeed a shrewd judge of literary talent. We simply remember Horace Liveright as a man with one uncanny trait, the ability to bet on a winner and still lose.

§ | *Ogden Nash*. When he left Harvard after only one year, Ogden Nash did have a career in mind: he wasn't merely drifting. The future poet hastened to New York where he worked as a bond salesman. In two years he sold exactly one bond, to his godmother.

§ | *Mr. Overton*. The following is a verbatim transcript of an adjustment request mailed to the editors of *Astounding Science Fiction* on March 1, 1952:

> Please cancel immediately the subscription and forward refund for the nine copies still due the subscriber to the agent listed below. Mr. Overton was killed while trying an experiment in the magazine.

§ | *Baron Harden-Hickey*. The Truth Seeker Company of New York City published in 1894 what may be the worst book in American literary history. The title was *Euthanasia; The Aesthetics of Suicide* by Baron Harden-Hickey. In theory the book is a gathering of quotations on the fine art of doing away with one's self, these from the greatest writers throughout history. In actuality Harden-Hickey "edited" and even composed a number of the passages. Basically his aim seems to have been to discredit religion and to provide a sort of handbook for the depressed. Suicide, after all, was the modern thing to do: the compiler notes in his preface, one might say cheerfully, that by 1894 people were committing suicide at the rate of one person every three minutes.

For whatever reasons finding first editions of *Euthanasia* today is extremely difficult (maybe you can take it with you). In any case, Dr. Charles F. Potter, former president of the national Euthanasia Society has his own ideas: "If I remember correctly there was a brief flurry of sales, and then the authorities suppressed it. They never seem to like books condoning suicide."

§ | *The New Republic's List*. Almost every literary magazine in this country has published at one time or another its listing of great books by neglected authors, or perhaps neglected books by great authors. One of the very first came from a questionnaire distributed by the editors of *The New Republic*. Here's an excerpt from what they printed as "Good Books That Almost Nobody Has Read":

John Dos Passos
  Laugh and Lie Down by Robert Cantwell
  Woman of Earth by Agnes Smedley
  Nobody Starves by Catherine Brody
  Forgotten Frontiers by Dorothy Dudley
  The American Jitters by Edmund Wilson
  The Disinherited by Jack Conroy
Sinclair Lewis
  Karl and the Twentieth Century by Rudolf Brunngraber
  Dynamite by Louis Adamic
  Nobody Starves by Catherine Brody
  The Child Manuela by Christa Winsloe
  The Human Body by Logan Clendenning
  The Glastonbury Romance by John Cowper Powys
  Night Over Fitch's Pond by Cora Jarrett
Edmund Wilson
  The Five Seasons by Phelps Putnam
Clara G. Stillman
  Rebels and Renegades by Max Nomad
  The Old Man Dies by Elizabeth Sprigge
  Laugh and Lie Down by Robert Cantwell
  Dorothy Wordsworth by Catherine Macdonald Maclean
  Flowering Judas by Katherine Anne Porter
John Chamberlain
  Flowering Judas by Katherine Anne Porter
  Orange Valley by Howard Baker
  American Humor by Constance Rourke
Thornton Wilder
  ". . . a fine idea, but I can't think of any more except the Keyserling *Meditations on South America*, and I don't even know if that was published in the United States." (Yes, Harpers, 1932).
Horace Gregory
  Saturday Night at the Greyhound by John Hampson
  Guardian Angel by Margery Latimer
  The Black Boxer by H. E. Bates
  Ideals by Evelyn Scott

    Poems, 1928—31 by Allen Tate
F. Scott Fitzgerald
    Miss Lonelyhearts by Nathanael West
    Sing Before Breakfast by Vincent McHugh
    I Thought of Daisy by Edmund Wilson
    Through the Wheat by Thomas Boyd
Conrad Aiken
    The Castle by Franz Kafka

§ | *At Scribner's.* Edward L. Burlingame was the editor of *Scribner's Magazine* from its very first days in 1887 until his retirement in 1914. Before that he had acted as general editor for the publishing house as a whole and prided himself on the gentleness of his manuscript rejections. He did have one sore loser however. When Burlingame refused to publish a Mr. Charles J. Guiteau, the frustrated author came to the Scribner offices late in June, 1881, threatening to kill Burlingame. The editor somehow saved himself, but on July 2 Guiteau shot President Garfield instead.

Burlingame also encountered the merely luckless. A woman once penned, "I was overjoyed to see the poem you accepted ten years ago in your last number. Since its acceptance I have bought every number, hoping to find it. I had bought 119 copies, and there it was in the 120th." (Scribner's had paid $10 for the poem: the magazine was 25¢ an issue. Net loss to the poet—around twenty dollars.)

And finally there was this from another woman: "My husband has always been a successful blacksmith. Now he is old, and his mind is slowly weakening so he has taken to writing poems, several of which I enclose herewith."

§ | *The Worst Poet.* Who was it who rhapsodized "I'd rather far have written 'Trees'/Than all its thousand parodies"?

Now there's a profound question for you, even something of a mystery. No doubt the worst poet in American English is an unknown parodist of Joyce Kilmer—unless of course it's Edgar Guest, the rhymster who tells us that it takes "a heap o'livin" to make a house a home. Dorothy Parker's evaluation of Guest was simply,

    I'd rather fail my Wasserman Test
    Than read the poems of Edgar Guest.

That's a hasty judgment, however, because there are at least several other nominations to be made for worst poet of American literature.

The first worst candidate must be Michael Wigglesworth, the Doggerel Dante of Puritan verse. After some two hundred stanzas of his "Day of Doom" one comes upon this particularized vision of the Last Judgment:

The Amorites and Sodomites
  although their plagues be sore,
Yet find some ease, compared to these
  who feel a great deal more.
Almighty God, whose iron rod,
  to smite them never lins,
Doth most declare His justice rare
  in plaguing these men's sins.

Is there a pun back there on *plagues*, or what?

Whatever the case, it was not until 1840 that an American writer felt inspired by what is surely the worst subject for a poem: in that year Solyman Brown published "Dentologia: A Poem on the Diseases of the Teeth." The poem was amply footnoted with the best health advice of the day and included as an appendix, a list of 300 qualified dentists who practiced throughout the country.

The most tedious and irritating poems certainly are "official" ones, American equivalents to the occasional poems scratched out by weary poets laureate of England. The "best" of these worst American "plaque" poems is by Emma Lazarus. It's cemented into the base of the Statue of Liberty:

The New Colossus

Not like the brazen giant of Greek fame,
With conquering limbs astride from land to land:
Here at our sea-washed, sunset gates shall stand
A mighty woman with a torch, whose flame
Is the imprisoned lightning, and her name
Mother of Exiles. From her beacon-hand
Glows world-wide welcome: her mild eyes command
The air-bridged harbor that twin cities frame.
"Keep, ancient lands, your storied pomp!" cries she
With silent lips. "Give me your tired, your poor,
Your huddled masses, yearning to breathe free.
The wretched refuse of your teeming shore.
Send these, the homeless, tempest-tost to me.
I lift my lamp beside the golden door!"

One conjectures from the examples cited above that the true nadir of American verse must be represented by a poet who combines twisted diction and the "right" subject. The Reverend William Cook came close to the mark in 1873 when he composed a poem about Indian corn beginning with these lines:

Corn, corn, sweet Indian corn,
    Greenly you grew long ago.
Indian fields well to adorn,
    And to parch or grind hah-ho!

While it is true that Cook had definite possibilities, his poetry was eclipsed, if that is the right word, by the work of Julia A. Moore, the Sweet Singer of Michigan—a woman so deadly in her poetizing that Mark Twain singled her out for special treatment in *Huckleberry Finn*. The "Ode to Stephen Dowling Bots, Dec'd" (by Emmeline Grangerford) is a direct parody of the death poems of Julia Moore. Somehow she managed to link a contorted style to an unfortunate subject (invariably the death of infants and children) with a high seriousness that would be comic if it were not so grotesque. Here, then, in full, is her "Little Andrew"—the worst poem ever written in American literature:

Andrew was a little infant,
And his life was two years old;
He was his parents' oldest boy,
And he was drowned, I was told.
His parents never more can see him
In this world of grief and pain,
And Oh! they will not forget him
While on earth they do remain.

On one bright and pleasant morning
His uncle thought it would be nice
To take his dear little nephew
Down to play upon a raft,
Where he was to work upon it,
And this little child would company be—
The raft the water rushed around it,
Yet he the danger did not see.

This little child knew no danger—
Its little soul was free from sin—
He was looking in the water,

When, alas, this child fell in.
Beneath the raft the water took him,
For the current was so strong,
And before they could rescue him
He was drowned and was gone.

Oh! how sad were his kind parents
When they saw their drowned child,
As they brought him from the water,
It almost made their hearts grow wild,
Oh how mournful was the parting
From that little infant son.
Friends, I pray you, all take warning,
Be careful of your little ones.

§ | *Don't Read It.* And, last, here's advice from Peter Andrews on how to spot literary losers before they slip into one's home. It's the reprint of an article Andrews did for *Horizon* in 1974:

The avalanche of books that threatens to engulf us all continues to grow apace. In a recent copy of *Publishers Weekly* I received the disquieting news that some 473 new titles were actually published in one week alone. They ranged from John Alden's *The American Steel Navy*, a photographic history of the U.S. Navy between the introduction of the steel hull in 1833 and the cruise of the Great White Fleet in 1907, to Ahmed Yacoubi's *The Alchemist's Cookbook*. And as sure as trees are being felled in the Pacific Northwest to create more books, next week will bring word of yet another 473 literary efforts.

In the face of this onslaught the reader is almost, but not entirely, defenseless. However, traditional methods such as skimming or speed reading are of little value in today's fast-moving society. Even a moment spent reading a book you don't want to is a moment lost forever. No. Bad books must be fought at the water's edge: at the very bookstore shelf itself. The reader must learn to master the art of Instant Rejection: the ability to look at nothing more than the dust jacket and pick out those little signs that tell him he doesn't want to read another word. I discovered the value of Instant Rejection quite by accident seven years ago at Brentano's, when I decided not to buy a book simply because the cover announced that it was "destined to become a classic of our time." Since then, I have not read one single classic of our time and I cannot tell you how much better I feel for it.

As I developed my skills I found that almost any part of the jacket can be used to form the basis of an I.R. For example, books with a colon in the title (as in *Bulgaria at the Crossroads: The Illusion and the Dilemma*) can always be safely skipped. Artwork should be checked, and the book immediately dropped at the first sign of an oil painting of a Southern mansion—especially if there is a lady in a ball gown standing in front. Even plugs from other writers can be grist for the mill. I have always tried to steer a middle course between the recommendations of both Earl and Edmund Wilson and have spared myself God knows how much heartache.

I have developed my system until it is now ready for publication as a public service. Keep one copy with you at all times and post another inside the medicine cabinet where the whole family can readily refer to it.

Do Not Read:

Any book entitled *Notes On* . . .

Any book by someone who has personally known Henry Kissinger, Judy Garland, the Kennedys, or Hugh Hefner.

Any book that promises to raise your consciousness or lower your weight.

Any book that "reads like a veritable 'Who's Who' of show business."

Any book by an author who has inherited the mantle of either Damon Runyon or Macaulay.

Any book of serious poetry by a Latin American author who has won the National Book Award in the past five years. (In the case of Nobel Prize winners, it is best to wait at least seven years.)

Any book by Norman Mailer that purports to be about women.

Any book illustrated by tarot cards or signs of the zodiac.

Any book by an ex-nun or an ex-prostitute. This is especially true if one has become the other.

Any compilation of the wit and wisdom of anyone.

Any book by an author over thirty who has his picture taken wearing jeans.

Any book on philosophy by a manual laborer or any book on manual labor by a philosopher.

Any university press book costing more than $8.50.

Any book on the funny things kids do.

Any book that is soon to become a major motion picture by Otto Preminger.

Any book set in a tumultuous period of America's history. Indeed, any book that is described as being tumultuous anywhere.

Any book that quotes a line from either Robert Frost or James Joyce in the title.

Any book of fairy tales for adults.

Any searing novel that finally brings homosexuality out of the closet.

Any book that promises to fill every moment of every day of your life.

Any book of "belles lettres" by an author who has not been dead for at least seventy-five years.

Any novel set in a kibbutz.

Any novel set in a plane, bus, train, ship, or any other conveyance where people from all walks of life meet and share one climactic moment.

Any novel that spans the life of three generations of a mighty family whose compelling story is told amid the holocaust of world war.

Although the list is long, be sure to keep plenty of blank paper handy because new categories are being added every day. And don't worry about what you might be missing. There are still plenty of great books around. For example, there is a compilation of jottings of mine to be published soon. Entitled *Badgers in the Bathtub*, it is the haunting story of a young boy coming of age during the construction of the Chicago World's Fair in 1893. Spun from the sheerest gossamer, its comic mask hides the serious social commentator underneath. Don't miss it. It makes *The Happy Hooker* read like *Little Women*.

Banned in Boston, and Elsewhere

One of the really curious features of American literary history has been the simultaneous flourishing of free speech and censorship. While most modern students know of certain political and religious intolerance during the country's earliest years, few appreciate the great numbers of books that have actually been banned in America right up to the present time.

Often it has been sensitivity to language that has sent the indignant in search of scissors or matches, as in 1833 when Noah Webster bowdlerized the Bible itself, eliminating verses guilty of using words like *stink* or *teat*. Almost a hundred years later the Western Society for the Prevention of Vice managed to get Theodore Dreiser's *The Genius* banned in many sections of the country because of the book's lewdness; censors were able to point out seventy-four scenes containing kissing, cussing, or cuddling. Then in 1929 librarians in Los Angeles removed all of Edgar Rice Burroughs's Tarzan books on grounds that the Lord of the Jungle was living in sin with his mate Jane (demonstrating clearly enough that they had not read the books).

With every book banning there is a story, amusing, outrageous, or sorrowful, depending on the victims and the effects of time's passing. A number of writers have achieved unique positions in American literature because of attempts to bar their work from sale, but what is really remarkable is a general ignorance of events behind the censorship itself. Some of these stories appear here separately before a general listing of books that have been banned in the United States.

§ | *Hinton Helper*. The most dangerous book ever printed in America was called *The Impending Crisis* by Hinton Rowan Helper. This all-but-forgotten volume was published in 1857 by Burdick Brothers. Although Helper seems to have foreseen the coming clash over slavery, his suggestions for eliminating the institution were so inflammatory that most Southern States immediately banned the book. In Helper's native North Carolina the Reverend Daniel Worth had to stand trial for owning the text. Pronounced guilty, Worth forfeited bail and fled the state rather than wait for the results of his appeal. Mobs took justice out of the courts in Arkansas where three men were actually hanged. Their crime, owning copies of *The Impending Crisis*.

§ | *The Satyricon*. For a prosecutor, if not for a literary historian, any given book is as American as its publisher, for it is he rather than the author who is the primary target of obscenity charges, it being easier to control the sale of dirty books than the writing of dirty books. In 1922 Petronius Arbiter's *Satyricon* became a grave concern to certain American prosecutors because an American publisher, Boni & Liveright, had just issued a new, thirty-dollar, two-volume limited edition of the book based on T. R. Smith's translation into contemporary English. It was this latter feature which disturbed the New York Society for the Suppression of Vice and hence the District Attorney's office.

The New York *Times* took the side one would expect and commented further on the futility of banning a book that had already survived for nineteen hundred years:

> It used to be assumed by courts which construed the law that persons who could read the classical languages were already corrupt beyond hope of redemption; hence the obscene classics were usually allowed to circulate without interference. Mr. Sumner has now attacked that interpretation of the law. And he is quite right, if one assumes—as he must—that in a work containing obscene passages nothing else is real, and that matter which might pervert some readers must be withheld from all readers.

When a minor magistrate found against the plaintiff, publisher Horace Liveright saw his opportunity to counterattack: he filed a libel suit against John Sumner for $25,000 intending to weaken his foe with exactly the same weapon used by the Society for the Suppression of Vice to wound so many publishers, namely long and expensive litigation. The struggle was a fierce one finally made bitter by District Attorney Joab A. Banton who tried twice to reopen the original case against Liveright. At last Banton went to the Grand Jury itself and asked it to return an indictment against the American *Satyricon*. Liveright, for his part, announced the intention of giving each member of the Grand Jury a free copy of the edition in question; but he was embarrassed to discover the *Satyricon* selling so briskly that he could not produce the twenty-odd copies from available stock. The alternative was for an assistant district attorney to read the two volumes to the assembled jurors, a noble aim which destroyed the prosecutor's case after several hours of droning by the reader and twitching by the listeners. The jurors deliberated at the end of a day's worth of reading, and what they found most revolting were thoughts of having to sit through an oral presentation of the entire manuscript: they voted to adjourn without further argumentation, without further reading, and without an indictment.

§ | *Mark Twain*. When *Huckleberry Finn* was banned from the public library of Concord, Massachusetts, in March, 1885, Samuel L. Clemens became the happiest writer in Christendom. He took it to be a victory that here in the last stronghold of purity in thought and expression the town fathers would judge Huck to be coarse, crude, and inelegant. Louisa May Alcott agreed with the puritans, finally making public this condemnation: "If Mr. Clemens cannot think of something better to tell our pure-minded lads and lasses, he had best stop writing for them." Still Mark Twain rejoiced, for he may have been the first American author to understand the benefits of being banned by the old regime. Even before 1885 Transcendentalism was bankrupt: Thoreau had been dead twenty years; Emerson was nearly senile; and Concord no longer served as a literary Mecca. Boston itself bowed to New York as the publishing capital of America, the bookish Brahmins having been replaced by Gilded Age capitalists. Clemens sensed, and rightly, that to be cursed by Louisa May Alcott amounted to a blessing in disguise.

Ironically, *Huckleberry Finn* had fared poorly before the banning: printing errors, production breakdowns, and legal problems all strangled early sales of the book. In great measure it was the free newspaper publicity from Concord that prevented an embarrassing failure. On March 18, 1885, Twain sent a "private" letter to his nephew and publisher Charles Webster beginning with these words:

> Dear Charley, The Committee of the Public Library of Concord, Mass., have given us a rattling tip-off puff which will go into every paper in the country. They have expelled Huck from their library as "trash suitable only for the slums." That will sell 25,000 copies for us sure.

Naturally this letter found its way into the newspapers, and the resulting controversy created even more publicity for Sam Clemens's stepchild.

Within two weeks another Concord organization, this one calling itself the Concord Free Trade Club, sent an apology to the author and an offer of honorary membership. Clemens accepted graciously—and publicly. This new position "endorses me," he said, "as worthy to associate with certain gentlemen whom even the moral icebergs of the Concord library committee are bound to respect." And on he went in the same vein and at considerable length. It was a public performance that the 1970s would have called a media event. By the first week in May, 1885, *The Adventures of Huckleberry Finn* had sold more than 50,000 copies.

§ | *Horatio Alger.* The private life of this best-selling author could have been taken directly from one of his own pulp novels of low life—could have been, except he would have been jailed for obscenity if he had written what he lived. In the literary sense Alger never made it to Boston, but he was banned in Brewster; and the circumstances had nothing at all to do with the wholesome plots of his fiction: it was Alger himself who was banned. He seems to have started out well enough at Harvard where fellow students called him "Holy Horatio," no doubt because of his single-minded pursuit of a divinity degree. He even managed to resist temptation in the form of a landlady who once showed up in his room stark naked and with suggestions on how to spend the evening. After that incident he decided to move where "there is more respect for decency." And he did.

The fall came during a trip to Paris after Alger had secured his divinity degree: it was there that a cafe singer transformed Holy Horatio into gay Lothario. In his diary he wrote, "I was a fool to have waited for so long. It was not nearly so vile as I had thought." Back in this country he continued his amorous exploits until he went too far for his congregation in Brewster, Massachusetts: in 1866 he was banned from his pulpit of the First Unitarian Parish for "unnatural familiarity with boys." With preaching no longer a viable option, he turned to writing.

After the success of his first book, *Ragged Dick*, Alger retired to a rural community named Peekskill, New York, where he searched for new novel ideas—or maybe novel new ideas. Anyway, he found them. Someone murdered a leading citizen of the town, and the hysterical widow described a short, chubby, baldheaded man she had noticed at the scene of the crime. Instantly police arrested the short, chubby, baldheaded stranger in town who kept insisting that he was the famous author Horatio Alger. A likely story they said. Sometime later the real murderer turned up, and embarrassed police freed Alger. The even more embarrassed widow tried to make amends with a dinner invitation and an introduction to her sister. Whether or not Alger enjoyed the dinner is a matter of conjecture; but as for the sister—a couple of weeks later she and the writer were living together in New York. The sister had a husband, however; and the uncharitable man soon hunted down the two lovers and sent the wife off to, of all places, Paris. Alger returned to his writing.

§ | *The Autobiography of Benjamin Franklin*. In many ways American editors of the eighteenth century showed a greater respect for their authors than has been shown in subsequent eras. The expurgation of Benjamin Franklin, for instance, seems to have increased over the years until he became in the early twentieth century one of the most censored and yet at the same time one of the most widely reprinted writers in American history. The reason is simple enough to understand: the myth of Benjamin Franklin had overgrown the man. Americans of later generations could not admit that a Founding Father wrote material that needed censoring, which by circular reasoning became justification for censoring whatever offended prevailing taste. Franklin gave offense with two essays particularly, "Advice on the Choice of a Mistress" and the "Letter to the Royal Academy of Brussels," neither of which was available during most of the nineteenth and early twentieth centuries. While these could be swept away, the autobiography itself was too famous and indeed too instructive to ban altogether. Editors simply removed certain passages.

The first version of Franklin's *Autobiography* appeared in 1791, but it was incomplete and based on inaccurate translations of an unauthorized French edition. It was William Temple Franklin, the statesman's grandson, who attempted the first definitive edition in 1818; and, interestingly enough, he retained many of the "damaging" passages which were expurgated in the future. For instance, the author himself mentions leaving Boston in 1723 because he "had got a naughty Girl with Child"; but William reports only that he "had an intrigue with a girl of bad character"; and most later editors do not include the incident at all. The point of course is that the great philosopher has tended to improve with age, principally because editors have spent so much time leading him not into temptation.

In 1725 Franklin lived in London with James Ralph, a fellow Philadelphian who was more attentive to the ladies than he was faithful to his wife. His mistress at the time was a milliner who had not gone unnoticed by the nineteen-year-old Benjamin. When Ralph went away from London on business, Franklin made his second try at becoming a founding father, lower case. "I attempted Familiarities," he reported in the autobiographical manuscripts, "which she repuls'd with a proper Resentment, and acquainted him with my Behavior. This made a Breach between us." By 1886 Franklin's indiscretion had disappeared from the autobiography entirely although Houghton Mifflin's edition of that year includes the fact that James Ralph had his affair with the milliner; hence the incident becomes a kind of comic aside rather than a moral issue. In D. H. Montgomery's edition of 1888 there's no mention of any London escapades, and so Ralph's character improves along with Franklin's. Slightly more honest, and allusive, was Professor Julian Abernethy who in 1892 hit upon the ultimate solution: he simply rewrote the passage. His version reads, "In the mean time another matter which gave him offense made a breach."

These editors and others were not so much liars as they were worriers, and they worried for a good reason. The greatest potential buyers of the *Autobiography* have always been school boards eager to use Poor Richard as a model for their young scholars—in which case mythology is far more important than actuality. So the editors edited, for money, for morality, and for the improvement of young minds which slowly grew closed to any but false pictures of Benjamin Franklin.

§ | *E. E. Cummings.* A clever author can sometimes avoid having his book censored by simply switching languages at critical points in his text. That's what happened after 1922 when E. E. Cummings's novel *The Enormous Room* offended John S. Sumner of the New York Society for the Suppression of Vice. A character in the book named Jean Le Negre originally used a common Anglo-Saxonism in referring to his father's death, and Sumner threatened to suppress the text unless that phrase were transformed into something more acceptable. Then, almost as an afterthought, Sumner ordered a secretary to ink out the word in every unsold copy of *The Enormous Room.*

When it came time for a second edition, Cummings shifted the English crudity into a downright elegant French, and Sumner was apparently as pleased as Presbyterian punch to see the change. Now Le Negre said, "Mon père est mort! Merde! Eh b'en! La guerre est finie." In the 1930s Modern Library kept the French for its edition of the novel, but not all publishers did: some of them used as copy-text volumes in which the secretary had inked out the offending four letters. The result was a really curious blank space in one of the lines (now back in its original English). What most readers took to be a typesetter's error was in reality John Sumner's only known contribution to American literature: it was, "My father is dead!   Oh well! The war is over."

§ | *Mein Kampf.* What should a free society do about books by authors who would do away with free society? In 1941 the United States decided that even an Adolf Hitler rated the protection of American publishing laws. The courts were trying to judge whether the 1925 edition of *Mein Kampf* qualified for international copyright, because in the year of publication Hitler had been classified as a "stateless German." The reasoning held that since he was the citizen of no country the author could not benefit from treaties and agreements protecting citizens of the various nations involved.

The court ruled, however, that Hitler did in fact qualify for the accumulated $22,666; but when the author did not appear for his check, it was seized by the Alien Property Custodian. Nevertheless, the trial of Adolf Hitler had an ironic and beneficial effect for a peculiarly diverse group of homeless authors. According to the *Mein Kampf* ruling, all the refugee writers of Europe secured international rights through the very man who had made them refugees.

§ | *George Metalious.* One of the most fretted-over books of the 1950s was Grace Metalious's *Peyton Place.* Thousands of libraries officially banned the book and then unofficially circulated it from behind the front desk. Such innocent deception represented an effective method for controlling readers rather than the book itself and at the same time allowed community leaders a great freedom of action. The earliest victim of community disapproval over *Peyton Place* was Grace Metalious's husband. George Metalious had been a mill hand until he struggled through college and became a teacher, but 1956 saw the publication of his wife's book and the ensuing scandal which cost him his job.

§ | *F. Scott Fitzgerald.* Books can be banned before they are published. One of Scott Fitzgerald's was burned. In spite of the fire, though, Charles Scribner's Sons published *This Side of Paradise* on March 26, 1920, and by so doing made Fitzgerald the youngest author ever to be published by that distinguished firm. He was also the boldest up to that time, but he would not have been an author at all if a sister of one of the salesmen had had her way.

While many of the readers at Scribner's thought that the Fitzgerald manuscript represented a major literary find, not everyone was sure; and in such cases the manuscript went almost automatically to a senior member of the sales department who had an uncanny ability to predict the success or failure of new books. The man's secret was his sister: she did the actual reading and predicting, and then he did the analyzing and evaluating back at the office—or some arrangement like that. So *This Side of Paradise* went home to the sister, and the brother returned shaking his head. Not only had the old lady disliked the book, she had even refused to touch it after a first reading. She reportedly picked it up with a pair of tongs and threw it into the fire as she demanded to be brought a Jane Austen to "cleanse her mind." There was no question about it: Scribner's could not afford to be associated with this author.

§ | *The Shubert War.* On rare occasions a vigilante group manages to ban a critic rather than an author, perhaps agreeing with Pope that a bad critic misleads while a bad writer merely bores. In any event, no such high-minded principles applied to the conflict between Alexander Woollcott and the Shubert theatre chain: it was purely and simply a case of hatred at first bite. The war started on March 17, 1915, when Woollcott, then drama critic for the New York *Times*, attended a performance of *Taking Chances* at the Thirty-Ninth Street Theatre on Broadway. The play had been poorly adapted from a not very successful French comedy, and Woollcott had the bad manners to say that in his newspaper column. The theatre owners, former clothing salesmen from upstate New York, were outraged because Woollcott had broken long-standing tradition by actually reviewing the play rather than writing a mere plot summary. Immediately the Shubert brothers banned Alexander Woollcott from all of their theatres and took out the following advertisement in the very issue of the *Times* which carried the fatal review:

> Do not believe everything you see in the notices today. And though some of the critics, lacking in humor, may try to make you believe that somewhere there is something just a little bit off the line in *Taking Chances*, the management is not taking any chances in extending its assurances to you that this impression is decidedly wrong. You will like *Taking Chances* just as the rest of the audience did last night, when the play scored one of the most sensational comedy hits ever known in an American theatre.
>
> The Management

Everyone knew that the play was neither sensational nor a hit, but the other "critics" had enough gumption to keep their mouths shut. When Woollcott appeared at the Maxine Elliott Theatre for the next Shubert opening, brother Jake himself barred the door. In all, the young critic tried twenty-two times to break the ban, and he failed twenty-two times. On April 3, 1915, Woollcott secured an injunction against the Shuberts in order to attend Paul M. Potter's *Trilby* and then gave the play a moderate review the next day saying that it was "well worth going to see—even if you have to get in by the use of an injunction." Of course these words were the equivalent of pouring gasoline on an already raging fire. The Shuberts appealed to a higher court claiming a right to ban anyone they pleased from their establishments; and, to everybody's amazement, the court agreed. The *Times* retaliated by cancelling all advertisements for Shubert theatres and with that achieved what appeared to be a stalemate.

In the meantime a California showbusiness tycoon named Oliver Morosco was preparing a dramatic resolution to the whole affair. For some time he had assigned the exclusive production rights of all his enterprises to the Shuberts—but throughout 1915 he had noticed an interesting statistic. Daily circulation for the New York *Times* had grown to 300,000, for the first time challenging the publishing empires of William Randolph Hearst and Joseph Pulitzer. Accordingly Morosco set forth a change in policy which assigned his production rights only to theatres that had no restrictions on their advertising. Back in New York the Shuberts got the message. Suddenly the legal maneuvering became, somehow, unimportant; and, why yes, of course Mr. Woollcott would receive his usual complimentary tickets to the very next Shubert opening.

§ | *The "Hatrack" Case.* Members of the New England Watch and Ward Society were incensed when the *American Mercury* published in September, 1925, an article called "Keeping the Puritans Pure." In fact, editor H. L. Mencken really should not have been surprised when the society demanded suppression of the magazine in April, 1926, for publishing the story of a small-town prostitute named "Hatrack." Mencken travelled to Boston where authorities had confiscated his magazine; and there, on Brimstone Corner of Boston Common, he arranged to sell a copy of the offending issue to the Reverend J. Franklin Chase. According to legend, Mencken bit into Chase's fifty-cent piece to see if it was good before turning over the magazine. In any event, Chase ordered the editor's arrest, and Mencken faced a potential two years in prison. Judge James Parmenter found that "no offense has been committed" in what became the major test of obscenity up to that time. After celebrating with Felix Frankfurter and a group of Harvard students Mencken found the next day that the United States Post Office was now barring the "Hatrack" *Mercury* from its mails. He sued. One court returned an injunction against the Post Office which a higher court eventually reversed. The physically and financially exhausted Mencken took his case no higher, and thus one of the most celebrated obscenity trials in American legal history ended in uncompromising ambiguity.

§ | *Boston Common Revisited.* Theodore Dreiser's *An American Tragedy* had not been on sale a month before it was banned in Boston. Nevertheless, publishers Boni and Liveright reasoned that they could make a stout defense of the work relying on the increased sophistication of the reading public: after all, the year was 1926. With the celebrated "Hatrack" case in mind, editor Donald Friede hastened north and on the same spot of ground used by Mencken sold a copy of Dreiser's book to a police officer. He was arrested. What the young defendant did not know was that Mencken, by incredible good fortune, had stood before the only liberal judge trying cases in the Boston district. Poor Friede had no such luck. Defense attorney Clarence Darrow was bested by a prosecutor asking jurors if they would like to see their daughters reading *that* and a judge apparently too repulsed to read all of *that* himself. The verdict, to no one's surprise, was guilty. Sentence, three months or three hundred dollars. Friede settled for the money and a train ticket south.

§ | *Ulysses.* On a blistering hot day in the summer of 1933, an agent of Random House ignited the most famous obscenity trial in American literary history with near-comic attempts to get himself arrested. When Joyce's American publisher decided to challenge earlier rulings on *Ulysses*, legal advisors suggested that a special copy of the book be "smuggled" into New York. Accordingly editors selected a French edition in which they themselves pasted favorable criticism of many literary masters: this tactic insured that the words of, say, Ford Madox Ford could be used as evidence at the trial rather than excluded as hearsay. On the day in question, though, Customs officials were embarrassingly cooperative: *Ulysses* was waved through without a shrug, and the man from Random had to insist on being arrested. The trial itself was something of an anticlimax, even though the ruling of the judge (there was no jury) represented a major turning point in American attitudes toward censorship. In January, 1934, Random House brought out the first American edition of Joyce's masterpiece, complete with Woolsey's famous decision. The book made a considerable amount of money for the author, for Random House, and for defense attorney Morris Ernst who had wisely asked for a share of the profits rather than a regular fee. Many citizens, though, convinced themselves that a thing of indescribable evil had been loosed upon the country, and Senator Reed Smoot of Utah spoke for them when he insisted that a ten minute review of *Ulysses,*

> indicated that it is written by a man with a diseased mind and a soul so black that he would even obscure the darkness of Hell. Nobody would write a book like that unless his heart was just as rotten as it could possibly be.

§ | Writers who have been banned in the United States number in the hundreds. The following is a select listing of the most notable:

Pierre Abelard
> 1930 U.S. Customs lifts ban on *Love Letters*.

Hans Christian Andersen
> 1954 In Illinois a special stamp is designed for *Wonder Stories:* "For Adult Readers" to make certain it is "impossible for children to obtain smut."

Sherwood Anderson
> 1930 *Dark Laughter* banned in Boston.

Anonymous
> 1927 *The Arabian Nights' Entertainment or the Thousand and One Nights* is banned. U.S. Customs seizes 500 sets.

Aristophanes
> 1930 Customs' ban of *Lysistrata* no longer enforced.

Balzac
> 1944 Concord Books features *Droll Stories* in a sale catalog. The Post Office declares the catalog obscene, and the company must block out the title.

Boccaccio
> 1922 A judge in Cincinnati fines a local bookseller $1000 for offering an expurgated edition of *Il Decamerone* for sale.
> 1926 Treasury Department bans *Il Decamerone*.
> 1927 A copy of *Il Decamerone* printed by Ashedene Press is mutilated by Customs and returned to Maggs Brothers, London, without the text.
> 1931 U. S. Customs ban on *Il Decamerone* lifted.
> 1934 *Il Decamerone* seized by Detroit police.
> 1935 Still banned in Boston.

Elizabeth Barrett Browning
> 1857 *Aurora Leigh* called "the hysterical indecencies of an erotic mind."

William Burroughs
> 1965 Boston finds *Naked Lunch* obscene.

James Branch Cabell
> 1920 The New York Society for the Suppression of Vice prosecutes *Jurgen*, but the publicity helps to make it a bestseller.

Erskine Caldwell
> 1935 The play version of *Tobacco Road* banned in Chicago.
> 1946 *God's Little Acre* banned in St. Paul.

1947 *God's Little Acre* banned in Denver.

1948 *God's Little Acre* seized in Philadelphia but wins a court fight.

1950 In a unanimous decision the Massachusetts Supreme Court bans *God's Little Acre*.

John Cleland

1821 When *Fanny Hill* is banned in Massachusetts, it becomes the first known obscenity case in the United States.

1963 *Fanny Hill* printed by Grove Press, but it takes a Supreme Court decision to allow its sale.

Samuel L. Clemens

1876 The Brooklyn and Denver public libraries ban *The Adventures of Tom Sawyer*.

1885 *The Adventures of Huckleberry Finn* banned by the Concord Public Library as "trash suitable only for the slums."

1905 The ban on Clemens's books is lifted from the children's room of the Brooklyn Public Library. Clemens replies later, "I wrote *Tom Sawyer* and *Huckleberry Finn* for adults exclusively, and it has always distressed me when I find boys and girls have been allowed access to them. The mind that becomes soiled in youth can never again be washed clean."

1957 Twain dropped from the list of approved reading for junior and senior high schools in New York state.

Charles R. Darwin

1925 In Dayton, Tennessee, John T. Scopes is fined one hundred dollars for teaching from *On the Origin of Species*. The state passes a law making it illegal to "teach any theory that denies the story of the Divine creation of man as taught in the Bible, and to teach instead that man was descended from a lower order of animals." This law remained in effect until 1967.

Theodore Dreiser

1900 An unknown number of copies of *Sister Carrie* appears before the publisher's wife intervenes and has the rest suppressed.

1916 The New York Society for the Suppression of Vice bans *The Genius*.

1930 *An American Tragedy* becomes required reading in a Harvard English course while at the same time a Boston Superior Court fines the publisher $300.

1958 *Sister Carrie* still banned in Vermont.

Faulkner

1948 Philadelphia police seize *Wild Palms, Mosquitoes,* and *Sanctuary:* it is almost a year before indictments are dismissed.

Flaubert
> 1954 The National Organization of Decent Literature bans *Madame Bovary*.

Nathaniel Hawthorne
> 1925 The National Board of Censorship forces the producers of the film version of *The Scarlet Letter* to change a few things; for one, Hester has to get married.

Ernest Hemingway
> 1930 *The Sun Also Rises* is banned in Boston.

> 1938 The only book suppressed during the year through the courts is *To Have and Have Not*.

> 1941 When *For Whom the Bell Tolls* is nominated for the Pulitzer Prize, Columbia University President Nicholas Murray Butler votes no; hence there is no Pulitzer Prize for fiction in 1940. The Post Office senses its cue and declares the book "unmailable."

> 1960 San Jose, California, bans *The Sun Also Rises* in all of its schools.

James Joyce
> 1918 Early installments of *Ulysses* printed in *The Little Review* are seized by the Post Office and burned.

> 1923 Random House defends *Ulysses* in court; Judge John Woolsey hands down his famous decision lifting the ban.

D. H. Lawrence
> 1922 John Sumner of the New York Society for the Suppression of Vice seizes *Women in Love* and declares it obscene.

> 1929 U. S. Customs bans *Lady Chatterley's Lover* and *Collected Paintings*.

> 1944 John Sumner seizes 400 copies of *Lady Chatterley's Lover* at the Dial Press in New York.

> 1959 The Post Office loses its case against *Lady Chatterley's Lover* after impounding all of Grove Press's copies.

Lenin
> 1940 In Oklahoma City vigilantes attack the bookshop of Mr. & Mrs. Robert Wood seizing copies of *The State and Revolution* along with the *Declaration of Independence* and the *United States Constitution* and selected works of fiction. At a later trial the Woods are sentenced to ten years in prison and fined $5,000, the only evidence against them being the works seized.

Sinclair Lewis
> 1927 *Elmer Gantry* banned in Boston.

1931 The Post Office forbids any catalog listing of *Elmer Gantry*.

Michelangelo

    1933 U. S. Customs "detains" *The Last Judgement* because it is part of "an obscene photo book."

Henry Miller

    1934 U. S. Customs bans *Tropic of Cancer*.

    1953 U. S. Court of Appeals continues the ban on both *Tropics*.

John O'Hara

    1941 *Appointment in Samarra* categorized "unmailable" by Post Office.

Eugene O'Neill

    1925 *Desire Under the Elms* closed by New York police.

    1929 When *Strange Interlude* is banned in Boston, it is moved to Quincy, Massachusetts.

Ovid

    1928 U. S. Customs still seizing and destroying *Ars Amatoria*.

Rabelais

    1930 The United States finally lifts the ban on all of his books except those "with obscene illustrations."

Bertrand Russell

    1929 *What I Believe* banned in Boston.

J. D. Salinger

    1955ff Perhaps the favorite target of modern American censors, *Catcher in the Rye*, has been banned somewhere in the United States yearly from 1955 to 1980.

Shakespeare

    1931 Jewish Organizations manage to ban the *Merchant of Venice* in Buffalo and Manchester, New York, high schools on grounds that the play is anti-Semitic. It is successfully banned in other schools as late as 1953.

Upton Sinclair

    1927 The Harding administration objects to comments in *Oil!*: immediately the book is banned in Boston.

Lillian Smith

    1944 *Strange Fruit* banned in Boston.

    1945 The Superior Court of Massachusetts confirms the earlier suppression of *Strange Fruit* and declares it a "menace to youth."

John Steinbeck

    1939 While the *Grapes of Wrath* is being burned in St. Louis; banned in Kern County, California; and successfully prosecuted in Kansas City, it is required reading at Princeton, Harvard, City College of New York, and the University of North Carolina.

Tolstoy

1890   The Post Office bans *The Kreutzer Sonata*, and Roosevelt says that the author is a "sexual and moral pervert."

Voltaire

1929   U. S. Customs "discovers" *Candide* and bars it even though it has been studied in American universities for years; copies were confiscated literally on their way to Harvard French classes.

Walt Whitman

1855   *Leaves of Grass* infuriates everybody: the Library Company of Philadelphia becomes the only known American library to buy a first edition in the year it is published.

Oscar Wilde

1895   *Salome* banned in Boston.

§ | *Kanawha County.* The most recent case of mass book banning taking place in this country involved a complicated series of events beginning with the 1970 campaign to suppress sex education in the schools of Kanawha County, West Virginia. A confrontation merely simmered until 1975 when some three hundred texts approved by a teacher committee got particularly close scrutiny from a fundamentalist group led by Mrs. Alice Moore. When the group moved to ban many of the titles, it got unexpected support from 3,500 coal miners who set up pickets throughout the county. Inexplicably, the wildcat strike swept into five other counties although the banned books were attacked only in the Kanawha County system. Even more puzzling was Rev. Marvin Horan's screaming "Pigs!" at policemen during a confrontation over books that sometimes referred to policemen as—"pigs." Listed among the "improper" books were those dealing with sex education, those by most major black authors, the *Iliad,* Plato's *Republic, Paradise Lost, Paradise Regained,* several novels by James Fenimore Cooper, *Moby-Dick, The Good Earth, The Old Man and the Sea, Catcher in the Rye, Animal Farm, Catch- 22,* and several language series by publishers Houghton Mifflin, Scott Foresman, D. C. Heath, and McDougal Littell. At this writing there remains no agreement on selection of textbooks to be used in the schools of Kanawha County.

Quotations

American Writers on American Writers

§ | *Henry Adams on Henry Adams.* "I want to look like an American Voltaire or Gibbon, but am slowly settling down to be a third-rate Boswell hunting for a Dr. Johnson."

§ | *. . . to William James.* "I have always said that you were far away the superior to your brother Henry, and that you could have cut him quite out, if you had turned your pen that way."

§ | *Conrad Aiken on William Faulkner.* "For if one thing is more outstanding than another about Mr. Faulkner—some readers find it so outstanding, indeed, that they never get beyond it—is the uncompromising and almost hypnotic zeal with which he insists on having a style, and, especially of late, the very peculiar style which he insists upon having."

§ | *. . . on E. A. Robinson.* "Mr. Robinson's method lies halfway between the tapestry effect of Morris and the melodrama of Wagner. Its chief excellence is an excellence of portraiture. And, again like James—of whom he is in many respects curiously a poetic counterpart—he particularly excels in his portraits of women."

§ | *Louisa May Alcott on Huckleberry Finn.* "If Mr. Clemens cannot think of something better to tell our pure-minded lads and lasses, he had best stop writing for them."

§ | *Richard Armour on Ezra Pound.* "It was Pound who thought up the name Imagists for the Imagists, who had been sitting around helplessly, wondering what to call themselves. But he himself soon left the Imagists and joined a more advanced group, the Vorticists. What attracted him to them was probably the mellifluous and descriptive name of their journal, *Blast*. He wished he had thought of it."

§ | . . . *on Ambrose Bierce.* "Some of Bierce's bitterness may have been caused by an unfortunate accident during the Civil War. In the Battle for Kennesaw Mountain, he received a musket ball through his head. Though the two holes eventually healed up, Bierce still felt hurt."

§ | . . . *on Henry James.* "Some find James hard to follow. It is not true, however, that a reader once wandered back and forth inside a pair of parentheses, unable to extricate himself, until he died of starvation. Never much concerned about plot, James developed his technique to such a point that he could write a full-length novel, such as *The Ambassadors,* in which nothing whatever happens. . . ."

§ | . . . *on James Russell Lowell.* "As a Harvard graduate and an editor for the *Atlantic Monthly*, it must have been difficult for Lowell to write like an illiterate oaf, but he succeeded."

§ | . . . *on Henry David Thoreau.* "Thoreau built himself a cabin on the shores of Walden Pond, near Concord, at a cost of $28.12½. At least that is what he told the county tax assessor when he came to appraise the place."

§ | . . . *on William Cullen Bryant.* "An unusual thing about Bryant is that he wrote his best poem, "Thanatopsis," when he was seventeen. Since he lived until he was eighty-four, and, try as he might, could never do quite as well again, he is not to be blamed for becoming a little morbid."

§ | . . . *on Sinclair Lewis.* "With the publication of *Main Street*, and even more with the publication of *Babbitt,* Lewis became a Successful Author, which meant that he drank heavily, was twice married and twice divorced, and was rude and insulting in public. He once made the mistake of being insulting in public to another author, Theodore Dreiser, who considered this plagiarism."

§ | *Joel Barlow on Thomas Paine.* "His private life disgraced his public character; certain immoralities, and low and vulgar habits, which are apt to follow in the train of almost habitual drunkenness rendered him a disgusting object for many of the latter years of his life, though his mental faculties retained much of their former luster."

§ | *Saul Bellow on F. Scott Fitzgerald.* "I often feel about Fitzgerald that he couldn't distinguish between innocence and social climbing."

§ | *Ambrose Bierce on Bret Harte.* "Bret Harte illuminated everything he touched. Now in shilling-shockers contracted for, years in advance at so many pounds a hundred words, he slaughters cowboys to make cockneys sit up or hashes up a short story to serve as jam between commercial sandwiches in sloppy popular magazines."

§ | . . . *on Stephen Crane.* "This young man has the power to feel. He knows nothing of war, yet he is drenched in blood. Most beginners who deal with the subject spatter themselves merely with ink. . . ."

§ | . . . *on James Whitcomb Riley.* ". . . affects the sensibilities like the ripple of a rill of buttermilk falling into a pig-trough. His pathos is bathos; his sentiment sediment, his 'homely philosophy' brute platitudes—beasts of the field of thought."

§ | *Morris Bishop on Ogden Nash.*

"Free from flashiness, free from trashiness
Is the essence of ogdenashiness.
Rich, original, rash, and rational
Stands the monument ogdenational!"

§ | *Maxwell Bodenheim on H. L. Mencken.* "H. L. Mencken suffers from the hallucination that he is H. L. Mencken—there is no cure for a disease of that magnitude."

§ | *The Boston Intelligencer on Leaves of Grass.* ". . . a heterogeneous mass of bombast, egotism, vulgarity, and nonsense."

§ | *Heywood Broun on Vachel Lindsay.* "Fundamentally, Mr. Lindsay is a remarkable poet; altogether he never comes to as much as he should. Probably he never had much of a chance. He grew up in the Babbit country. He was, when young, a Babbit himself, and to this day he has not ceased trying to transmute the activities of Babbitry into the stuff of dreams and fantasy."

§ | *Edgar Rice Burroughs on Edgar Rice Burroughs.* "I am sorry that I have not led a more exciting existence, so that I might offer a more interesting biographical sketch; but I am one of those fellows who has few adventures and always gets to the fire after it is out."

§ | *Truman Capote on Saul Bellow.* "Saul Bellow is a rarity among American novelists. He is not a child prodigy. I say *is* not because most of our "marvelous boys" have, in the face of time, stalwartly refused to age, have instead become elder statesmen—child prodigies, senile innocents, imaginary boys in real bull rings . . . . What is so remarkable about Bellow's career is that, while continuing to grow as a writer, he has risked transaction, each time out, with different uncharted territory of the novel."

§ | *. . . on Jack Kerouac.* "That's not writing—that's typing."

§ | *. . . on Truman Capote.* "I move in all worlds. I'm not snobbish, but I like people who are accomplished, people who are terribly brilliant or terribly amusing or terribly beautiful. I do *not* have an addiction to rich people. I have a lot of friends because they have great taste. One of the first things that interests me in anybody is the spectrum of their tastes. I call it the pursuit of excellence. An artist can't be a snob—they cancel each other out. But still, you wouldn't want to eat just a *rather* good oyster."

§ | *Phoebe Cary on John Greenleaf Whittier.*

"Thou hast battled for the right
  With many a brave and trenchant word,
And shown us how the pen may fight
  A mightier battle than the sword."

§ | *Raymond Chandler on Ernest Hemingway.* "Having just read the admirable profile of Hemingway in the *New Yorker* I realize that I am much too clean to be a genius, much too sober to be a champ, and far, far too clumsy with a shotgun to live the good life."

§ | *The Chicago Times on The Gettysburg Address.* "The cheek of every American must tingle with shame as he reads the silly, flat, and dishwatery utterances of the man who has to be pointed out to intelligent foreigners as the President of the United States."

§ | *Malcolm Cowley on John Dos Passos.* "As a result of the family situation he spent a lonely childhood in luxury hotels, always moving from city to city, always feeling himself the alien, always speaking the language with a foreign accent whether he was in France or Italy or Belgium—or in England, where he first went to school, or later among rich Americans at the Choate School in Connecticut—and never feeling at home except on trains or ocean steamers, where he could spend most of his time with a book held close to his gollywog glasses."

§ | . . . *on William Faulkner.* "There in Oxford (Mississippi), Faulkner performed a labor of imagination that has not been equalled in our time, and a double labor: first, to invent a Mississippi county that was like a mythical kingdom, but complete and living in all its details; second; to make his story of Yoknapatawpha County stand as a parable or legend of all the Deep South."

§ | *Hart Crane on Edmund Wilson.* "It is so damned easy for such as he, born into easy means, graduated from a fashionable university into a critical chair overlooking Washington Square, etc. to sit tight and hatch little squibs of advice to poets not to be so 'professional' as he claims they are. . . ."

§ | *E. E. Cummings on Ezra Pound.* "Pound is humane, but not human."

§ | *John Dos Passos on Hart Crane.* "Someone told me that when Hart finally met his end by jumping overboard from the Havana boat the last his friends on deck saw of him was a cheerful wave of the hand before he sank and drowned. That last friendly wave was very like Hart Crane."

§ | . . . *on E. E. Cummings.* "His mind was essentially extemporaneous. His fits of poetic fury were like the maenadic seizures described in Greek lyrics."

§ | . . . *on Theodore Dreiser.* "It was the ponderous battering ram of his novels that opened the way through the genteel reticences of American nineteenth century fiction for what seemed to me to be a truthful description of people's lives. Without Dreiser's treading out a path for naturalism none of us would have had a chance to publish even."

§ | . . . *remembering Edmund Wilson.* "There appeared a slight sandy-headed young man with a handsome clear profile. He wore a formal dark business suit. The moment we were introduced, while we were waiting for the elevator, Bunny gave an accent to the occasion by turning, with a perfectly straight face, a neat somersault."

§ | *Theodore Dreiser on William Dean Howells.* "He appeals to me as possessing a deeply religious nature unanchored to any religious belief."

§ | *Max Eastman on Mabel Dodge Luban.* "She has neither wit nor beauty, nor is she vivacious or lively minded or entertaining. She is comely and good-natured, and when she says something, it is sincere and sagacious, but for the most part she sits like a lump, and says nothing."

§ | *T. S. Eliot on T. S. Eliot.*

> "How unpleasant to meet Mr. Eliot!
> With his features of clerical cut,
> And his brow so grim
> And his mouth so prim
> And his conversation, so nicely
> Restricted to What Precisely
> And If and Perhaps and But."

§ | . . . *on Marianne Moore.* "Miss Moore is, I believe, one of the few who have done the language some service in my lifetime."

§ | . . . *on Henry James.* "The current of English literature was not appreciably altered by his work during his lifetime; and James will probably continue to be regarded as the extraordinarily clever but negligible curiosity."

§ | *Ralph Waldo Emerson on Edgar Allan Poe.* "Oh, you mean the jingleman!"

§ | . . . *on Nathaniel Hawthorne.* "Nathaniel Hawthorne's reputation as a writer is a very pleasing fact, because his writing is not good for anything, and this is a tribute to the man."

§ | . . . *on Amos Bronson Alcott.* "A. is a tedious archangel."

§ | . . . *on Henry David Thoreau.* "No truer American existed than Thoreau. His preference of his country and condition was genuine, and his aversion from English and European manners and tastes almost reached contempt. He listened impatiently to news or *bon-mots* gleaned from London circles; and though he tried to be civil, these anecdotes fatigued him. The men were all imitating each other, and on a small mold."

"Had his genius been only contemplative, he had been fitted to his life, but with his energy and practical ability he seemed born for great enterprise and for command; and I so much regret the loss of his rare powers of action, that I cannot help counting it a fault in him that he had no ambition. Wanting this, instead of engineering for all America, he was the captain of a Huckleberry-party. Pounding beans is good to the end of pounding empires one of these days; but if, at the end of years, it is still only beans!"

§ | . . . *on Leaves of Grass.* "The most extraordinary piece of wit and wisdom that America has yet contributed."

§ | *Clifton Fadiman on William Faulkner.* "Mr. Faulkner, of course, is interested in making your mind rather than your flesh creep."

§ | . . . *on Ambrose Bierce.* "Born in a log cabin, Ambrose Bierce defied Alger's Law and did not become President."

§ | *William Faulkner on Henry James.* ". . . the nicest old lady I ever met."

§ | *Edna Ferber on Alexander Woollcott.* "I want to be alone on this trip. I don't expect to talk to a man or a woman—just Aleck Woollcott."

§ | *Eugene Field on Hamlin Garland.* "Mr. Garland's heroes sweat and do not wear socks; his heroines eat cold huckleberry pie and are so unfeminine as not to call a cow 'he.' "

§ | *F. Scott Fitzgerald on Sherwood Anderson.* "As a matter of fact Anderson is a man of practically no ideas—but he is one of the very best and finest writers in the English language today. God, can he write."

§ | . . . *on Thomas Wolfe.* "His end was so tragic that I am glad I knew him in carefree and fortunate times. He had that flair for the extravagant and fantastic which has been an American characteristic from Irving and Poe to Dashiell Hammett."

§ | *. . . on Edith Wharton*. "Mrs. Wharton, do you know what's the matter with you? You don't know anything about life."

§ | *. . . on Ernest Hemingway*. "He's a great writer. If I didn't think so I wouldn't have tried to kill him. . . . I was the champ and when I read his stuff I knew he had something. So I dropped a heavy glass skylight on his head at a drinking party. But you can't kill the guy. He's not human."

§ | *Robert Frost on E. A. Robinson*. "Robinson was a prince of heartaches amid countless achers of another part. The sincerity he wrought was all sad. He asserted the sacred right of poetry to lean its breast to a thorn and sing its dolefullest. Let weasels suck eggs. I know better where to look for melancholy. A few superficial irritable grievances, perhaps, as was only human, but these are forgotten in the depth of griefs to which he has plunged us."

§ | *Margaret Fuller on Amos Bronson Alcott*. "He is a philosopher of the palmy times of ancient Greece—a man whom the worldings of Boston hold in as much horror as the worldings of Athens held Socrates."

§ | *Hamlin Garland on William Dean Howells*. "It requires more insight and more creative intelligence to write twenty successful novels—as Mr. Howells has done—without a single crime or unnatural vice in any of them, than to write a score of romances made up of murder, adultery, suicide, manslaughter, and all the other indispensable elements of the present-day romance."

§ | *. . . on Stephen Crane*. "With all his endowments he was not an admirable character. He gave out the effect of being an alley cat as far as habit went. And during the days when I first knew him in New York City he was living like an outcast. Although not a drinking man, he smoked incessantly and sometimes was thought to have used a drug of some kind."

§ | *Julian Hawthorne on Nathaniel Hawthorne*. "My father was two men, one sympathetic and intuitional, the other critical and logical; altogether they formed a combination that could not be thrown off its feet."

§ | *Nathaniel Hawthorne on Women Writers*. "America is now wholly given over to a damned mob of scribbling women, and I should have no chance of success while the public taste is occupied with their trash—and should be

ashamed of myself if I did succeed. What is the mystery of these in-
numerable editions of the 'Lamplighter,' and other books neither better nor
worse?—worse they could not be, and better they need not be, when they
sell by the 100,000.''

§ | . . . *on Henry Thoreau.* "He is as ugly as sin, long-nosed, queer-
mouthed, and with uncouth and somewhat rustic, although courteous
manners, corresponding very well with such an exterior. But his ugliness is
of an honest and agreeable fashion, and becomes him much better than
beauty. . . .''

§ | . . . *on William Cullen Bryant.* ". . . a very pleasant man to associate
with, but rather cold, I should imagine, if one should seek to touch his heart
with one's own.''

§ | *Paul Hamilton Hayne on Henry James.* "Just here I must pause to
comment upon the immense change which has taken place in the taste of
novel readers. Tens of thousand now believe that there is but *one* Divinity, or
potent inspirer of art in fiction, and that Mr. Henry James is his prophet.
This deity is 'Aesthetic Realism'—this art should have for its motto the
Knife-grinder's exclamation, 'Story! God bless your honor, I have none to
tell!' ''

§ | *Ben Hecht on H. L. Mencken.* "He edited a magazine called *The Smart Set*
which is like calling Cape Kennedy 'Lovers' Lane.' ''

§ | *Lillian Hellman on Dorothy Parker.* "But she was, more than usual, a
tangled fishnet of contradictions: she liked the rich because she liked the way
they looked, their clothes, the things in their houses, and she disliked them
with an open and baiting contempt; she believed in socialism but seldom,
except in the sticky sentimental minutes, could stand the sight of a working
radical; she drank far too much, spent far too much time with ladies who
did, and made fun of them and herself every inch of the way; she faked
interest and sympathy with those who bored her and for whom she had no
feeling, and yet I never heard her hit mean except where it was, in some
sense, justified. . . .''

§ | . . . *on Dashiell Hammett.* "He had patience, courage, dignity in those
last, awful months. It was as if all that makes a man's life had come together
to prove itself: suffering was a private matter and there was to be no invasion

of it. He would seldom even ask for anything he needed, and so the most we did—my secretary and Helen, who were devoted to him, as most women always had been—was to carry up the meals he barely touched, the books he now could hardly read, the afternoon coffee, and the martini that I insisted upon before the dinner that wasn't eaten."

§ | *Ernest Hemingway on Ezra Pound.* "Ezra was the most generous writer I have ever known and the most disinterested. He helped poets, painters, sculptors and prose writers that he believed in and he would help anyone whether he believed in them or not if they were in trouble. He worried about everyone. In the time when I first knew him he was most worried about T. S. Eliot who, Ezra told me, had to work in a bank in London and so had insufficient time and bad hours to function as a poet."

§ | *. . . on F. Scott Fitzgerald.* "His talent was as natural as the pattern that was made by the dust on a butterfly's wings. At one time he understood it not more than the butterfly did and he did not know when it was brushed or marred. Later he became conscious of his damaged wings and of their construction and he learned to think and could not fly any more because the love of flight was gone and he could only remember it when it had been effortless."

§ | *. . . on Gertrude Stein.* "Looked like a Roman emperor and that was fine if you liked your women to look like Roman emperors. But Picasso painted her, and I could remember her when she looked like a woman from Friuli."

§ | *Thomas Wentworth Higginson on Ralph Waldo Emerson.* "It must be left for future generations to determine Emerson's precise position even as a poet. There is seen in him the tantalizing combination of the profoundest thoughts with the greatest possible variation in artistic work—sometimes more boldness and almost waywardness, while at other times he achieves the most exquisite melody touched with a certain wild grace. He has been likened to an aeolian harp, which now gives and then perversely withholds its music."

§ | *. . . on Amos Bronson Alcott.* "Then, what Mr. Alcott called conversations, in his earlier days, were such startling improvisations, so full of seemingly studied whim and utter paradox, that those who went to learn remained to smile. There was plenty of thought in them, and much out-of-the-way literary knowledge; but, after all, the theories of race, food, genesis, and what not, left but little impression on the public mind."

§ | . . . *on John Greenleaf Whittier.* "Of his poetry it may thus safely be said that it has two permanent grounds of fame: he was the Tyrtaeus of the greatest moral agitation of the age, and he was the creator of the New England legend. He was also the exponent of a pure and comprehensive religious feeling; but this he shared with others, while the first two branches of the laurel were unmistakably his own."

§ | . . . *on Walt Whitman.* "Probably no poet of equal pretensions was ever so entirely wanting in the sentiment of individual love for woman; not only has he given us no love-poem, in the ordinary sense of the term, but it is as difficult to conceive of his writing one as of his chanting a serenade beneath the window of his mistress. His love is the blunt, undisguised attraction of sex to sex; and whether his appetite is directed toward a goddess or a streetwalker, a Queensberry or a handmaid, is to him absolutely unimportant."

§ | . . . *on Sidney Lanier.* "Lanier was a critic of the best kind, for his criticism is such as a sculptor receives from a brother sculptor, not such as he gets from the purchaser on the one side or the marble worker on the other."

§ | *Oliver Wendell Holmes on Nathaniel Hawthorne.* "Ah, well! I don't know that you will ever feel that you have really met him. He is like a dim room with a little taper of personality burning on the corner of the mantel."

§ | . . . *on John Greenleaf Whittier.* "Best loved and saintliest of our singing train."

§ | . . . *on Henry Adams.* "When I happened to fall in with him on the street, he could be delightful, but when I called at his house and he was posing to himself as the old cardinal he could turn everything to dust and ashes. After a tiresome day's work one didn't care to have one's powers of resistance taxed by discourse of that sort, so I called rarely."

§ | . . . *on Timothy Dexter.* "As an inventor of American style he goes far beyond Mr. Whitman, who, to be sure, cares little for the dictionary. I am afraid that Mr. Emerson and Mr. Whitman must yield the claim of declaring American literary independence to Lord Timothy Dexter, who not only taught his countrymen that they need not go to the Herald's College to authenticate their titles of nobility, but also that they were at perfect liberty to spell just as they liked, and to write without troubling themselves about stops of any kind."

§ | *William Dean Howells on Stephen Crane.* "Here is a young writer sprung into life fully armed."

§ | *. . . to Sarah Orne Jewett.* "Your voice is like a thrush's in the din of all the literary noises that stun us so."

§ | *. . . on Mark Twain.* "Once I remember seeing him come into his drawing-room at Hartford in a pair of white cowskin slippers, with the hair out, and do a cripple colored uncle to the joy of all beholders. Or, I must not say all, for I remember also the dismay of Mrs. Clemens, and her low despairing cry of 'Oh, Youth!' That was her name for him among their friends, and it fitted him as no other would, though I fancied with her it was a shrinking from his baptismal Samuel, or the vernacular Sam of his earlier companionship. He was a youth to the end of his days, the heart of a boy with the head of a sage. . . ."

§ | *. . . on John Greenleaf Whittier.* "There is a great inequality in his work, and I felt this so strongly that when I came to have full charge of the Magazine, I ventured once to distinguish. He sent me a poem, and I had the temerity to return it, and beg him for something else. He magnanimously refrained from all show of offence, and after a while, when he had printed the poem elsewhere, he gave me another. By this time, I perceived that I had been wrong, not as to the poem returned, but as to my function regarding him and such as he."

§ | *. . . on Oliver Wendell Holmes.* "His novels all belonged to an order of romance which was as distinctly his own as the form of dramatized essay which he invented in the *Autocrat*. If he did not think poorly of them, he certainly did not think too proudly, and I heard him quote with relish the phrase of a lady who had spoken of them to him as his 'medicated novels.' "

§ | *. . . on Harriet Beecher Stowe.* "As for the author of *Uncle Tom's Cabin* her syntax was such a snare to her that it sometimes needed the combined skill of the proofreaders and the assistant editor to extricate her. Of course nothing was ever written into her work, but in changes of diction, in correction of solecisms, in transposition of phrases, the text was largely rewritten in the margin of her proofs. The soul of her art was present, but the form was so often absent, that when it was clothed on anew, it would have been hard to say whose cut the garment was of in many places."

§ | . . . *on Booker T. Washington.* "He has lived heroic poetry, and he can, therefore, afford to talk simple prose."

§ | *Henry James on Louisa May Alcott.* "If Miss Alcott's experience of human nature has been small, as we should suppose, her admiration of it is nevertheless great."

§ | . . . *to Edith Wharton.* "Your only drawback is not having the homeliness and the inevitability and the happy limitation and the affluent poverty of a country of your own."

§ | . . . *on Nathaniel Hawthorne.* ". . . thoroughly American in all ways, in none more so than in the vagueness of his social distinction. He liked to fraternize with plain people, to take them on their own terms, and put himself, if possible, into their shoes."

§ | . . . *on Edgar Allan Poe.* "With all due respects to the very original genius of the author of *Tales of Mystery*, it seems to us to take him with more than a certain degree of seriousness is to lack seriousness one's self."

§ | . . . *on Walt Whitman.* "It exhibits the effort of an essentially prosaic mind to life itself, by prolonged muscular strain, into poetry."

§ | . . . *on Henry Thoreau.* ". . . literally the most childlike, unconscious and unblushing egoist it has ever been my fortune to encounter in the ranks of manhood."

§ | . . . *on James Russell Lowell.* "He was strong without narrowness, he was wide without bitterness and glad without fatuity."

§ | *Randall Jarrell on Wallace Stevens.* "Stevens's poetry makes one understand how valuable it can be for a poet to write a great deal. Not much of that great deal, ever, is good poetry; but out of quantity can come practice, naturalness, accustomed mastery. . . . Stevens has learned to write at will, for pleasure; his methods of writing, his ways of imagining, have made this possible for him as it is impossible for many living poets—Eliot, for instance."

§ | . . . *on Robert Frost.* "No other living poet has written so well about the actions of ordinary men. . . ."

§ | . . . *on John Crowe Ransom.* "In John Crowe Ransom's best poems every part is subordinated to the whole, and the whole is accomplished with astonishing exactness and thoroughness."

§ | . . . *on Marianne Moore.* "She shows us that the world is more poetic than we thought."

§ | . . . *on Robert Lowell.* "More than any other poet Robert Lowell is the poet of shock: his effects vary from crudity to magnificence, but they are always surprising and always his own—his style manages to make even quotations and historical facts a personal possession."

§ | *Thomas Jefferson on Noah Webster.* "I view Webster as a mere pedagogue, of very limited understanding."

§ | *Sidney Lanier on Edgar Allan Poe.* "The trouble with Poe is that he did not know enough."

§ | . . . *to Walt Whitman.* "Although I entirely disagree with you in all points of your doctrine as is involved in those poetic exposures of the person which your pages so unreservedly make, yet I feel sure that I understand you therein, and my dissent in these particulars becomes a very insignificant consideration in the presence of that unbounded delight which I take in the bigness and bravery of all your ways and thoughts. It is not known to me where I can find another modern song at once so large and so naive: and the time needs to be told few things so much as the absolute personality of the person, the sufficiency of the man's manhood *to* the man, which you have propounded in such strong and beautiful rhythms."

§ | *Sinclair Lewis on Theodore Dreiser.* "Dreiser more than any other man, marching alone, usually unappreciated, often hated, has cleared the trail from Victorian and Howellsian timidity and gentility in American fiction to honesty and boldness and passion of life."

§ | . . . *on Willa Cather.* "Her style is so deftly a part of her theme that to the uncomprehending, to the seeker after verbal glass jewels, she is not perceivable as a 'stylist' at all."

§ | . . . *on Ernest Hemingway.*

> "Mister Ernest Hemingway
> Halts his slaughter of the kudu
> To remind you that you may
> Risk his sacerdotal hoodoo
> If you go on, day by day,
> Talking priggishly as you do
> Speak up, man! Be bravely heard
> Bawling the four-letter word!
> And wear your mind décolleté
> Like Mister Ernest Hemingway."

§ | *Vachel Lindsay on O. Henry.*

> "This was that dubious hero of the press
> Whose slangy tongue and insolent address
> Were spiced to rouge on Sunday afternoon
> The man with yellow journals round him strewn.
> We laughed and dozed, then roused and read again,
> And vowed O. Henry funniest of men.
> He always worked a triple-hinged surprise
> To end the scene and make one rub his eyes."

§ | *Jack London on Ambrose Bierce.* "Bierce could bury his best friend with a sigh of relief and express satisfaction that he was done with him."

§ | *Henry Wadsworth Longfellow on William Cullen Bryant.* "He was my master in verse. . . ."

§ | *Amy Lowell on Walt Whitman.* "Whitman was like a prophet straying in a fog and shouting half-truths with a voice of great trumpets. He was seeking something, but he never knew quite what, and he never found it.

He vanishes in the mist, and his words float back, dim, superb, to us behind him.''

§ | *James Russell Lowell on Ralph Waldo Emerson.*

"But to come back to Emerson (whom, by the way
I believe we left waiting),—he is we may say,
A Greek head on right Yankee shoulders, whose range
Has Olympus for one pole, for t'other the Exchange;
He seems, to my thinking (although I'm afraid
The comparison must be, long ere this, have been made),
A Plotinus-Montaigne, where the Egyptian's gold mist
And the Gascon's shrewd wit cheek-by-jowl coexist;
All admire, and yet scarcely six converts he's got
To I don't (nor they either) exactly know what;
For though he builds glorious temples, 'tis odd
He leaves never a doorway to get in a god."

§ | *. . . on William Cullen Bryant.*

"There is Bryant, as quiet, as cool, and as dignified,
As a smooth, silent iceberg, that never is ignified,
Save when by reflection 'tis kindled o'nights
With a semblance of flame by the chill Northern Lights."

§ | *. . . on James Fenimore Cooper.*

"Here's Cooper, who's written six volumes to show
He's as good as a lord: well, let's grant that he's so;
If a person prefer that description of praise,
Why, a coronet's certainly cheaper than bays;
But he need take no pains to convince us he's not
(As his enemies say) the American Scott."

§ | *. . . on Edgar Allan Poe.*

"There comes Poe, with his raven, like Barnaby Rudge,
Three-fifths of him genius and two-fifths sheer fudge,
Who talks like a book of iambs and pentameters,
In a way to make people of common sense damn metres,
Who has written some things quite the best of their kind,
But the heart somehow seems all squeezed out by the mind. . . ."

§ | . . . *on James Russell Lowell.*

"There is Lowell, who's striving Parnassus to climb
With a whole bale of *isms* tied together with rhyme,
He might get on alone, spite of brambles and boulders,
But he can't with that bundle he has on his shoulders,
The top of the hill he will ne'er come nigh reaching
Till he learns the distinction 'twixt singing and preaching."

§ | . . . *on Margaret Fuller.*

"She always keeps asking if I don't observe a
Particular likeness 'twixt her and Minerva."

§ | . . . *on Leaves of Grass* ". . . a solemn humbug."

§ | *Archibald MacLeish on E. E. Cummings.* "There are very few people who deserve the word poet. Cummings was one of them."

§ | . . . *on Clifford Odets.* "Now the point I am trying to make is not that Clifford Odets is a good playwright nor that his work is better than anything else in New York. The first fact is pretty widely known and the second is obvious."

§ | *Norman Mailer on Truman Capote.* "Truman Capote I do not know well, but I like him. He is as tart as a grand aunt, but in his way he is a ballsy little guy, and he is the most perfect writer of my generation; he writes the best sentences word for word, rhythm upon rhythm."

§ | . . . *on Henry Miller.* "Compared to Melville, Miller's secondary work is more impressive and considerably more varied. There is not one Henry Miller, but twenty, and fifteen of those authors are very good. Of course when Miller is bad, he may be the worst great writer ever to be bad."

§ | . . . *on Henry James.* "The cruellest criticism ever delivered of Henry James is that he had a style so hermetic his pen would have paralyzed if one of his characters had ever entered a townhouse, removed his hat, and found crap on his head (a matter, parenthetically, of small moment to Tolstoy let us say, or Dostoyevsky, or Stendhal)."

§ | *Edgar Lee Masters on Mark Twain.* "The genius from Missouri was sensitive and tremulous, he was griefstricken and remorseful, he was superstitious and overbelieving, yet skeptical. In some particulars he loved the beautiful, but he was vulgar. He had a certain affection for his fellows, yet he distrusted and even despised them."

§ | *Carson McCullers on Katherine Anne Porter.* "She may be the greatest female writer in America now—but just wait until next year."

§ | *. . . on Carson McCullers.* "I have *more* to say than Hemingway, and God knows, I say it *better* than Faulkner."

§ | *Herman Melville on Nathaniel Hawthorne.* ". . . Nathaniel Hawthorne is a man as yet utterly mistaken among men. Here and there, in some quiet armchair in the noisy town, or some deep nook among the noiseless mountains, he may be appreciated for something of what he is. But unlike Shakespeare, who was forced to the contrary course by circumstances, Hawthorne (either through simple disinclination, or else from inaptitude) refrains from all the popularizing noise and show of broad farce, and blood-smeared tragedy; content with the still, rich utterances of a great intellect in repose, and which sends few thoughts into circulation, except they be arterialized at his large warm lungs, and expanded in his honest heart."

§ | *. . . on Ralph Waldo Emerson.* "I could readily see in Emerson, notwithstanding his merit, a gaping flaw. It was, the insinuation, that had he lived in those days when the world was made, he might have offered some valuable suggestions."

§ | *H. L. Mencken on Theodore Dreiser.* "I spent the better part of forty years trying to induce him to reform and electrify his manner of writing, but so far as I am aware with no more effect than if I had sought to [get him to] take up gold or abandon his belief in non-Euclidian arcana."

§ | *. . . on Ambrose Bierce.* "For all our professed delight in and capacity for jocosity we have produced so far but one genuine wit—Ambrose Bierce— and save to a small circle, he remains unknown today."

§ | *. . . on Ralph Waldo Emerson.* ". . . the cod-fish Moses."

§ | . . . *on O. Henry*. "I give him up. Either he is the best storyteller in the world today, or the worst. Sometimes I think he is the one and sometimes I am convinced that he is the other. Maybe he is both."

§ | . . . *on Willa Cather*. "One finds in every line of her writing a sure-footed and civilized culture; it gives her an odd air of foreignness. . . ."

§ | . . . *on James Branch Cabell*. "All efforts to make him popular will fail inevitably; he is far too mystifying a fellow to enchant the simple folk. . . ."

§ | . . . *on Sherwood Anderson*. "Of all American novelists, past or present, Sherwood Anderson is probably the one whose struggle to express himself was the most interesting."

§ | . . . *on Lewis' Babbitt*. "I know of no American novel that more accurately presents the real America. It is a social document of high order."

§ | . . . *on James' What Maisie Knew*. "—a perfect comedy, a riotous and delightful piece of Olympian foolery. . . ."

§ | *Henry Miller on Henry David Thoreau* "Viewed from the heights of our decadence, he seems almost like an early Roman. The word virtue has meaning again, when connected with his name."

§ | *George Jean Nathan on Eugene O'Neill*. "The truth about O'Neill is that he is the only American playwright who has what might be called 'size.' There is something relatively distinguished about even his failures; they sink not trivially but with a certain air of majesty like a great ship, its flags flying, full of holes."

§ | *Frank Norris on William Dean Howells*. "We ourselves are Mr. Howells's characters, so long as we are well behaved and ordinary and bourgeois, so long as we are not adventurous or not rich or not unconventional. If we are otherwise, if things commence to happen to us, if we kill a man or two, or get mixed up in a tragic affair, or do something on a large scale, such as the amassing of enormous wealth or power or fame, Mr. Howells cuts our acquaintance at once. He will none of us if we are out of the usual."

§ | *Flannery O'Connor on Henry James*. "There is no literary orthodoxy that can be prescribed as settled for the fiction writer, not even that of Henry

James, who balanced the elements of traditional realism and romance so admirably within each of his novels."

§ | *. . . on Southern Writers.* "In the South there are more amateur authors than there are rivers and streams. It's not an activity that waits upon talent. In almost every hamlet you'll find at least one lady writing epics in Negro dialect and probably two or three old gentlemen who have impossible historical novels on the way. The woods are full of regional writers, and it is the great horror of every serious Southern writer that he will become one of them."

§ | *. . . on Hawthorne.* "Hawthorne knew his own problems and perhaps anticipated ours when he said that he did not write novels, he wrote romances."

§ | *. . . on Teaching Southern Literature.* "When I went to college twenty years ago, nobody mentioned any good Southern writers to me later than Joel Chandler Harris, and the ones mentioned before Harris, with the exception of Poe, were not widely known outside the region. As far as I knew, the heroes of Hawthorne and Melville and James and Crane and Hemingway were balanced on the Southern side by Br'er Rabbit—an animal who can always hold up his end of the stick, in equal company, but here too much was being expected of him."

§ | *O. Henry on Walter Hines Page.* "Page could reject a story with a letter that was so complimentary and make everybody feel so happy that you could take it to a bank and borrow money on it."

§ | *Dorothy Parker on the Algonquin Round Table.* "These were no giants. Think of who was writing in those days—Lardner, Fitzgerald, Faulkner, and Hemingway. Those were the real giants. The Round Table was just a lot of people telling jokes and telling each other how good they were."

§ | *Dorothy Parker on Dorothy Parker.* "If I had any decency, I'd be dead. Most of my friends are."

§ | *Edgar Allan Poe on William Gilmore Simms.* ". . . immeasurably the best writer of fiction in America."

§ | *. . . on writers in general.* "The most 'popular,' the most 'successful' writers among us (for a brief period at least) are, ninety-nine times out of a hundred, persons of mere address, perseverance, effrontery—in a word, busy-bodies, toadies, quacks."

§ | . . . *on Henry Wadsworth Longfellow.* "His didactics are all out of place. He has written brilliant poems, by accident; that is to say, when permitting his genius to get the better of his conventional habit of thinking, a habit deduced from German study."

§ | . . . *on Nathaniel Hawthorne.* "For example, Mr. Hawthorne, the author of *Twice-Told Tales*, is scarcely recognized by the press or by the public, and when noticed at all, is noticed merely to be damned by faint praise. Now, my opinion of him is, that although his walk is limited, and he is fairly to be charged with mannerism, treating all subjects in a similar tone of dreamy *innuendo*, yet in his walk he evinces extraordinary genius, having no rival either in America or elsewhere; and this opinion I have never heard gainsaid by any one literary person in the country. That this opinion, however, is a spoken and not a written one, is referable to the facts, first, that Mr. Hawthorne is a poor man, and, secondly, that he is *not* an ubiquitous quack."

§ | . . . *on Edward Coote Pinckney.* "It was the misfortune of Mr. Pinckney to have been born too far south. Had he been born a New Englander, it is probable that he would have been ranked as the first of American lyrists, by that magnanimous cabal which has so long controlled the destinies of American Letters, in conducting the thing called *The North American Review*."

§ | *Katherine Anne Porter on Eudora Welty.* "Miss Welty escaped also a militant social consciousness, in the current radical-intellectual sense, she never professed communism, and she has not expressed, except implicitly, any attitude at all on the state of politics or the condition of society. But there is an ancient system of ethics, an unanswerable, indispensable moral law in which she is grounded firmly, and this, it would seem to me is ample domain enough. . . ."

§ | . . . *on Gertrude Stein.* "Miss Stein had no problems: she simply exploded a verb as if it were a soap bubble, used chthonian grammar long before she had heard it named (and she would have scorned to name it), was a born adept in occult hypnosis of language without even trying. Serious young men who were having a hard time learning to write realized with relief that there was nothing at all to do if you just relaxed and put down the first thing that came into your head. She gave them a romantic name, the Lost Generation, and a remarkable number of them tried earnestly if unsuccessfully to live up to it."

§ | . . . *on Ezra Pound*. "Ezra detested the 'private life,' denied that he ever had one, and despised those who were weak enough to need one. He was a warrior who lived on the battlefield, a place of contention and confusion, where a man shows all sides of himself without taking much thought for appearance."

§ | . . . *on Willa Cather*. "To her last day Willa Cather was the true child of her plain-living, provincial farming people, with their aristocratic ways of feeling and thinking; poor, but not poverty-stricken for a moment; rock-based in character, a character shaped in an old school of good manners, good morals, and the unchallenged assumption that classic culture was their birthright; the belief that knowledge of great art and great thought was a good in itself not to be missed for anything; she subscribed to it all with her whole heart. . . ."

§ | *Noah Porter on Walt Whitman*. "A generation cannot be entirely pure which tolerates writers who, like Walt Whitman, commit, in writing, an offence like that indictable at common law of walking naked through the streets."

§ | *Marjorie Kinnan Rawlings on Ernest Hemingway*. "He is so great an artist that he does not ever need to be on the defensive. He is so vast, so virile, that he does not ever need to hit anybody. Yet he is constantly defending something that he, at least, must consider vulnerable."

§ | *Gertrude Stein to Ernest Hemingway*. "That's what you all are. All of you young people who served in the war. You are a lost generation."

§ | . . . *on Gertrude Stein*. "Think of the Bible and Homer, think of Shakespeare and think of me."

§ | . . . *on Ezra Pound*. "A village explainer, excellent if you were a village, but if you were not, not."

§ | *John Steinbeck on Ernie Pyle*. "There are really two wars, and they haven't much to do with each other. There is the war of maps and logistics, of ballistics, armies, divisions, and regiments—and that is General Marshall's war.

Then there is the war of homesick, weary, funny, violent, common men, who wash their socks in their helmets, complain about the food, whistle at Arab girls, or any girls for that matter, and lug themselves through as dirty a business as the world has ever seen, and do it with humor and dignity and courage—and that is Ernie Pyle's war. He knows it as well as anyone and writes about it better than anyone else."

§ | *Harriet Beecher Stowe on Harriet Beecher Stowe.* "I no more thought of style or literary excellence than the mother who rushes into the street and cries for help to save her children from a burning house thinks of the teachings of the rhetorician or the elocutionist."

§ | *Allen Tate on Emily Dickinson.* "Her poetry is a magnificent personal confession, blasphemous and, in its self-revelation, its honesty, almost obscene. It comes out of an intellectual life towards which it feels no moral responsibility. Cotton Mather would have burnt her for a witch."

§ | *. . . on Edgar Allan Poe.* "If he was a madman, he was also a gentleman."

§ | *Edward Thompson Taylor on Ralph Waldo Emerson.* "Mr. Emerson is one of the sweetest creatures God ever made; there is a screw loose somewhere in the machinery, yet I cannot tell where it is, for I never heard it jar. He must go to heaven when he dies, for if he went to hell, the devil would not know what to do with him. But he knows no more of the religion of the New Testament than Balaam's ass did about the principles of Hebrew grammar."

§ | *Henry David Thoreau on Amos Bronson Alcott.* "Alcott is a geometer, a visionary, the Laplace of ethics, more intellect, less of the affections, sight beyond talents, a substratum of practical skill and knowledge unquestionable, but overlaid and concealed by a faith in the unseen and impracticable."

§ | *. . . on Leaves of Grass.* "As for the sensuality in Whitman's *Leaves of Grass*, I do not so much wish that it was not written, as that men and women were so pure that they could read it without harm."

§ | *. . . on Ralph Waldo Emerson.* "Emerson says that he and Agassiz and Company broke some dozens of ale-bottles, one after another, with their bullets, in the Adirondack country, using them for marks! It sounds very Cockneyish. He says that he shot a peetweet for Agassiz, and this, I think he said, was the first game he ever bagged. He carried a double barrelled gun—rifle and shotgun—which he bought for the purpose, which he says received much commendation—all parties thought it a very pretty piece. Think of Emerson shooting a peetweet (with shot) for Agassiz, and cracking an ale bottle (after emptying it) with his rifle at six rods!"

§ | *. . . on Margaret Fuller*. "Wheresoever her eye rests, our indolence and indulgence, our way of life and want of heroic action are shamed."

§ | *Henry Timrod on Edgar Allan Poe*. "The theory of Poe leads directly to the conclusion (and this he boldly avows) that Tennyson is the noblest Poet who ever lived; since no other poet that ever lived possessed so much of that ethereality and dim suggestiveness which Poe regards, if not as the sole, at least as the highest characteristic of a poem. I am constrained to add that while the theory leads to the conclusion that Tennyson is the noblest of poets, it leads as surely to the conclusion that Poe is the next noblest."

§ | *Mabel Loomis Todd on Emily Dickinson*. "His sister Emily is called in Amherst 'the myth.' She has not been out of her house for fifteen years. One inevitably thinks of Miss Haversham in speaking of her. She writes the strangest poems, & very remarkable ones. She is in many respects a genius. She wears always white, & has her hair arranged as was the fashion fifteen years ago when she went into retirement. She wanted me to come & sing to her, but she would not see me. She has frequently sent me flowers & poems & we have a very pleasant friendship in that way."

§ | *Mark Twain on James Fenimore Cooper*. "Cooper's gift in the way of invention was not a rich endowment; but such as it was, he liked to work it, he was pleased with the effects, and indeed he did some quite sweet things with it. In his little box of stage properties he kept six or eight cunning devices, tricks, artifices for his savages and woodsmen to deceive and circumvent each other with, and he was never so happy as when he was working these innocent things and seeing them go. A favorite one was to make a moccasined person tread in the tracks of the moccasined enemy, and thus hide his own trail. Cooper wore out barrels and barrels of moccasins working that trick. Another stage property that he pulled out of his box pretty frequently was his broken twig. He prized his broken twig above all the rest of his effects, and worked it the hardest. It is a restful chapter in any book of his when somebody doesn't step on a dry twig and alarm all the reds and whites for two hundred yards around. Every time a Cooper person is in peril, and absolute silence is worth four dollars a minute, he is sure to step on a dry twig. There may be a hundred handier things to step on, but that wouldn't satisfy Cooper. Cooper requires him to turn out and find a dry twig; and if he can't do it, go and borrow one. In fact, the Leatherstocking series ought to be called the Broken Twig Series."

§ | *. . . on Bret Harte.* "In the early days I liked Bret Harte, and so did the others; but by and by I got over it; so did the others."

§ | *. . . on Joel Chandler Harris.* "He was the bashfulest grown person I have ever met. When there were people about he stayed silent and seemed to suffer until they were gone. But he was lovely nevertheless, for the sweetness and benignity of the immortal Remus looked out from his eyes and the traces and sincerities of his character shone in his face."

§ | *. . . on Thomas Bailey Aldrich.* "The justification for an Aldrich Memorial Museum for pilgrims to visit and hallow with their homage may exist, but to me it seems doubtful. Aldrich was never widely known; his books never attained a wide circulation; his prose was diffuse, self-conscious and barren of distinction in the matter of style. . . ."

§ | *. . . on Mark Twain.* "When I was younger, I could remember anything, whether it had happened or not; but my faculties are decaying now and soon I shall be so I cannot remember any but the things that never happened. It is sad to go to pieces like this but we all have to do it."

§ | *. . . on George Washington Cable.* "Cable's gifts of mind are greater and higher than I had suspected. But—that 'But' is pointing toward his religion. You will never, never know, never divine, guess, imagine, how loathsome a thing the Christian religion can be made until you come to know and study Cable daily and hourly."

§ | *. . . on Benjamin Franklin.* "What an adroit old adventurer the subject of this memoir was! In order to get a chance to fly his kite on Sunday he used to hang a key on the string and let on to be fishing for lightning."

§ | *Carl Van Doren on William Dean Howells.* ". . . an author so prolific during the sixty years between his earliest book and his latest that he amounts almost to a library in himself, as an editor and critic so influential that he amounts almost to a literary movement."

§ | *Gore Vidal on Carson McCullers.* "Unlike too many other 'legends,' she was as real as her face."

§ | *. . . on Ernest Hemingway.* "Ernest Hemingway in *A Farewell to Arms* did a few good descriptions, but his book, too, is a work of ambition, in which can be seen the beginning of the careful, artful, immaculate idiocy of tone that since has marked both his prose and his legend as he has declined into that sort of fame which, at moments I hope are weak, Mailer seems to crave."

§ | *. . . on Norman Mailer.* "Despite a nice but small gift for self-destruction, he is uncommonly adroit, with an eye to the main chance. . . ."

§ | *Robert Penn Warren on William Faulkner.* "If respect for the human is the central fact of Faulkner's work, what makes that fact significant is that he realizes and dramatizes the difficulty of respecting the human."

§ | *. . . on Theodore Dreiser.* "Theodore Dreiser once said that his philosophy of love might be called 'Varietism.' But there was one mistress to whom he remained faithful, after his fashion, all his life. That mistress was the bitch goddess Success. He knew all her failings and falsities. He knew that her sweetest kiss would turn to ashes on the tongue. But he could never forget her face. All his stories are about her."

§ | *. . . on Melville's Poetry.* "It must be admitted that Melville did not learn his craft. But the point is that the craft that he did not learn was not the same craft which some of his more highly advertised contemporaries did learn with such glibness of tongue and complacency of spirit."

§ | *Booker T. Washington on Frederick Douglass.* "The life of Frederick Douglass is the history of American slavery epitomized in a single human experience. He saw it all, lived it all, and overcame it all."

§ | *George Whitman (brother of Walt) on Leaves of Grass.* "I saw the book, but I didn't read it at all—didn't think it worth reading. Mother thought as I did."

§ | *Walt Whitman on Sidney Lanier.* "Never simple, never easy, never in one single lyric natural and spontaneous for more than one stanza, always concealing his barrenness and tameness by grotesque violence to language and preposterous storm of sound, Lanier appears to me to be as conclusively not a poet of genius as any man who ever lived, labored, and failed."

§ | . . . *on James Russell Lowell.* "Lowell was not a grower—he was a builder. He *built* poems: he didn't put in the seed, and water the seed, and send down his sun—letting the rest take care of itself: he measured his poems—kept them within the formula."

§ | . . . *on Walt Whitman.* "I am as bad as the worst, but thank God I am as good as the best."

§ | *Richard Wilbur on Edgar Allan Poe.* "Poe's mind may have been a strange one; yet all minds are alike in their general structure; therefore, we can understand him, and I think he will have something to say to us as long as there is civil war in the palaces of men's minds."

§ | *William Carlos Williams on Marianne Moore.* "It is a talent which diminishes the tom-toming on the hollow men of a wasteland to an irrelevant pitter-patter. Nothing is hollow or waste to the imagination of Marianne Moore."

§ | *Tennessee Williams on Gore Vidal.* ". . . I was quite taken by his wit as well as his appearance. We found that we had interests in common and spent a lot of time together. Please don't imagine that I'm suggesting that there was a romance. We merely enjoyed conversation and a lot of laughing together."

§ | . . . *on Ernest Hemingway.* "He was exactly the opposite of what I expected. I had expected a very manly, super-macho sort of guy, very bullying and coarse spoken. On the contrary, Hemingway struck me as a gentleman who seemed to have a very touchingly shy quality about him."

§ | . . . *on Truman Capote.* "In those days Truman was about the best companion you could want. He had not turned bitchy. Well, he had not turned *maliciously* bitchy. He was full of fantasies and mischief."

§ | . . . *on William Faulkner.* "I felt a terrible torment in the man. He always kept his eyes down. We tried to carry on a conversation but he would never participate. Finally he lifted his eyes once to a direct question from me, and the look in his eyes was so terrible, so sad, that I began to cry."

§ | *Edmund Wilson on Sidney Lanier.* "And yet there was something that commends our respect, even our admiration. In his life he was, in a real sense, heroic; his passion for art was intense; it sustained him through many miseries; and the work that he was doing at the time of his death seems to show that he was becoming a first-rate artist."

§ | *. . . on Ambrose Bierce.* ". . . he detested the melodrama that the Northerners had made of the Civil War. On one of his visits to the South, he found, in a little West Virginia valley, a graveyard of Confederate soldiers who had fallen in one of the battles in which he had taken part, and he wrote of them—in a piece called *A Bivouac with the Dead*—with a tenderness that was very rare with him. . . ."

§ | *. . . on Oliver Wendell Holmes.* "It is Holmes's special distinction—which perhaps makes him unique among judges—that he never dissociates himself from the great world of thought and art, and that all his decisions are written with awareness of both their wider implications and the importance of their literary form."

§ | *. . . on George Washington Cable.* "George Cable emerges in New Orleans as a phenomenon which could not have been predicted and of which, as a matter of fact, neither Northerners nor Southerners knew what to make."

§ | *. . . on Carl Sandburg.* ". . . there are moments when one is tempted to feel that the cruelest thing that has happened to Lincoln since he was shot by Booth has been to fall into the hands of Carl Sandburg."

§ | *. . . on Henry B. Fuller.* ". . . a unique and distinguished writer who does not deserve to be dumped in the drawer devoted to regional novelists for a chapter in academic literary history."

§ | *. . . on Harold Frederic.* "Henry Fuller was a discreet homosexual and at the same time something of a puritan. But the appetite of Harold Frederic for attractive women was indomitable and persistent. It appears in Frederic's work as well as his publicly irregular life. In his novels, he violated the genteel conventions by allowing sex often to figure in its rawest, least romantic form, though he makes an effort to veil it from the more squeamish of his readers."

§ | . . . *on Ernest Hemingway.* "It always surprised me that the more or less imaginary Hemingway, the myth about himself that he managed to create by the self-dramatization of his extensive publicity and, in his fiction, by the exploits of some of his heroes, should have imposed on the public to the extent that it did."

Writers on the Profession of Writing

§ | *Erskine Caldwell.* "I think that you must remember that a writer is a simple-minded person to begin with and go on that basis. He's not a great mind, he's not a great thinker, he's not a philosopher; he's a story-teller."

§ | *John Ciardi.* "You don't have to suffer to be a poet. Adolescence is suffering enough for anyone."

§ | *John Dos Passos.* "If there is a special hell for writers, it would be the forced contemplation of their own works."

§ | *R. W. Emerson.* "If a man have genius for painting, poetry, music, architecture, or philosophy, he makes a bad husband and an ill provider."

"Talent alone cannot make a writer. There must be a man behind the book."

§ | *John Farrar.* "Great editors do not discover or produce great authors; great authors create and produce great publishers."

§ | *William Faulkner.* "The only environment the artist needs is whatever peace, whatever solitude, and whatever pleasure he can get at not too high a cost."

"A writer is congenitally unable to tell the truth and that is why we call what he writes fiction."

§ | *Benjamin Franklin.* "Write with the learned. Pronounce with the vulgar."

§ | *Robert Frost.* "Poetry is a way of taking life by the throat."

§ | *Margaret Fuller*. "It does not follow that because many books are written by persons born in America that there exists an American literature. Books which imitate or represent the thoughts and life of Europe do not constitute an American literature. Before such can exist, an original idea must animate this nation and fresh currents of life must call into life fresh thoughts along its shores."

§ | *Nathaniel Hawthorne*. "I don't want to be a doctor, and live by man's diseases; nor a minister to live by their sins; nor a lawyer to live by their quarrels. So I don't see there's anything left for me but to be an author."

§ | *Ben Hecht*. "I'm a Hollywood writer; so I put on a sports jacket and take off my mind."

§ | *Ernest Hemingway*. "We are all apprentices in a craft where no one ever becomes a master."
"No classic resembles any previous classic, so do not be discouraged."

§ | *Lillian Hellman*. "Decision by democratic majority is a fine form of government, but it's a stinking way to create."

§ | *Oliver Wendell Holmes*. "A lecturer is a literary strumpet, subject for a greater than whore's fee to prostitute himself."

§ | *Robinson Jeffers*. "I write verses myself, but I have no sympathy with the notion that the world owes a duty to poetry, or any other art. Poetry is not a civilizer, rather the reverse, for great poetry appeals to the most primitive instincts. It is not necessarily a moralizer; it does not necessarily improve one's character; it does not even teach good manners. It is a beautiful work of nature, like an eagle or a high sunrise. You owe it not duty. If you like it, listen to it; if not, let it alone."

§ | *Gypsy Rose Lee*. "Royalties are nice and all that but shaking the beads brings in money quicker."

§ | *John P. Marquand*. "You don't get better by worrying. You get better by writing and you have to do it every day—for hours."

§ | *Groucho Marx*. "Practically everybody in New York has half a mind to write a book—and does."

§ | *H. L. Mencken.* "The impulse to create beauty is rather rare in literary men. . . . Far ahead of it comes the yearning to make money. And after the yearning to make money comes the yearning to make a noise."

"Poetry is a comforting piece of fiction set to more or less lascivious music."

§ | *George Jean Nathan.* "Perhaps the saddest lot that can befall mortal man is to be the husband of a lady poet."

§ | *Thomas Paine.* "A man may write himself out of a reputation when nobody else can do it."

§ | *Dorothy Parker.*

> "Authors and actors and artists and such
> Never know nothing, and never know much.
> Sculptors and singers and those of their kidney
> Tell their affairs from Seattle to Sydney.
> Playwrights and poets and such horses' necks
> Start off from anywhere, and end up at sex.
> Diarists, critics and similar roe
> Never say nothing and never say no.
> People Who Do Things exceed my endurance;
> God, for a man that solicits insurance!"

"The only 'ism' Hollywood believes in is plagiarism."
"He is a writer for the ages—the ages of four to eight."

§ | *Katherine Anne Porter.* "Most people don't realize that writing is a craft. You have to take your apprenticeship in it like anything else."

§ | *John Crowe Ransom.*

> "God have mercy on the sinner
> Who must write with no dinner,
> No gravy and no grub,
> No pewter and no pub,
> No belly and no bowels,
> Only consonants and vowels."

§ | *Carl Sandburg.* "Poetry is the achievement of the synthesis of hyacinths and biscuits."

§ | *John Steinbeck*. "The profession of book-writing makes horseracing seem like a solid, stable business."

§ | *Mark Twain*. "A classic is something that everybody wants to have read and nobody wants to read."

§ | *E. B. White*. "Writing is an act of faith, not a trick of grammar."

Writers on Critics

§ | *Josh Billings*. "Silence is one of the hardest arguments to refute."

§ | *Jim Bishop*. "A good writer is not, per se, a good book critic. No more so than a good drunk is necessarily a good bartender."

§ | *Samuel L. Clemens*. "The trade of critic, in literature, music, and the drama is the most degraded of all trades."

"The public is the only critic whose opinion is worth anything at all."

"Only kings, editors, and people with tapeworm have the right to use the editorial 'we.' "

"It is the will of God that we must have critics, and missionaries, and congressmen, and humorists, and we must bear the burden."

"The critic's symbol should be the tumble-bug; he deposits his egg in somebody else's dung, otherwise he could not hatch it."

§ | *Ralph Waldo Emerson*. "It is not observed that . . . librarians are wiser men than others."

§ | *William Faulkner*. "The artists who want to be writers, read the reviews; the artists who want to write, don't."

§ | *Lillian Hellman*. "Cynicism is an unpleasant way of saying the truth."

§ | *Oliver Wendell Holmes*. "Nature, when she invented, manufactured, and patented her authors, contrived to make critics out of the chips that were left."

§ | *Washington Irving*. "Critics are a kind of freebooters in the republic of letters, who, like deer, goats, and diverse other graminivorous animals, gain subsistence by gorging upon buds and leaves of the young shrubs of the forest, thereby robbing them of their verdure and retarding their progress to maturity."

§ | *Henry James*. "The practice of 'reviewing' . . . has nothing in common with the art of criticism."

§ | *Henry Wadsworth Longfellow*. "Critics are sentinels in the grand army of letters, stationed at the corners of newspapers and reviews, to challenge every new author."

"Some critics are like the chimney-sweepers; they put out the fire below, and frighten the swallows from the nests above; they scrape a long time in the chimney, cover themselves with soot, and bring nothing away but a bag of cinders, and then sing out from the top of the house as if they had built it."

§ | *James Russell Lowell*. "Nature fits all her children with something to do;/He who would write and can't write can surely review."

"A wise scepticism is the first attribute of a good critic."

§ | *John P. Marquand* to Herman Wouk (after publication of *The Caine Mutiny*). "The critics will be waiting for you with meat cleavers the next time around."

§ | *George Jean Nathan*. "The drama critic who is without prejudice is on the plane with the general who does not believe in taking human life."

§ | *Dorothy Parker*. "You can lead a horticulture, but you can't make her think."

§ | *John Steinbeck*. "One man was so mad at me that he ended his letter, 'Beware. You will never get out of this world alive.' "

§ | *E. B. White*.

> "The critic leaves at curtain fall
> To find, in starting to review it,
> He scarcely saw the play at all
> For watching his reaction to it."

§ | *Alexander Woollcott*. "Unbridled enthusiasm, incredible elasticity, and tumultuous overpraise are distinguishing marks of the whole platoon. The dramatic critics of New York, ranging as they do from the late twenties to the early eighties, and extraordinarily varied in their origins, education, intelligence, and personal beauty, are alike in one respect. They are all be-troubled Pollyannas."

"It is probably not necessary for a critic to be insane to survive all those opening nights, but I assure you that it helps."

Last Words

§ | *Henry Adams*. Apparently to his secretary. "Dear child, keep me alive."

§ | *Louisa May Alcott*. "Is it not meningitis?"

§ | *Thomas Bailey Aldrich*. "In spite of all I am going to sleep."

§ | *Josh Billings*. "My doctors east ordered a rest of brain, but you can see I do not have to work my brain for a simple lecture: it comes spontaneously."

§ | *Hart Crane*. Dived from a passenger ship to drown himself. "Good-bye, everybody!"

§ | *Stephen Crane*. "Robert, when you come to the hedge that we must all go over, it isn't so bad. You feel sleepy, and you don't care. Just a little dreamy anxiety, which world you're really in, that's all."

§ | *Emily Dickinson*. There are conflicting versions of her last words. One is, "I must go in, the fog is rising." Another, supposedly in reference to a drink of water she was offered, is, "Oh, is that all it is?"

§ | *Ralph Waldo Emerson*. To Amos Bronson Alcott. "Good-bye my friend."

§ | *F. Scott Fitzgerald*. When Sheila Graham offered him some Hershey candy bars, he said, "Good enough: they'll be fine." Suddenly he stood to grab at the mantel before him and then fell.

§ | *Benjamin Franklin*. His daughter helped him to change position in bed to which Franklin said, "A dying man can do nothing easy."

§ | *Joel Chandler Harris*. "I am about the extent of a tenth of a gnat's eyebrow better."

§ | *Oliver Wendell Holmes*. About an oxygen tent being prepared for him. "A lot of damn foolery."

§ | *Robert E. Howard*. Typed a couplet before committing suicide.

> "All fled—all done, so lift me on the pyre;
> The feast is over and the lamps expire."

§ | *William Dean Howells*. Writing about Henry James. "Our walks by day were only in one direction and in one region. We were always going to Fresh pond, in those days a wandering space of woods and water where people skated in winter and boated in summer."

§ | *Washington Irving*. "Well, I must arrange my pillows for another night. When will this end?"

§ | *Henry James*. "So here it is at last, the distinguished thing."

§ | *Thomas Jefferson*. Died July 4, 1826, fifty years exactly after the signing of his great document and fell unconscious after asking, "Is it the fourth?"

§ | *Jack London*. Written to his daughter, Joan. "I leave California Wednesday following. Daddy."

§ | *Cotton Mather*. "Is this dying? Is this all? Is this all I feared when I prayed against a hard death? Oh, hear this! I can bear it! I am going to where all tears will be wiped from my eyes."

§ | *Herman Melville*. Spoke exactly the same last words as his own character Billy Budd. "God bless Captain Vere!"

§ | *Edgar Allan Poe*. "Lord, help my poor soul."

§ | *William Sydney Porter*. "Turn up the lights. I don't want to go home in the dark."

§ | *Damon Runyan*. "You can keep the things of bronze and stone and give me one man to remember me just once a year."

§ | *Gertrude Stein*. There are several published versions of these last words—"The answer? What is the answer?" Pause. "In that case, what is the question?"

§ | *Henry David Thoreau*. Words purportedly sounding like, "Moose. Indian."

§ | *Mark Twain*. To his daughter Clara. "Good-bye. If we meet. . . ."

§ | *Booker T. Washington*. "Take me home. I was born in the South; I have lived and labored in the South; and I wish to die and be buried in the South."

§ | *Daniel Webster*. "Wife, children, doctor, I trust on this occasion I have said nothing unworthy of Daniel Webster."

§ | *John Greenleaf Whittier*. To the nurse pulling the shades in his room. "No! No!"

§ | *Thomas Wolfe*. Dying after a brain operation, answered his sister who'd called his name. "All right, Mable. I'm coming. . . ."

Realities

§ | *Introduction*. It is probably true in some sense that every fictional character has been inspired at least in some minuscule way by a real person. Such observation is neither astonishing nor particularly helpful to students and scholars who must deal in specifics, but as Irving Wallace points out in a fascinating history called *The Fabulous Originals,* when an author bases his characters on recognizable models, he interests more than biographers—he flavors his writing in a way to interest all of those who know the story of his "originals." In this chapter are short essays on some real people who have appeared in disguise throughout American letters.

§ | *Mary*. There are those who assume that all of the Mother Goose poems are simply nonsense rhymes. Not so, say certain scholars who claim that the Mary who "had a little lamb" was a real child. Her name was Mary Elizabeth Sawyer, a Massachusetts schoolgirl who took responsibility for one of two lambs which had been abandoned by a ewe. When the lamb accompanied Mary to school, she slipped it under a desk, covering it with her shawl until a suspicious teacher expelled the unwanted visitor. According to the story, another visitor to the school, this one a student named Rawlston or Rallston, gave Mary Sawyer the first two or three verses of the immortal poem and apparently faded into obscurity without knowing of his contribution to world literature.

§ | *Evangeline*. On September 5, 1755, the governor of Nova Scotia issued a proclamation to the French colonists of the island. King George II had ordered that the Acadians be dispersed and that "their lands and tenements, cattle of all kinds, and live stock [be] forfeited to the Crown. . . ." Five days later the evacuation began, separating parents and children, husbands and wives, maids and lovers. Some of the colonists found refuge on Prince Edward Island; a few settled on New Brunswick's coast; and still others wandered into the interior of the United States. It was this latter group that greatly interested a friend of Nathaniel Hawthorne.

According to several sources, Hawthorne, in the company of a learned clergyman, once visited Henry Wadsworth Longfellow at Craigie House. During dinner the clergyman tried to interest Hawthorne in the tale of a young Acadian girl who had been separated from her lover in the dispersal of 1755: after searching for some years in the Mississippi Valley she had at last found her young man, now grown old, dying in a hospital. Although Longfellow seemed profoundly moved by the tale, Hawthorne remained cool toward using the idea in one of his own works. At last Longfellow ventured that it might make a good poem, and immediately his guest surrendered any literary claims on it.

Over the next several months Longfellow read what histories of Nova Scotia he could find and gathered more information on the families which had been moved; he even wrote to Hawthorne suggesting that the Acadian wanderings would make a fine background for a gothic romance, but Hawthorne insisted that he had no interest. So Longfellow returned to his poem of the young girl, whom he now called Evangeline, and made her the single most famous heroine in American literature during the nineteenth century.

§ | *Charlotte Temple.* Scholars know nothing definite about the young woman who inspired Susanna Haswell Rowson's eighteenth century bestseller: only a few names and a sentimental anecdote have survived since the first American publication of the novel in 1794. The title of this book is *Charlotte Temple: A Tale of Truth*, but the name of the real heroine was Charlotte Stanley. Even though the plot betrays an obvious debt to *Pamela* and *Clarissa*, Mrs. Rowson added just enough truth from the lives of Charlotte Stanley and another real person, Colonel John Montresor of the Royal Engineers, to make *Charlotte Temple* a sensation in its own day. Apparently the sorrow and sentiment appealed to succeeding generations too, for in its first one hundred years the book went through two hundred editions. When Miss Stanley died, her body was laid to rest in New York's Trinity churchyard; and soon the grave became a meeting place for lovers and then a major tourist attraction. Sometime during the nineteenth century an anonymous admirer of Mrs. Rowson struck out the name *Stanley* on the gravestone and changed it to read *Charlotte Temple*.

§ | *Mrs. Beauchamp, Miss Rogers, and Mrs. Stanard.* Contemplating the death of a beautiful woman moved Edgar Allan Poe to write some of his best work and some of his worst. In at least two cases he wrote about real women. With the first instance, John Pendleton Kennedy, his benefactor and friend, wrote in 1835 that Poe "is at work upon a tragedy but I have turned him to drudging upon whatever may make money." However, Poe did not abandon the play although it never made money and never secured a place in literary histories. It was called *Politian*.

Considerably before Kennedy's letter, newspapers across the country had given broad play to what became known as the "Kentucky Tragedy," a lurid murder and suicide involving the Attorney General of the state. What Poe undoubtedly read was an account of Jeroboam O. Beauchamp killing Attorney General Solomon P. Sharp, who had seduced Mrs. Beauchamp. The remorseful wife committed suicide and Beauchamp himself attempted suicide shortly before he was hanged. Thomas Holley Chivers used the case for his *Conrad and Eudora,* and so did William Gilmore Simms for his *Beauchamp.* Poe changed the events to a classical setting and used the devices of Elizabethan revenge tragedy; however, *Politian* could not compete with the newspapers, and Poe turned elsewhere in his desperate battle against poverty.

In 1837 and '38 Poe frequented the tobacco shop of John Anderson, located at 319 Broadway in New York: there he could mingle with his more successful contemporaries such as James Fenimore Cooper, and there he met the beautiful salesgirl Mary Cecilia Rogers. One can only imagine his thoughts some three years later when Poe read that the body of Mary Rogers had been found in the Hudson River on July 28, 1841: she had been battered and strangled. Newspapers exploited the case for more than two months; and police interviews of Bowery gangs, suitors, abortionists, and a sailor led nowhere. Interest in the brutal slaying faded only when another sensational murder took its place some nine weeks later.

Poe saved clippings of the crime but did not begin work on his sequel to the "Murders in the Rue Morgue" until 1842. It was then that he attempted to unravel in fiction the mystery that still puzzled the police in fact. Poe knew all the suspects in the case including Daniel Payne, an alcoholic cork cutter who at one time intended to marry Miss Rogers; and he knew also of the mysterious temporary disappearance of Mary Rogers in October of 1838, although it is unclear whether he knew of the girl's note claiming that she had been seduced by a naval officer "well known aboard his ship." Of course he could not examine other clues such as the trampled bushes where the death struggle was supposed to have taken place; but in his story Poe unhesitatingly assigned guilt to the naval officer, pointing out among other things that the time between Mary's first disappearance and the murder was three years, the length of ordinary cruises aboard U. S. men-of-war.

Poe claimed to know the identity of the real sailor but never revealed it. It was not until 1880 that his biographer John H. Ingram mentioned the name Spencer in connection with the case, this without substantiation of any sort. According to William K. Wimsatt there were only three Spencers who were United States naval officers in 1841. One was old and ill; one was in Ohio when Mary Rogers died; and one had just returned to New York aboard the brig *Somers*: his name was Philip Spencer, son of Secretary of War John Canfield Spencer. No one ever questioned this young man, and perhaps no one ever suspected him; but along with the most popular suspect in the case, Daniel Payne, Spencer came to a violent end. Captain Alexander Mackenzie ordered the young officer hanged from the main yardarm of the *Somers* for conspiracy to mutiny. Earlier, on October 8, 1841, Daniel Payne made his way to the thicket where Mary Rogers had struggled with her attacker; and there he committed suicide with an overdose of laudanum. Eventually the case of Mary Rogers lost significance and today survives only as Poe's "The Mystery of Marie Roget."

There are other fabulous originals in the works of Edgar Allan Poe. One of them was Jane Stith Stanard, the mother of the poet's schoolmate Robert Stanard. She was almost old enough to have been Poe's own mother; and when she died insane at the age of thirty-one, the previously orphaned boy fell into a deep depression. In his mind he had already idealized her beauty, and soon he transferred his sentiments to poetic expression. The result was "To Helen" where Jane Stanard represents a classic beauty not subject to death or the ravages of time. Poe claimed to have been fifteen when he wrote these first lines of the poem:

> Helen, thy beauty is to me
>   Like those Nicean barks of yore,
> That gently, o'er a perfumed sea,
>   The weary, wayworn wanderer bore
>   To his own native shore.

Professor Lewis Leary discovered two real men who appear as part of the fantastic setting of "Ulalume." In this poem Poe conjures up images from

"the dim lake of Auber" and the "ghoul-haunted woodland of Weir."
Actually Weir might well have had some connection to woodlands in Poe's
mind since in real life he was Robert Walter Weir, a painter of the Hudson
River School who was famous for his landscapes. Auber, on the other hand,
must have been Daniel-Francois-Esprit Auber, a composer whose "Le Lac
des Fées" may have lingered with Poe long enough to become the dim lake
in that "misty mid region of Weir."

§ | *The Spy.* John Jay, a friend and distant neighbor of James Fenimore
Cooper, did not entirely approve of the author's first effort at novel writing.
For a second attempt Jay suggested writing about a Revolutionary War hero
named Enoch Crosby. Cooper listened, at first respectfully, and then with
fascination, to a remarkable tale of espionage and loneliness during the
harshest years of the war. In December, 1821, there appeared Cooper's
retelling of this history, perhaps America's first best-selling novel: it was
called *The Spy: A Tale of the Neutral Ground.*

Enoch Crosby was a shoemaker who wandered about New York's
Westchester county gathering information on Tory organizations and
British troop movements. Occasionally he reported to a Mr. Harper, better
known at the time as General George Washington. Throughout his career as
an apparent British sympathizer and friend of Tories, Crosby was hated by
his own family and an outcast among his real friends; several times he barely
escaped hanging by aroused patriots.

From the moment of publication Cooper's book was a popular success
in England as well as America; but although the author acknowledged a
debt to John Jay, he never publicly revealed the identity of the novel's spy,
Harvey Birch. It was not until 1827 that the true Harvey Birch came to be
known as Enoch Crosby, a seventy-seven year old farmer still living in
Carmel, N.Y. An enterprising dramatist brought Crosby to the Lafayette
Theatre where *The Spy* was appearing on stage, and the old gentleman sat
quietly through the play, writing later that he was "much gratified with the
performance."

It was at the play also that the original spy got his first real taste of
gratitude from the children of those who had shunned him fifty-odd years
before: the ovation for him was wild and long. Finally in 1831 Crosby
became more generally known through *The Spy Unmasked; or, Memoirs of
Enoch Crosby, the Hero of Mr. Cooper's Tale of the Neutral Ground; Being an
Authentic Account of the Secret Services Which He Rendered His Country During the
Revolutionary War (Taken from His Own Lips, in Short-Hand).*

James Fenimore Cooper celebrated too, for he had at last proved
himself an author of note. But at the moment a grateful country was

remembering Crosby, Cooper was forgetting him: he had turned his attention to another book, this one called *The Last of the Mohicans.*

§ | *The Blithedale Romance.* Nathaniel Hawthorne and Sophia Hawthorne invested $1,000 in a socialistic utopia where they lived from April to November 1841. There at Brook Farm the husband and wife worked in admirably disguised disharmony with Bronson Alcott and other Concord Transcendentalists, that is until the strain became too great and the as-yet-unproved author returned to ordinary life. The community itself eventually dissolved, but it reappeared in Hawthorne's third novel, *The Blithedale Romance.*

W. D. Howells and other critics admired the book for its realistic analysis of Brook Farm, and today literary historians conjecture to what degree Emerson, Alcott, and others are truly represented in the book. The most striking figure of *The Blithedale Romance,* however, is Zenobia, Hawthorne's portrait of Margaret Fuller. Easily the most accomplished of the American Bluestockings, Margaret Fuller read a number of ancient and modern languages with ease, edited the Transcendentalist *Dial,* gained the admiration of Emerson and Thoreau with her lectures, and became the first book reviewer for the New York papers.

She also preached the doctrines of free love and aggressively campaigned for the rights of women. She was ambitious, deliberately shocking in conversation, opinionated in all matters, and free with her references to sex. It was this side of Fuller that Hawthorne detested, and it is this side which dominates the character of Zenobia in the novel. Hawthorne's repulsion from the real woman was so intense that he even includes a pointed allusion to her death which occurred two years before publication of the novel. In *Blithedale* Zenobia drowns herself at the end of a tragic love affair while in real life Margaret Fuller perished off the coast of Fire Island as she sailed back to this country with her illegitimate child. Although Margaret Fuller disappeared, the body of the child washed ashore. Henry David Thoreau and several other of her friends made trips to the vicinity of the shipwreck in hopes of recovering her body, but Margaret Fuller evidently died with the Italian nobleman who was first her lover and then her husband. As for the details of Zenobia's death, Hawthorne took them from another real incident which he first recorded in his notebooks: this was the drowning of a young woman named Martha Hunt in the Concord River during 1843.

§ | *Herman Melville.* Melville and a friend actually deserted the whaling ship *Acushnet* and lived through the adventures that were subsequently written into *Typee*. It was not until the publication of the novel in 1846, moreover, that "Toby," the shipmate, learned Melville had survived his stay with the cannibals. In 1854 the former named his newborn son Herman Melville Greene; and the flattered author mailed to the baby an engraved spoon, apparently a standard gift to Melville's namesakes.

Based on truth or not, the revision of *Typee* did pose one difficulty. In 1845 the author was forced to drop a sentence that had greatly offended proofreaders. Melville had described the boarding of the *Dolly* by young women from Nukuheva in these words:

> All of the nymphs succeeded in getting up the ship's side, where they hung dripping with the brine and glowing from the bath, their jet-black tresses streaming over their shoulders, and half enveloping their otherwise naked forms. . . .
>
> Their appearance perfectly amazed me; their extreme youth, the light clear brown of their complexions, their delicate features, and inexpressibly graceful figures, their softly molded limbs, and free unstudied action, seemed as strange as it was beautiful. . . .
>
> Our ship was now given up to every species of riot and debauchery. Not the feeblest barrier was interposed between the unholy passions of the crew and their unlimited gratification.

That last sentence was the one that had to go.

The story of Owen Chase supplied the basis for another Melville sea story. In 1819 the whaler *Essex* sank with most of its crew, having been rammed by a maddened whale. Chase and five crewmen began a ninety-one day ordeal in an open boat, travelling some four thousand miles before they were rescued by a British vessel. Chase eventually returned to Nantucket in June of 1821 and there published *Narrative of the Most Extraordinary and Distressing Ship Wreck of the Whaleship Essex*. Melville read the book and recalled some of the incidents later when he turned to writing himself.

§ | *Walden.* Henry Thoreau's experiment at Walden Pond lasted the two years from 1845 to 1847. Although the incidents he describes in his famous book are true, there is nonetheless a studied anonymity about most of the characters except Thoreau himself. For instance, few people today can correctly identify "the landlord and waterlord" of the domain as Ralph Waldo Emerson. It was indeed Emerson who owned the lot where Thoreau built his cabin, yet the author of *Walden* never refers to him by name. In fact there are several notable figures and a few townspeople whom Thoreau labels rather than names in his text.

Among Thoreau's visitors, "the one who came farthest" was Ellery Channing, and "the one who came oftenest" was Emerson. The "long-headed farmer" who "donned a frock instead of a professor's gown" was neighbor Edmund Hosmer. The one who came with his "cast iron man" was Nathaniel Hawthorne, and the "last of the philosophers" was Amos Bronson Alcott, father of Louisa May Alcott. The "honorable raisers" of the cabin's frame were Emerson, Hosmer, Alcott, and several more. Finally, the artist who sketched the cabin for the title page of *Walden* was Sophia Thoreau, Henry's sister.

The cabin itself survived until 1868. James Clark bought it in September, 1849, moving it by ox team to his family farm just outside Concord. The Clarks used it to store grain, and quickly the hut fell into disrepair. In 1868 they dismantled part of it, using the roof to cover a pigsty. 1875 saw the remaining boards made into a shed on the side of the Clark barn; and when that collapsed, the boards went into the repair of the barn. Ellery Channing was outraged by the neglect of what he considered to be a shrine. Although Thoreau had no direct descendants, it is still pleasant to know that the Clark barn eventually became the property of Ralph Waldo Emerson's grandson—so that once more an Emerson landlord protected what remained of Thoreau's cabin.

§ | *Uncle Tom's Family.* Harriet Beecher Stowe's sensational novel so seized the popular imagination of the mid-nineteenth century that there grew up a sort of cottage industry which capitalized on the most memorable features of the book. Mrs. Stowe attempted to satisfy the demand for factual information with *A Key to Uncle Tom's Cabin*, but it did not seem to supply exactly what the public wanted. Fairs and exhibitions came closer by displaying dozens of hastily-constructed "original" cabins purporting to be the home(s) of the real Uncle Tom.

From time to time a character from the book would appear with his or her own version of the true story. One such was the Reverend John Rankin who died in Ironton, Ohio, on March 18, 1886, claiming to be the generous husbandman who hid the real Eliza and her child in his home before sending them toward safety. There is at least some indication that other characters too had real-life counterparts. According to contemporary records the real little Eva was still alive close to the turn of the century: she was originally a Letcher who married into the famous Kennedy family of Virginia and Kentucky. Her husband's slave Louis Clark was the model for George Harris in the novel and supposedly told Mrs. Stowe what became the plot for *Uncle Tom's Cabin*. Mrs. Kennedy's son was St. Clair, and General Kennedy was altered into Simon Legree.

For a time the author said little about Uncle Tom himself, although it was popularly circulated that he was an aged negro Mrs. Stowe met in

Indianapolis during a visit to the home of her brother, the Reverend Henry Ward Beecher. Finally on July 27, 1882, she mailed this letter to the editor of the Indianapolis *Times*:

Dear Sir:—In reply to your inquiries, I will say that the character of Uncle Tom was not the biography of any one man. The first suggestion of it came to me while in Walnut Hills, Ohio. I wrote letters for my colored cook to her husband, a slave in Kentucky. She told me that he was so faithful, his master trusted him to come alone and unwatched to Cincinnati to market his farm product. Now this, according to the laws of Ohio, gave the man his freedom, since if any master brought or sent his slave into Ohio he became free, *de facto*. But she said her husband had given his word as a Christian, his master promising him his freedom. Whether he ever got it or not I know not. It was some four or five years later, when the Fugitive Slave Law made me desirous of showing what slavery was, that I conceived the plan of writing the history of a faithful Christian slave. After I had begun the story I got, at the Anti-Slavery Rooms, in Boston, the autobiography of Josiah Henson, and introduced some of his most striking incidents into my story. The good people of England gave my simple good friend, Josiah, enthusiastic welcome as the Uncle Tom of the story, though he was alive and well and likely to live long, and the Uncle Tom of the story was buried in a martyr's grave. So much in reply to your inquiries. I trust that this plain statement may prevent my answering any more letters on this subject.

Truly yours,

H. B. Stowe

§ | *Barbara Frietchie.* Mrs. E.D.E.N. Southworth was probably a more famous writer than John Greenleaf Whittier when she suggested that he write a poem about the dramatic confrontation between an old woman of Frederick, Maryland, and the conquering troops of Stonewall Jackson. Whittier wrote his poem; and when it became a national sensation, he wrote to Mrs. Southworth, "If it is good for anything, thee deserves all the credit." The title of the poem was "Barbara Frietchie," after the name of the real woman who inspired it.

Not only did Whittier's verse become part of the national literature, more interestingly it became part of the national heritage. Largely because of sentiment generated by the poem, Barbara Frietchie's house was designated a Civil War monument. Here Whittier has her scold the Confederates for dishonoring the Stars and Stripes, and here her bravery stirs the Southern gallantry of Stonewall Jackson:

"Who touches a hair on yon gray head,
Dies like a dog! March on!" he said.

The problem, of course, is that the incident never took place. The real Barbara Frietchie was bedridden in September, 1862, when the Southern forces marched past her home, and the legendary Jackson was visiting friends nearby instead of riding with the column. A now-anonymous old woman apparently did berate certain Rebels, but she was ignored until her identity merged with the real Barbara Frietchie, who was indeed well enough to wave a flag and cheer the Northern troops who came through Frederick when the Confederates were gone.

In a way Whittier's poem was better than the truth, for it created a legend. Publication in the *Atlantic Monthly* gave "Barbara Frietchie" a national following. Even Southerners admired the crusty old lady, and generations of school children have memorized the thirty stanzas celebrating patriotism and honor. Today the house still stands, a product of the poem.

§ | *The Man Without a Country.* A man who aroused a storm of hatred in the 1860s, even the malice of Abraham Lincoln, became the subject of one of the most famous short stories in American literary history. His name was Clement Laird Vallandigham, an Ohio lawyer with a number of ties to the South and lacking the discretion to hide them. Generations of school children read of Vallandigham after his death, but they knew him only as "the man without a country," the peculiarly cursed villain of Edward Everett Hale's sombre tale.

According to the story the wretched protagonist cursed his country and insisted that he never wanted to hear of the United States again. In truth Vallandigham did just that. As a Congressional Representative from the Third Ohio District, Vallandigham operated as a Copperhead, or a Northerner who opposed the North's cause during the Civil War. He called Lincoln a despot. He supported the South's right to secede. He ignored specific orders to cease "declaring sympathy for the enemy."

It is not surprising that Vallandigham lost his re-election effort and a later campaign for governor, but still the rebel did not modify his stand. In early May, 1863, he actually called for the overthrow of the Lincoln government. Spies for General Ambrose Burnside recorded his words and arrested him. Vallandigham was ordered confined until the end of the war. On May 19, 1863, Abraham Lincoln changed the sentence to banishment within the Confederacy.

While in exile the self-declared martyr accepted the Democratic nomination for governor of Ohio and made his way to Canada to more easily manage his "campaign." So hated was the man that Edward Everett Hale hastily composed "The Man Without a Country" as a propaganda piece to help defeat Vallandigham in this race. James T. Fields agreed to publish the story immediately before the election in the *Atlantic Monthly*. As it happened, Hale did not meet his deadline, and Vallandigham still lost the race by a substantial margin.

In 1865 Ticknor & Fields published "The Man Without a Country" in book form, and Hale found himself a famous author. Vallandigham, on the other hand, returned to Ohio anonymously and began practicing law. Early in 1871 he undertook the defense of Thomas McGehan, accused in the shooting death of a gambler. The laywer obtained a pistol and tried to show how the gambler could have shot himself in the scuffle: in demonstrating, Vallandigham jerked the pistol from his vest and accidentally fired a bullet into his own stomach. He died the next morning.

§ | *The Aspern Papers.* The publishing scoundrel of Henry James's *The Aspern Papers* was a real man, and the events of that novella reflect real happenings in Florence, Italy, during the year 1879. The eighty-two year old Clare Clairmont, former mistress of Lord Byron, lived then at 43 Via Romana in Florence and with her were a middle-aged niece and a cache of manuscripts from the pen of Percy Bysshe Shelley. It was this latter which attracted the attention of Captain Edward Augustus Silsbee, a man determined to have the mementoes at any cost.

In 1887 Henry James first heard from poet Eugene Lee-Hamilton the story of Silsbee's leaving his home in Salem, Massachusetts, and travelling to Florence in a bold attempt to ingratiate himself with the aging woman. Silsbee managed to rent rooms at 43 Via Romana. In time he conversed with the Clairmonts, even became friendly with the old woman. For the most part Silsbee simply waited for an opportunity to get his hands on the papers, his great fear being that Clare Clairmont would die while he was away from the house; and indeed that is exactly what happened. Hearing of Clare's death on March 19, 1879, Silsbee scurried back to Florence from a vacation, and seeing no other tactic now available, offered outright to buy the papers from Paula Clairmont, the surviving niece.

The charming pirate was not prepared for Paula's reply however; she offered to simply give him the papers in exchange for marriage. The proposal must have stunned Silsbee, for he left Florence immediately, taking with him a notebook of Shelley's poems and a letter Shelley had written to Clare. The letter he kept, and the notebook he later gave to Harvard in spite of bitter accusations of theft.

James was so fascinated by the story that he began refining it into artistic form almost immediately and published what he called *The Aspern*

Papers in the *Atlantic Monthly* during the months March–May, 1888. Juliana Bordereau represents Clare Clairmont. Tina is Paula Clairmont. In the 1908 preface to his work James finally acknowledged the source of his novella and that he changed very little of what he heard.

There is a difference in endings though. And in this case reality cannot compare to the master's touch. The fictionalized Silsbee recoils from marriage but later decides to pay even that price for the papers. He returns to Tina with his acceptance, but James has him return too late. Tina has burned the manuscripts:

" 'Destroyed them?' I wailed.

" 'Yes; what was I to keep them for? I burnt them last night, one by one, in the kitchen.'

" 'One by one?' I coldly echoed it.

" 'It took a long time—there were so many.' "

§ | *Andrews and Stoddard.* One of the most unpopular books ever published in America had, paradoxically, a long and successful sales life and became itself a character in a Henry James novel. It appeared first in 1836 under the title *Grammar of the Latin Language* by Ethan A. Andrews and Solomon Stoddard, but the schoolboys who were whipped through its paradigms and declensions referred to the book universally by the last names of its authors. The book made another appearance though, this time in Henry James's *The Bostonians.* In his novel the author pictures a little boy, apparently driven berserk by the rigors of the Roman tongue, finally lashing out at his enemies: the teacher, the mother, and Andrews and Stoddard. So delightful was the episode to one of Andrews' heirs that, on finishing this installment of *The Bostonians* in the July, 1885, *Century,* she immediately wrote to the publishers withdrawing her objections to another edition of the book. With Andrews and Stoddard properly personified and negotiations completed, Houghton Mifflin in 1888 started the now revised *Grammar of the Latin Language* on its second fifty years.

§ | *The Perfectly Ordinary Unoriginal.* Sometimes readers demand and then create the original of a character when there really never was a prototype or model. That happened in 1883, and the public controversy ruined the career of a Wisconsin farm girl who became too closely identified with her own poems. The story is this: in 1883 Ella Wheeler, of Johnson Centre, Wisconsin, published a forgettable book of verses called *Poems of Passion.* To the modern eye these poems appear to be stilted, artificial, and almost wholly without passion; but what mattered to the nineteenth century audience was that suggestive title and the immoral possibilities of lines like, "A new life dawned for him once he caressed me." Clearly the author of such poetry was an adventuress or perhaps even a fallen woman schooled in the very arts she wrote about.

The truth was that Ella Wheeler had travelled outside of Johnson Centre only two or three times in her entire life, and the poems she wrote were merely imitations of the sentimental rubbish then so popular. Even her phraseology was derivative of authors like E.D.E.N. Southworth and Swinburne. Nevertheless, the public furor over this scarlet woman raged only slightly behind the demand for her scandalous book. One Milwaukee newspaper described her as the poet who "out-Swinburnes Swinburne and out-Whitmans Whitman"—a bloodcurdling condemnation for the 1880s. Since no decent girl could afford to associate with a "half-tipsy wanton," as the New York *Sun* referred to her, Miss Wheeler lost most of her friends; and she indefinitely postponed marriage because the man to whom she was engaged risked even greater humiliation than her own by taking an "experienced" woman for his blushing bride.

For a time *Poems of Passion* sold briskly, but this very success transformed Ella Wheeler into a bitter and lonely woman. There is a further irony, however. In this same book there is a poem called "Solitude," which attracted almost no attention during the controversy over the poet. It is not a remarkable poem, and not one person in a thousand has ever heard the title. But it does contain two lines that everyone knows well, even today, and somehow these seem more descriptive of Ella Wheeler's life than anything else she wrote:

> Laugh, and the world laughs with you;
> Weep, and you weep alone. . . .

§ | *Ephraim Tutt.* There was no fabulous original of Ephraim Tutt, and that fact resulted in one of the strangest law suits in publishing history. The story begins in the 1920s when a writer named Arthur Train created a New England lawyer named Ephraim Tutt. Although Train is virtually unknown today, his character enjoyed a tremendous popularity in the *Saturday Evening Post* until after World War II. Train's mistake lay in attempting to capitalize on that popularity. In 1943 the author published *Yankee Lawyer: The Autobiography of Ephraim Tutt* in which he created a full life for Tutt, complete with illustrations originally drawn for the *Post*.

The effect was sensational. Thousands of readers who had assumed that Tutt was fictional now believed that he was a real man. Many wrote to ask him for legal advice, and several women proposed marriage. Although this gullibility seemed perfect for exploitation in further advertising schemes, things backfired in March, 1944. A Philadelphia lawyer, this time a real one named Lewis R. Linet, filed suit against Arthur Train and his publisher charging fraud and deceit. Mr. Linet demanded $50,000—one dollar for himself and one dollar for each of the other 49,999 people who bought the autobiography only to discover that it was "spurious fiction."

Although rival publishers insisted that Linet's suit was part of an even larger publicity scheme, it was not. The case really did go to trial with former ambassador to England John W. Davis defending the author and publisher. Davis based his argument on earlier publications like Defoe's *Journal of the Plague Year* and Swift's *Gulliver's Travels,* both of which purport to be true biographies. Of course the verdict was evident from the first; but what is particularly sad about the case is that Arthur Train died before the trial ended, never knowing that Ephraim Tutt would win his greatest courtroom battle.

§ | *Erle Stanley Gardner.* There is no question that the most famous lawyer in the world is no real man at all but a fictional character who maintains his practice in Los Angeles. He was born of another California lawyer named Erle Stanley Gardner, whom many insiders take to be the original of his creation, Perry Mason. In physical appearance the two do not match, but Dorothy B. Hughes points out in *The Case of the Real Perry Mason* that the courtroom antics now familiar to millions of readers did befuddle real officials around Ventura, California, before they befuddled Hamilton Burger and Lieutenant Tragg in Gardner's books.

A perfect example of the author's Perry Masonic shenanigans occurred shortly before World War I when Ventura County police arrested some twenty residents of a nearby Chinatown for running an illegal lottery. Gardner was enraged when he learned that the county itself had more or less conspired to arrest the twenty Chinese, fine them each $100, and thus pay off a $2,000 public debt; and along with Paul W. Schenck, at the time a far more experienced lawyer than the author, Gardner took the case. The prosecution used one fancy legal maneuver after another in building its case. Gardner, on the other hand, turned away from his Blackstone.

Knowing that the police most likely would not be able to distinguish one Chinese face from another, Gardner went to the Chinatown and shuffled the businessmen who had been charged to addresses different from their own. So when police arrived at the laundry, they arrested a baker; at the baker's, they arrested a grocer; at the grocery, they arrested a druggist; and so on and so forth. All of the victims protested loudly that they were not the men named on the arrest warrants, but of course the police would not listen.

Once in court, the young defense lawyer merely relaxed and waited for the prosecutor to walk far enough into the trap for Gardner to spring up with indignant shouts of false arrest. It was this sort of poetic justice rather than legalistic posturing that inspired the author and ended with the multiple "cases of . . ." Perry Mason being translated into some thirty languages.

The incident above made Gardner a local hero and assured him the entire legal practice for the Chinese community. A touching postscript to this story occurred some years later when Gardner became a salesman before settling on a career as an author. His partnership with Joe Templeton lasted only long enough for a recession to wipe out their automotive parts business: the two lost their final $5.42 at a shooting gallery where they went for one last fling. The following day though Gardner received a letter from the First National Bank of Oxnard, California: it seemed that an anonymous Chinese gentleman had deposited $200 to an account bearing the name of Erle Stanley Gardner. Whenever the bankrupt Gardner drew on the account, another deposit occurred, always in cash, always by a Chinese whom the cashier could not recognize. Until Gardner got on his feet again as a successful novelist, the magic account remained at a constant $200.

§ | *An American Tragedy.* When Theodore Dreiser published his famous naturalistic novel in 1925, many people remembered newspaper accounts of the original case. Few do now. The real American tragedy began on July 11, 1906, at Big Moose Lake in upstate New York when tourists came upon an overturned boat and floating bits of clothing. Volunteers dragged the lake and in time produced the body of twenty-year-old Grace Brown, a native of South Otselic, New York. Her companion's body, suggested by a floating straw hat, was never recovered.

Miss Brown had indeed been accompanied by a young man who had signed them both into the Glenmore Hotel using the name of Carl Graham. Police did not grow suspicious, though, until the examining physician announced that Grace Brown was pregnant and that she had been killed by a savage blow to the head, not by drowning. Carl Graham was suddenly much wanted by the authorities. Police learned also that the young woman had worked for three years at the Gillette Shirt Factory in Courtland, New York, where she dated Chester Gillette, nephew of the firm's owner. When experts compared samples of Chester Gillette's handwriting with Carl Graham's signature, they concluded that the two belonged to the same man.

Gillette was arrested without difficulty and went on trial November 16, 1906, for first degree murder. He confessed to knowing Grace Brown and even to exchanging promises of marriage for sex, but he claimed that her death was an accident. The prosecutor, on the other hand, used 106 witnesses to prove his case, that Gillette used Grace Brown for a time and then decided to do away with his encumbrance when he began climbing socially. It took the jury four hours to agree with the prosecution. Early in 1907 Chester Gillette went to the electric chair.

An American Tragedy did not appear until eighteen years after Gillette's execution, but Dreiser handsomely acknowledged his debt to the newspapers. In addition, Dreiser drew on the life of another real person, himself. Unlike Chester Gillette the Clyde Griffiths of the novel had a childhood of brutal poverty very similar to Dreiser's own. Also interesting to consider is the novel's version of the death, which there is not first degree murder at all. Although Griffiths does plan murder, the fictionalized Grace Brown actually dies when she slips and strikes her head on the rowboat's gunwale: nevertheless, circumstantial evidence is so overwhelmingly against the luckless protagonist that he dies, like his prototype, in the electric chair.

§ | *F. Scott Fitzgerald.* On Thursday, October 24, 1929, a matter of economics ended the Jazz Age. According to some critics it also ended the career of the self-styled "Spokesman for the Jazz Age," Scott Fitzgerald. While it is true that he never produced another *Great Gatsby,* Fitzgerald did continue to write for another decade, producing short stories, screenplays, and a very good novel; but for his continued use of autobiographical material he paid a terrific psychological price. Individual pieces of *The Crack-Up*, for instance, betray Fitzgerald's own crack-up, the result of alcohol and an unstable relationship with his wife Zelda, herself a victim of mental distress.

In 1934 he published *Tender Is the Night* where Zelda appears as Nicole Warren, a psychiatric patient. Fitzgerald actually read his own wife's hospital folders to create a case history for Nicole. This exploitation is not as cruel as it is sad because both Zelda and Scott had a sense of being the truly fabulous originators of Scott's characters. According to the title of his second novel they were both extraordinarily beautiful and damned, prophetic words verified years later in a letter to Zelda which Fitzgerald could not bring himself to mail:

> You were going crazy and calling it genius—and I was going to ruin and calling it anything that came to hand. And I think everyone far enough away to see us outside of our glib presentations of ourselves guessed at your almost megalomanical selfishness and my insane indulgence in drink. Toward the end nothing much mattered.

> I wish the *Beautiful and Damned* had been a maturely written book because it was all true. We ruined ourselves—and I have never honestly thought that we ruined each other.

§ | *Mad Maude.* In November, 1936, a character from one of Thomas Wolfe's short stories appeared in the offices of Charles Scribner's Sons and demanded publication of an essay she had written. Editors there thought the woman was insane, and in fact she may well have been. Her name was Marjorie Dorman, and she had served as Wolfe's landlady for a time while he was living in Brooklyn. Unfortunately, she had also served as the original of "Mad Maude" Whittaker in his story "No Door." Mad Marjorie recognized herself and started an uproar which eventually ended the famous relationship between Wolfe and Maxwell Perkins. In a way Miss Dorman was justified in her demands, because Wolfe had written fairly explicitly of her father and sisters, all mentally handicapped; and he had described Marjorie's own periodic insanity and her struggle to keep the family together. Apparently her article corrected "misconceptions" in the story and relieved some of the hurt caused by achieving fame in such an ignoble manner.

The tempest began when Perkins refused the essay. A month later she sued. What had at first seemed to be mildly amusing eventually caused Wolfe to panic. The reason was this: quite nearly all of his writing was autobiographical. If Marjorie Dorman secured judgment against Wolfe, it would open the door to endless lawsuits by the originals of characters in his earlier works. Therefore, the publishers wisely, and with Wolfe's full knowledge and consent, decided to settle the matter quietly and out of court. The Dormans got $3,000 of the $125,000 they sued for, and Wolfe's legal fees came to another $2,000. Considering what was at stake, the settlement represented a bargain for the author. Nevertheless, there were further complications. It was about this same time that gossipers in the literary community popularized Wolfe's "dependence" on Perkins's editing; and the writer felt obliged to assert his independence or, more specifically, that he could publish successfully without Perkins. What Wolfe needed was a pretext for leaving Scribners, and of course the Dorman incident supplied a ready made one. Soon he was telling friends that the firm had neglected his defense against insane charges brought by an insane woman; and by the end of December, 1936, Thomas Wolfe had formally broken his ties with Charles Scribner's Sons.

§ | *Alexander Woollcott.* For two decades following World War I the most powerful literary arbiter in America was a man whose name has been virtually forgotten in the two decades just past. The name was Alexander Woollcott, drama critic for the New York *Times*, biographer, essayist, radio commentator, and minister extraplenipotentiary from the Algonquin Round Table. Although his major contribution to literary criticism was the rigor he brought to the analysis of modern drama—before him reviews had been mere advertisements—the public clearly perceived him as an American Oscar Wilde, breaking social conventions, creating literary ones, and nurturing an entire generation of new authors including William Faulkner, Eugene O'Neill, John Steinbeck, and George S. Kaufman.

In 1939 Kaufman and Moss Hart presented a play called *The Man Who Came to Dinner*, which revolved around the insulting pronouncements (Woollcott pronounced; he never conversed) of Sheridan Whiteside. Audiences everywhere immediately recognized Alexander Woollcott as the title character because there was so little difference between his private life and his public "role" as presented in the play and as acted every day by Woollcott himself. Everything about him was outrageous, in the then complimentary sense of the word, even his physical appearance. After a case of mumps left him sterile as a young man, the later Woollcott became fat and effeminate. Opening nights on Broadway might find him affecting broad-brimmed hat, polished black cane, and a flowing cape. It was all part of his act; and since it was also a very large part of *The Man Who Came to Dinner*, delighted audiences gave the play a handsome run.

Woollcott died in 1943. There was a memorial service at Columbia University, and then the body was cremated. But even in death the titanic imp managed one final outrage. Since Aleck had wanted to be buried on the campus of his beloved Hamilton in Clinton, New York, immediately after the service friends mailed his ashes to the college. In time he arrived—late as usual and sixty-seven cents postage due.

§ | *The Citizens of Raintree County.* Ross Lockridge committed suicide in 1948, the result, most people say, of a depression brought on by the constant rewriting of his famous novel. That's true in a sense, but it's also an oversimplification of Lockridge's anxieties. In another sense he was killed by his own characters in *Raintree County,* nearly all of whom were fabulous originals who threatened the author's ties to his family.

The real Raintree County is Henry County in Indiana, twenty-odd miles east of Indianapolis; and likewise the towns and farms and buildings had real counterparts; and so did the characters; and the language was real and earthy; and many of the incidents really happened. In fact, it was the combination of fictive technique and actuality that worried Lockridge from the first. Not long before Houghton Mifflin published the book he wrote the following to a friend:

> For the time being, and until my family have read *Raintree County* (which will not be until advance copies exist and shortly before publication) there can

be *no reference* at all to the existence of family materials in the book and . . . no statement of *any* kind must appear that my grandfather influenced the character of John Wickliff Shawnessy.

Therefore at the risk of belaboring the point *ad nauseam* let me repeat that *absolutely* no official statement from any source can be released for the present in any way involving my family in *Raintree County.*

I assure you that an unwise early use of this stuff could conceivably cause untold anguish for me and trouble for us all. I know what I am talking about.

Poor Lockridge did know what he was talking about. When *Life* magazine excerpted "The Great Footrace," response from his family was stony silence. The bawdy, blasphemous dialogue had badly hurt the author's parents in Bloomington, and it seemed certain that the whole novel would be a scandal precisely because he had succeeded where so many authors fail; ironically he had made Raintree County too real. In spite of a surface reconciliation with his father and a promise from his mother to read the whole novel before passing judgment, the author fell into deeper and deeper depressions over what he had done. The characters haunted him now, refusing to hide behind even the thinnest veil of fiction.

So Lockridge began revising the 600,000 words of his novel. It is at this point that the popular accounts pick up his biography, saying only that he was depressed over rewriting his earlier drafts. The truth is that Lockridge had been struggling with his own characters for years, and the incident with his parents simply proved to him how real the characters of *Raintree County* really were. The author revised the manuscript until March 6, 1948, when he walked to his garage, locked the door, and turned on the ignition of his car.

§ | *Lt. Roberts.* One of the few good things to come out of World War II was Tom Heggen's novel *Mr. Roberts.* The young naval officer of the title represents an admixture of Heggen's friends Doug Whipple and Chuck Roberts, hence Lieutenant Doug Roberts of the fictitious *U.S.S. Reluctant.* The author himself served in the Pacific aboard the *U.S.S. Virgo* and engineered several of the feats credited to Mr. Roberts in the novel. Right before the invasion of Okinawa, the *Virgo* anchored in the Philippines to take on marines. For some reason, boredom perhaps, Heggen declared war on his own commanding officer and later wrote some of the skirmishes into his book. The most famous became Mr. Roberts's battle of the palms.

One day in April, 1945, the captain ordered a work party ashore to dig up a palm tree which he then potted and placed on the bridge where he could admire the foliage. Tom Heggen, for his part, saw the tree as symbolic, evidence of the captain's power to give arbitrary orders; and when his first opportunity arose, Heggen casually heaved the tree overboard. Captain Randall was outraged. Immediately he sent another work party ashore with orders to dig up two more palm trees, to pot them, and to place one on either side of the bridge. That done, he stationed a marine guard beside both palms.

The Heggelian mind, though, proved equal to the challenge. Guessing correctly that the guards would sneak away to watch a movie being shown on deck, Tom and a friend crept up to the bridge one evening, seized the palms, and heaved them into the blue. Guessing further that the captain's suspicions might settle on the right man, Heggen put into operation an ingenious Phase Two of his plan. He descended below decks and persuaded a machinist's mate to create a medal from an old shell casing, which he in turn delivered to a fellow conspirator. When the ship's officers gathered for dinner twenty-four hours later, an ensign presented the medal to a completely innocent and thoroughly bewildered young officer named Ed Fahl. As Fahl examined his prize, the captain's flunkies smiled to themselves, for they knew they had their man. The inscription read, *"The Order of the Palm, for service above and beyond the call of duty in the face of the enemy."*

§ | *Two Archbishops. Death Comes for the Archbishop* by Willa Cather is a fictional rendering of the careers of Bishop Lamy and Father Macheboeuf in the New Mexico Territory of the 1850s.

§ | *Martin Eden.* Jack London's novel *Martin Eden* draws its incidents from the author's own life.

§ | *The Kingfish.* Robert Penn Warren's *All the King's Men* won both a Pulitzer Prize as a novel and an Academy Award as a movie: it was based on the career of Louisiana Governor Huey Long.

§ | *The Robe.* Lloyd C. Douglas insisted that the fabulous original of his bestseller *The Robe* (1942) was not to be found specifically in the life of Jesus but in another novel, *Ben-Hur* by Lew Wallace.

§ | *Little Women.* The little women of Louisa May Alcott's famous book were the four Alcott girls—Anna, Louisa, Elizabeth, and Abby. Mrs. Alcott was Marmee.

§ | *In Paradise.* John Peale Bishop, who wrote *Act of Darkness* in 1935, was a classmate of Fitzgerald's at Princeton and appears as Tom D'Invilliers in *This Side of Paradise.*

§ | *Major Joppolo.* John Hersey's *A Bell for Adano* had been selling well for a year when a man sued the author claiming that he was the prototype for Major Joppolo and that Hersey had defamed him in the novel: Hersey said that Major Joppolo was based on no real man.

§ | *The Mortons.* In 1789 William Hill Brown published *The Power of Sympathy,* sometimes called the first American novel. The book appeared anonymously because it was a scandal in the family of Brown's next door neighbors, the Mortons, which formed the basis of the plot. Some authorities still list Mrs. Sarah Morton as the author of *The Power of Sympathy,* but that is not likely, considering that the Mortons bought and burned every copy of the novel that they could find.

§ | *Master Cedric.* The character and physical description of Cedric Errol in *Little Lord Fauntleroy* came from Frances Burnett's own son Vivian. The illustrator for the first edition (Reginald Birch) copied a photograph of the boy wearing the now stereotyped black velvet knickers, white lace collar, white cuffs, and white sash.

§ | *Parson Hooper.* Parson Hooper of Hawthorne's "The Minister's Black Veil" shared his eccentricity with a real clergyman named Joseph Moody, known as "Handkerchief Moody," of York, Maine. When Moody was a young man, he killed a friend by accident: from the day of that funeral to the day of his own the minister kept his face covered with a black veil.

§ | *Whittier's Response.* The long sermon of Whittier's "Massachusetts in Virginia" was triggered by a real incident, the seizure in Boston of a fugitive slave named George Latimer. Latimer's owner was James B. Grey of Norfolk, Virginia, who eventually allowed the slave to be purchased into freedom.

§ | *Tilbury, Maine.* The Tilbury Town of Edwin Arlington Robinson's poetry was in reality Gardiner, Maine.

§ | *Ramon Fernandez.* Wallace Stevens insisted that he made up the name Ramon Fernandez, whom he calls upon in "The Idea of Order at Key West" to interpret the "glassy lights" in fishing boats. Perhaps, but the real Ramon Fernandez, a French critic, was at the height of his literary influence when Stevens wrote the poem in 1934.

§ | *Twain's Characters.* The protagonist of Mark Twain's *The Tichborne Claimant* was a real man, Arthur Bull Orton, a butcher boy from Australia: he claimed to be Sir Roger Tichborne, drowned off the coast of Brazil in 1854. Huckleberry Finn's real name was Tom Blankenship, a boyhood friend of Clemens. Tom Sawyer seems to have had no specific prototype, but Sidney Sawyer, according to the *Autobiography*, was Sam's brother Henry.

§ | *Tarzan's Dirigible.* The great dirigible of Edgar Rice Burrough's *Tarzan at the Earth's Core* was given the author's own telephone number—0-220.

§ | *Hammett.* The tough-guy detective portrayed in much of Dashiell Hammett's fiction may characterize Hammett himself, a Pinkerton detective for eight years.

§ | *The Prison Ship.* Philip Freneau's "British Prison Ship" is based on the poet's own capture while on board the *Aurora* in May, 1780: he was held captive on the British prison ship *Scorpion* and later on the *Hunter*.

§ | *Sleepy Hollow.* The characters in Washington Irving's "The Legend of Sleepy Hollow" were drawn from real lives: lovely Katrina Van Tassel was Katrina Van Alen; the bully Brom Bones was Bron Van Alstyne; and Ichabod Crane was travelling schoolmaster Jesse Merwin.

§ | *Laura Dickey.* In Emily Dickinson's poem "The Last Night That She Lived" (J 1100) the young woman alluded to is Mrs. Laura Dickey, who died in her parent's home on May 3, 1866; the parents, Mr. and Mrs. L. M. Hills, lived next door to the Dickinsons in Amherst.

§ | *Pearl.* Hester Prynne's illegitimate daughter Pearl in *The Scarlet Letter* grew out of Hawthorne's study of his own daughter Una.

§ | *Stephen Crane.* The unnamed battle in Crane's *The Red Badge of Courage* was the Battle of Chancellorsville. Also based on fact is Crane's "The Open Boat": Crane himself was the correspondent who survived the wreck of the *Commodore* which was transporting munitions to Cuban insurgents.

§ | *The Financier.* The financier in Theodore Dreiser's novel of the same name was in real life a tycoon named Charles T. Yerkes.

§ | *The Glencairn.* The name of the real ship from Eugene O'Neill's *S. S. Glencairn* group was the *Ikalis,* a British tramp manned by a crew from Liverpool.

§ | *Mrs. Newsome.* The prototype for Mrs. Newsome and other forceful dowagers in novels by Henry James was Mrs. Jack Gardener of Boston.

§ | *Frances Longfellow.* The one "long dead" in Longfellow's "Cross of Snow" was his second wife Frances Appleton Longfellow: the poem was not discovered until after the poet's death and first published in an 1886 biography written by Longfellow's brother.

§ | *The Constitution.* "Old Ironsides" by Oliver Wendell Holmes must be credited with saving the then forgotten frigate *U. S. S. Constitution:* the poem also confirmed the ship's nickname so strongly that the official name faded into obscurity.

§ | *Ichabod.* The Ichabod of John Greenleaf Whittier's poem similarly titled is Daniel Webster, who shocked the Abolitionist party by supporting the Fugitive Slave Bill.

§ | *Main Street.* The main street of Sinclair Lewis's famous novel ran through the center of Sauk Center, Minnesota.

§ | *Rebecca Nurse.* Maule's curse in *The House of the Seven Gables* was actually spoken by a woman named Rebecca Nurse who had been condemned to death as a witch by Hawthorne's ancestor Judge John Hathorne (sic).

§ | *Longfellow's Children.* The children in Longfellow's "The Children's Hour" were his own: Alice, Edith, Allegra. The little girl who "had a little curl" was Longfellow's infant daughter Alice, according to the son Ernest Longfellow; biographer Blanche R. Tucker claims it was Edith.

§ | *Ghosts.* The house in James Thurber's "The Night the Ghost Got In" was a real residence, 77 Jefferson Avenue, Columbus, Ohio. Thurber once replied to an editor of the Columbus Dispatch, "I deliberately changed the address for the simple reason that there *was* a ghost. . . ."

§ | *The Sun Also Rises.* According to several biographers the characters in Hemingway's famous novel of the lost generation were based on real people. For example, a formerly close friend named Harold Loeb appears in *The Sun Also Rises* as the offensive Robert Cohn. Although Loeb had introduced Hemingway to publisher Horace Liveright and even delivered the manuscript of *In Our Time* across the Atlantic, he angered the author by sleeping with a woman Hemingway considered part of his own entourage. The latter was Lady Duff Twysdon, the Brett Ashley of *The Sun Also Rises*. Jake Barnes, of course, is a modified self-portrait. For details of other real-life characters in Hemingway one should read *A Moveable Feast* (New York: Charles Scribner's Sons, 1964).

§ | *John Sartoris.* The real John Sartoris was William Faulkner's great-grandfather, Colonel William C. Faulkner. Although the Colonel changed his name to *Falkner* sometime after 1850, William changed back to *Faulkner* around 1918. In 1880 Col. Falkner published *The White Rose of Memphis,* a novel which became more famous than many works by his great-grandson in a like period of time. Throughout the middle years of the nineteenth century Col. Falkner lived through the adventures which were later written into *Sartoris* and *The Unvanquished,* and he did in fact die just as the younger Faulkner wrote: in 1889 J. H. Thurmond (Redmond in the novels) gunned him down on a street in Ripley, Mississippi.

Hoaxes, Forgeries, Frauds, Thefts

§ | *Introduction*. It doesn't seem proper somehow to write about the "slimy" underside of American letters. There is an underside all right; but it is rather genteel compared to some undersides, and a literary underside ought for the sake of propriety to be "musty" rather than slimy anyway. In the case of American literature, the hoaxers and forgers and thieves and professional riff-raff make up a colorful lot at the least, frequently displaying more sparkle and originality than respectable bookmen, compilers of almanacs for instance. Here then, are the stories on some of the under-writers of the national letters.

§ | *Thomas Paine*. The most ambitious theft in American literary history was not of a book, but a body. In 1819 an Englishman named William Cobbett removed Thomas Paine's body from its resting place in New Rochelle, New Jersey, apparently intending to transport it to Britain. English magistrates, however, refused to allow burial of the traitor on English soil; and to this day the location of Paine's corpse is a mystery.

The great propagandist had come to America in 1774. Then, on January 10, 1776, he published his famous pamphlet *Common Sense* and for a time enjoyed a popularity as broad as Franklin's or Jefferson's. Furthermore, Paine's usefulness as a professional revolutionary elevated him to a sort of world citizenship and made easy his rise to power in France during that country's revolution. He became a member of the National Convention and was the only person to vote against the execution of Louis XVI. Unknown to most readers, though, is the fact that Paine's fall from grace was as dramatic as his ascent. Because he favored the overthrow of all monarchy, the British indicted him as a traitor on May 21, 1792. Because he advocated the French brand of revolution, the Americans took him to be an atheist and a degenerate. Because he opposed the Reign of Terror, the French accused him of betraying their cause and jailed him in the Luxembourg.

It was the American ambassador to France, James Monroe, who secured Paine's release from prison; and it was in Monroe's own home that Paine recovered and completed *The Age of Reason* in 1795. In 1802 he resettled in America and then died on his farm seven years later, still in disgrace. Only six people attended the funeral. Exactly why William Cobbett exhumed the body in 1819 is a matter of some controversy, but certainly no one cared very much at the time. Today the consensus is that Cobbett intended to make amends for his earlier attacks on Paine by returning the body to its native soil. If that is the case, the English as a whole were not so forgiving. The magistrates made their ruling, which Cobbett may or may not have obeyed; and no less than Lord Byron expressed the outrage of the ordinary citizens:

> In digging up your bones, Tom Paine,
>   Will Cobbett has done well;
> You visit him on earth again,
>   He'll visit you in hell.

§ | *A Pickle for the Knowing Ones.* Possibly the most unusual work ever published by an American author is the second edition of a monograph written by Lord Timothy Dexter of Newburyport, Massachusetts. Literary historians have never been able to decide whether this little book is hoax, lunacy, or avant-garde; so this seems as good a place as any to describe it. An eccentric of the first order, Dexter prided himself on cultivating the finest garden in Newburyport, on owning forty life-sized wooden statues of famous people, and on developing the only workable plan for a world government. It was this latter which he put into the first edition of his book *A Pickle for the Knowing Ones: or Plain Truth in a Homespun Dress by Timothy Dexter, Esq.*, printed in Salem, Massachusetts, 1802.

Those who received copies of this rare volume (Dexter gave them away) were astonished to begin a book made up entirely of one sentence. It contained not a single punctuation mark. Capitalization appears to have been at random but must have occurred according to a system known only to the author, and spelling was more or less phonetical (using Dexter's phonetics of course). Because of the mechanical complexity of such a book, few readers could agree on the details of its content; but in general it might be described as an outright demand for brotherly love—instantly, and among all of the world's "nasions," the world government to follow later.

The second edition of this jewel retained all the peculiarities of the first and added one more, a page of punctuation for the fastidious:

> fourder mister printer the Nowing ones complane of my book the fust edition had no stops I put A nuf here and thay may peper and solt it as they please

```
,,,,,,,,,,,,,,,,,,,,,,,,,,,,,,,,,,,,,,,,,,,,,,,,,,,,,,,,,,,,,,,,,,,,,,
,,,,,,,,,,,,,,,,,,,,,,,,,,,,,,,,,,,,,,,,,,,,,,,,,,,,,,,,,,,,,,,,,,,,,,
,,,,,,,,,,,,,,,,,,,,,,,,,,,,,,,,,,,,,,,,,,,,,,,,,,,,,,,,,,,,,,,,,,,,,,
;;;;;;;;;;;;;;;;;;;;;;;;;;;;;;;;;;;;;;;;;;;;;;;;;;;;;;;;;;;;;;;;;;;;;;;;
;;;;;;;;;;;;;;;;;;;;;;;;;;;;;;;;;;;;;;;;;;;;;;;;;;;;;;;;;;;;;;;;;;;;;;;;
::::::::::::::::::::::::::::::::::::::::::::::::::::::::::::::::::::::::
....................................................................
...............!!!!!!!!!!!!!!!!!!!!!...............................
....................!!!!!!!!!!!!!!!!!!!!...........................
......................!!!!!!!!!!!!!...............................
.....................................!...............................
,,,,,,,,,,,,,,,,,,,,,,,,,,,,,,,,,,,,,,,,,,,,,,,,,,,,,,,,,,,,,,,,,,,,,,
...................????????????????????............................
```

§ | *The Knickerbocker Hoax.* There must be some significance to the fact that the first work of American literature to gain recognition abroad had at its origin a certain lighthearted fraud. It began with this curious piece in the *New York Evening Post:*

DISTRESSING

> Left his lodgings some time since, and has not yet been heard of, a small elderly gentleman, dressed in an old black coat and cocked hat, by the name of Knickerbocker. . . .

The date was October 27, 1809.

Soon afterward there appeared further items, in the same paper, stating that a man answering this quaint description had in fact been observed in a "fatigued and exhausted" condition resting beside one of the roads leading away from New York City. Why should he appear to be so travel-weary? The answer, suggested by the *Post* ten days later, came in the form of an action by the landlord of the Independent Columbian Hotel: Mr. Knickerbocker's debts to this hotel and his hasty departure from same necessitated a sale to the general public of a "very curious kind of written book" left behind in the otherwise vacant room of the old gentleman. The landlord, after all, had to recover what losses he could.

Exactly one month after the original notices, someone presented what seemed to be the logical consequence of all that had come before, a publisher's advertisement for the book "found in the chamber of Dr. Diedrich Knickerbocker, the old gentleman whose sudden and mysterious disappearance has been noticed." The title was to be *A History of New York*.

Of course the real author behind the book and newspaper hoax was Washington Irving. The advertisement, however, was no empty promise: he did indeed publish the satirical history, and curious readers did indeed make him a success. Within a year Irving earned $2,000 from this survey of New York "from the Beginning of the World to the End of the Dutch Dynasty." It was a gentle satire which gained the author an immediate popularity, and the renown of the "old gentleman" grew so quickly that "Knickerbocker" became a name applied first to New Yorkers of Dutch ancestry and then to New Yorkers in general. Nevertheless, the book, author, and the nickname did not become popular among the Dutch themselves. Descendants of the people Irving admired so much read his book as a continuation of the advertising hoax, seeing mockery and hidden scorn on every page. To them the *History* was a tasteless failure.

§ | *Clement Clarke Moore.* In 1882 a little known professor of Oriental and Greek literatures at the General Theological Seminary of New York City composed a poem which was destined to become the most famous stolen property in North American history. Clement C. Moore wrote this jingle as a Christmas present for his three daughters and originally entitled the piece "An Account of a Visit from St. Nicholas" although today most people incorrectly call it by its first line. There was never any intention to publish the poem, and unquestionably the learned Dr. Moore would have been chagrined at the possibility of being remembered for a nursery rhyme.

Fortunately, someone stole the poem and gave a copy to editor Orville Holley of the Troy, New York, *Sentinel* where he published it anonymously on December 23, 1823. To this day no one can positively identify the thief because Holley referred to this source only as "a lady of this city." As anyone might guess, the "Visit from St. Nicholas" became extremely popular and appeared yearly in newspapers across the country, sometimes with attribution to this author or to that one. When the New York *Courier* issued a plea in 1829 for the real poet to identify himself, Mr. Holley replied with a piece in his own paper implying that he knew about Moore. Among other things he mentions this pun:

> We have been given to understand that the author of the verses belongs, by birth and residence, to the city of New York, and that he is a gentleman of *more* merit as a scholar and a writer than many more of more noisy pretensions.

This implication, in turn, suggests that the thief was at heart an honest woman. She may have been Harriet Butler, daughter of Dr. David Butler, who was in 1822 rector of St. Paul's church in, significantly, Troy, New York. We do know that Miss Butler was visiting the Moore family when "A Visit from St. Nicholas" got its first reading to the Moore children, and she may well have copied the poem before returning home. Harriet Butler would have known, too, that the distinguished Moore would not have wanted his name associated with what he considered to be a piece of trivia, which explains why Orville Holley refused to release the poet's name even though he seems to have known it. It was not until 1844 that the sixty-three year old Professor Moore first acknowledged the poem by including it in a volume of his collected works, a concession he certainly never would have made without the happy interference of Harriet Butler—or someone.

§ | *Jared Sparks.* When does fraud have a beneficial effect on scholarship? Rarely. But from time to time the exposure of fraud will lead to greater accuracy or more careful preservation of an author's work. It helps if the subject-author is important and if the scandal is a rollicking one in high places, the beneficial effect being directly proportional to public shock at the tampering. That's why Jared Sparks has been so useful in the field of American biography. In a way, we owe him a great debt.

Sparks was first a Unitarian minister, then an editor of the *North American Review*, and finally a biographer of George Washington. It was in this latter capacity that he made his contribution, and what Sparks contributed was considerable. With Washington's correspondence (*Works*, 1834) he added whole sentences, struck out unflattering passages, and altered the sense of many phrases: much of this edited material he then inserted into a new biography (1837) in order to present a "real" Washington similar in every respect to Parson Weems's saint-like figure. Thus, two of the first biographies of Washington ever written and two of the most popular ever written, Weems's of 1800 and Sparks's of 1837, were mutually supporting and equally fraudulent; but no one questioned the authority until mid-century.

By 1847 Sparks had become a powerful and admired figure in American letters, Harvard having made him professor of history eight years earlier. He could therefore ignore snivelling criticisms when a volume of correspondence by Washington's friend Joseph Reed used texts of some Washington letters which differed substantially from the texts Sparks had published. He could not ignore, however, the English historian Lord Mahon who repeated the charges of inconsistency in his *History of England* (1851). Sparks admitted that he had made "corrections" but not that he had done anything wrong. He was merely preserving, he said, a picture of Washington he knew to be true.

The ensuing debate gained volume and importance because of the potential damage to Harvard, not because of the potential damage to Washington; and the public was clearly interested in establishing that the former minister had lied, not that the former President had. Still, Sparks's fall from a high place did have one beneficial effect on scholarship, the strengthening of a principle that readers now take for granted. Never again, until the time of Clifford Irving, would an American biographer try to create an American myth rooted so firmly in emended evidence.

§ | *Rufus Wilmot Griswold.* The most malicious hoaxer of American letters, and unfortunately one of the most successful, was an ex-minister named Rufus W. Griswold, a literary parasite who first met his victim in 1841. When Griswold travelled to Philadelphia soliciting contributions to his *Poets and Poetry of America*, Edgar Allan Poe submitted "The Haunted Palace," "The Coliseum," and "The Sleeper." The book appeared in due time, and Poe reviewed it favorably in *Graham's* magazine. A later review bearing Poe's name had mixed comments but was still generally favorable. And still later an anonymous review of January 28, 1843, ravaged the anthology. Griswold convinced himself that Poe wrote this latter attack.

Immediately after Poe's death in 1849 there appeared in one of the New York papers a blistering evaluation of the poet's career and character which was signed only "Ludwig." Of course Ludwig and Rufus Griswold were the same. To malign the dead poet once was not enough however; the unctuous Griswold approached Poe's mother-in-law, Mrs. Clemm, and offered to become Poe's literary executor. The elderly dame readily agreed, recalling only that Griswold's name had been mentioned about the house from time to time. So, by an almost incredible irony, Poe's letters and manuscripts fell into the hands of his worst enemy.

In the meantime the Poe legend had got its start: already the name Poe stood for the brilliant but degenerate orgiast addicted to drugs and inhuman imaginings. Then when Griswold's 1850 edition of the works appeared, one saw clear evidence among the published letters to support the sordid picture. Certain passages verified the portrait of Poe as a back-stabbing, perverse genius who nonetheless was incapable of functioning in the real world. What people did not suspect of course was that Griswold had tampered with the correspondence, adding passages that damned Poe, striking out what presented him in a charitable light, and completely destroying some letters. It was almost a hundred years later that Professor Arthur Hobson Quinn of the University of Pennsylvania completed his own work on the correspondence and demonstrated the nature of Griswold's fraud. Nevertheless, Griswold's picture of Poe is so colorful that the public remains unwilling to abandon it even today: that it is a fraud disturbs almost no one.

§ | *Mother Goose.* In the middle of the nineteenth century, Boston became the center of a controversy involving the best-loved children's rhymes in English. According to the legend, or hoax, a printer named Thomas Fleet first published *Mother Goose's Melody* in 1719. By the 1860s Fleet's descendants and supporters were arguing that many of the poems were American in origin as was Mother Goose herself.

Supposedly the famous rhymster was Elizabeth Foster Goose (or Vergoose or Vertigoose) who had been born in 1665. One of her daughters married Thomas Fleet, a printer in Boston's Pudding Lane; and it was Fleet who actually compiled *Songs for the Nursery, or Mother Goose's Melodies for Children.* On the title page appeared a goose, long-necked and open-mouthed.

The mystery here is that collectors have never turned up a copy of Fleet's book. The publisher's descendant, John Fleet Eliot, circulated an article in 1860 describing one of the ghost volumes which had been seen by Edward A. Crowninshield in the library of the American Antiquarian Society in Worcester, Massachusetts. Although years later publishers Munroe and Francis would claim to have based their *Mother Goose's Quarto* on an original Fleet text, Crowninshield himself died before he could substantiate the authenticity of the American Mother Goose.

Scholars can indeed verify the existence and much biographical information concerning the Goose and Fleet families of the seventeenth century, but their literary productions represent more of a problem. Still, there are collectors who treasure the possibility of locating the 1719 text even though numerous searches of the library of the American Antiquarian Society have failed to turn up what would certainly be one of the great finds of the century.

§ | *The Cyclopedia of American Biography*. For sheer creative energy few hoaxes match the efforts of a now anonymous scholar or scholarly group who contributed to the 1886 and 1888 editions of Appleton's *Cyclopedia of American Biography*. Nothing unusual surfaced from these volumes until 1919 when Dr. John Hendley Barnhart, bibliographer of the New York Botanical Garden, uncovered biographies of fourteen botanists who never existed. Immediately the staff of Sabin's *Dictionary of Books Relating to America* along with experts in all fields began to examine the once-prestigious reference work: by 1936 they had discovered a total of eighty-four completely counterfeit entries, but to date no one knows the identity of the brilliant hoaxer. Although the editors of the *Cyclopedia* lost a certain amount of credibility, the books themselves retained a high price: they became instant collectors' items.

§ | *Plagiarists*. The aristocrats of literary crime are the plagiarists, those who steal words and ideas rather than mere things. In the nineteenth century charges of plagiarism shuttled among gentlemen authors with the elaborate solemnity of preparations for a duel, although it was the occasion for a full-fledged war when Poe accused Longfellow of pilfering. The problem of course has always been to make the charges stick: for instance, anybody who's read both Poe and Thomas Holley Chivers can see that one of them "influenced" the other, but just who took what from whom isn't clear. The ambiguity of these situations was such that the gentlemen duelists could remain gentlemen, even friends, while their seconds exchanged shots in the magazines of the day. It is much to Chivers's credit, for example, that he was lending his antagonist money even after Poe had made his charges.

With the turn of the century, though, the romance drained out of plagiarism: it's money and malice that seem to characterize modern "borrowing." In the past five years, for example, three bestselling authors— Alex Haley (*Roots*), John Gardner (*The Life and Times of Chaucer*), and Gail Sheehy (*Passages*)—answered charges of plagiarism more with defiance than with embarrassment or contrition. In 1942 Joseph Campbell and Henry M. Robinson started a particularly nasty fight by publishing in the *Saturday Review* an accusation that Thornton Wilder's *The Skin of Our Teeth* was plagiarized from Joyce's *Finnegan's Wake* (there's a similarity in characters). Of all the modern crooks though, the most hard boiled seemed to be the compilers of cook books, many of whom use canned recipes from earlier works: according to Karen Hess, writing for *Harper's* on this topic, the last honest cookbook appeared in the nineteenth century. Ms. Hess insists that for really original recipes one must turn to *Modern Cookery for Private Families*, published in 1845.

As a matter of routine many contemporary publishers send galley proofs of their new books to reading services for checks on possible plagiarism. Probably the most famous such agency is the Virginia Kirkus Bookshop Service in New York, which has reviewed thousands of books over the years. In 1953, for instance, Miss Kirkus herself sent to the editors of Little, Brown a review of their upcoming *Position Unknown* by Robert E. Preyor. It was an old review, not a current one at all; but Miss Kirkus insisted that it applied as well this time as when she first read the book under the title of *Island in the Sky*, published by Viking in 1944 and written by Ernest K. Gann.

The only plagiarists to display any real style in modern times have been the poets, and the most forward of these was a woman identified only as Mrs. X in an article written by John Ciardi in 1961 and published by *Saturday Review*. It seems that Mrs. X submitted for publication a word-for-word copy of Richard Wilbur's "Museum Piece," and Ciardi puzzled over what sort of rejection piece to send, whether or not to take the whole incident as a joke. Finally he wrote the following:

> Dear Mrs. X:
> Regarding your poem, Museum Piece—I find it very rich and moving, and I can think of few recent poems I would more happily publish. Certainly, however, a special rate is indicated for so rich a poem.
>
> Do please let me know what price you would like for it. Some special token is certainly indicated.
>
> Let me thank you again for one of the best poems to be submitted to us in some time. I shall hope for the real pleasure of seeing more such poems.
>
> Sincerely,
> John Ciardi

Mrs. X was no joker, or at least her intentions were not humorous. She did indeed expect *Saturday Review* to publish her poem; but, perhaps to demonstrate her faith in the editors' honesty, she decided to leave the rate of payment to them. True poetry is of the soul.

§ | *The American Claimant.* Surely the most unlucky author in American literature was a man named John Luckey McCreery. While there is overwhelming evidence that he wrote one of the most popular poems of the nineteenth century, he met with nothing but scorn and ridicule during the forty years in which he tried to establish his right to the title. The name of this disputed poem was "There Is No Death," and it became one of those combinations of sentiment and religiosity with which the Victorians loved to grace their tombstones. The frequently chiselled first verse reads as follows:

> There is no death! The stars go down
> To rise upon some other shore,
> And bright in Heaven's jeweled crown
> They shine for evermore.

Although these words appear on McCreery's own tombstone in Washington, D.C., the claim that he actually wrote them seemed preposterous, because the poem had been printed for decades in anthologies and always credited to Owen Meredith. Meredith, whose real name was Edward Robert Lytton Bulwer, first Earl of Lytton, was a British poet widely read throughout this country in McCreery's day. To all appearances the latter was merely an American plagiarist. Bulwer never claimed he wrote the poem, however; and it never appeared in any of his collected works.

The first hint of a controversy appeared in 1869. In the March 1 issue of the Dubuque *Herald*, McCreery published an article maintaining that he had written the poem ten years earlier and had first printed it in the *Delaware County Journal* of Delhi, Iowa. He claimed further that a Eugene Bulmer copied "There Is No Death" afterwards and published it in the Chicago *Independence Offering* under his own name. Then when the Wisconsin *Farmer's Advocate* reprinted the piece, editors there decided that "Bulmer" had been a misprint and accordingly changed the author to "E. Bulwer," hence the insistence in 1869 that the poem belonged to Owen Meredith (who died in 1873).

What immeasurably damaged McCreery's case is the fact that he varied his story over the years. One version has him writing the poem in 1863 and publishing it first in *Arthur's Home Magazine* for July, 1863 (Volume 22, page 41), although in every case he has the poem stolen by Eugene Bulmer and a false attribution to E. Bulwer. On the other hand, no other author has ever claimed "There Is No Death," and it can indeed be found in *Arthur's Home Journal* under the name of J. L. McCreery. There is, in addition, no record of a claim for McCreery's standing offer of $1,000 to anyone proving that a rival author composed the poem. Nevertheless, readers, publishers, and critics in England and America simply refused to believe that a rural

Midwestern newspaper editor wrote some of the best known lines in both countries. Ironically, the one man who did not dispute McCreery's authorship also proved just how luckless the poet could be. In 1868 President-elect Ulysses S. Grant denied McCreery a job as his official stenographer on grounds that a President needed a man about who understood public business rather than poetry. John Luckey McCreery finally died in 1906 without the Presidential appointment, without credit for his poem, and yet without knowing that no writer other than the mysterious Eugene Bulmer would ever claim to have composed his poem.

§ | *Bulmer Redivivus.* While the claims of James L. McCreery seem to call for a sympathetic hearing, believing that exactly the same injustice befell another American poet seems to call for an exotic and peculiar credulity. The poet this time is a woman named Mrs. Lizzie York Case, and the obviously derivative title of her poem is "There Is No Unbelief." In truth, there is nothing remarkable about the work, and it was never especially popular except among preachers and English teachers who felt compelled to have children memorize the following sentiments:

> There is no unbelief;
> Whoever plants a seed beneath the sod
> And waits to see it push away the clod,
> He trusts in God.

In the minds of most people there was never any controversy about this poem: it was simply another work by the already famous Owen Meredith. On August 1, 1905, however, Lizzie York Case came out with an article maintaining that she had written the poem thirty-seven years earlier and had first published it in the Detroit *Free Press.* She claimed further that a Eugene Bulmer copied "There Is No Unbelief" afterwards and published it in the Chicago (sic) *Farmer's Advocate.* Then when "some paper in Wisconsin" reprinted the piece, editors there decided that "Bulmer" had been a misprint and accordingly changed the author to "E. Bulwer," hence the insistence in 1905 that the poem belonged to Owen Meredith (who had died in 1873).

What immeasurably damaged Mrs. Case's case is the fact that she seemed to have stolen her coincidences directly from James Luckey McCreery. Perhaps she had read one of his accounts somewhere and unconsciously appropriated the story for her own use since the odds against duplicate thefts by the mysterious Bulmer are astronomical. It was painfully obvious to everyone that the aged Mrs. Case was herself a thief, and so even in 1905 the quoting clergymen who were responsible for the poem's Sunday School popularity had to credit Meredith with authorship.

On the other hand, no other author has ever claimed "There Is No Unbelief," and it appears nowhere in the collected works of Edward Bulwer. It was newspapers and anthologies that kept the poem alive and Mrs. Case's incredible story that convinced readers she was lying about her early publication. Everyone simply assumed, and no one checked.

But in the morgue of the Detroit *Free Press*, there can be found—in the issue of August 18, 1878—a poem. Its title, "There Is No Unbelief." Its author, undeniably, Mrs. Lizzie York Case.

§ | *The Archives Caper.* Secured in the National Archives Building of Washington, D. C. are priceless bits of the American heritage including the Declaration of Independence and the United States Constitution, all protected by elaborate security. Or at least that's what the guidebooks say. Librarians grew uneasy in 1963, however, when autograph and manuscript dealers in New York, Boston, Philadelphia, Detroit, and Kansas City began offering for sale documents belonging to the national holdings. A hasty series of checks revealed that certain rare manuscripts were indeed missing from the Archives although no one could estimate the extent of the pilfering. A year-long investigation began.

The first break in the case occurred when a Colonel Andrew Barnett of Kansas City attempted to trade fifty handwritten letters of Harry S. Truman to a knowledgeable New York dealer. The expert had become suspicious at the handsome cache because a letter in Truman's manuscript is rarer than one by Washington. It was New York postal inspector Gerard Mailloux and special agent Arthur Nehrboss of the F.B.I. working together who eventually connected this attempted sale to a number of seemingly unrelated ones across the country. Over time the identity of Colonel Barnett and several other names solidified into their true form, Samuel George Matz, a child abuser, petty criminal, and bigamist from Cleveland, Ohio. Unfortunately for authorities, Matz also had the uncanny senses of a cornered animal: he remained at large for months with an intensive search going on all around him. Time and again he frustrated police by last minute escapes or lucky changes of address. Once in Cincinnati he and his current wife were arrested for shoplifting, only to be released moments before the cops learned of the major warrants for him issued by the F.B.I.

Detroit police finally arrested Matz when a manuscript expert of the Detroit Public Library reported some of the astonishing bargains offered to him by a Mrs. R. McClaferty. A search of the Matz-Barnett-McClaferty apartment turned up seven stuffed suitcases of priceless documents! Included in the recovery were letters by Lincoln, Jackson, Monroe, Woodrow Wilson, Franklin D. Roosevelt, Dwight D. Eisenhower, and John F. Kennedy along with one letter by Lincoln written on April 14, 1865, the day of his assassination. Ten more boxes of documents surfaced later.

What is even more remarkable is that the Matzes's robbery of the National Archives is the only known successful attempt, but their method was simplicity itself. Late in 1962 Matz and his wife posed as visiting scholars to the archives, taking the names of Dr. and Mrs. Robert Bradford Murphy. They worked steadily for days seemingly at high-level research on rare documents. Although the guards checked briefcases and parcels as visitors left the building, these gentlemen were too courteous to examine the pocketbook of Mrs. Murphy; and each day the hefty purse carried keys, cosmetics, and priceless manuscripts out of the building.

There was a certain simplicity in their trial also: it lasted only a few days, ending in a guilty verdict and a sentence of ten years for each.

§ | *The Spectra Hoax.* The best con game in town is the one that swindles the swindlers. In a sense that's what happened in 1916 when the great *Spectra* hoax ended with some victims and the hoaxers themselves being further taken in by Earl Roppel, "The Ploughboy Poet of Tioga County." *Spectra* was a book purportedly written by Emanuel Morgan and Anne Knish, he an American expatriate and she a Byronic Hungarian who had settled in Pittsburgh. Together they had founded a new literary movement and published their book as a harbinger of what was to come in American literature. In truth, Morgan was Witter Bynner, and Knish was Arthur Davison Ficke, two gifted parodists who felt that their spoof of modern literature had succeeded when *Spectra* got sympathetic reviews.

Malcolm Cowley and Damon Foster, on the other hand, did not appreciate the implied attack on contemporary poets and set about hoaxing the hoaxers. On June 15, 1916, they composed a number of poems which they attributed to their creation, the ploughboy poet Earl Roppel. Later Cowley and Foster dispatched these poems to the authors of *Spectra*, asking for "the opinion of someone I feel knows what poetry is on my poems which enclosed please find." Then in a moment of inspired deviltry, they made revisions and mailed Roppel's complete poetical works to Amy Lowell and Conrad Aiken, again asking for evaluation. What each victim received was a packet of inane verses inspired by the writings of Bynner and Ficke, perhaps best represented by the poem entitled "Moon Light":

> Last night when I was in our surrey,
>   Driving home with my best girl,
> I saw the moon run down the fence-row
>   Like a fat squirrel.

First to take the bait was Conrad Aiken, who sent low-keyed encouragement and an autographed copy of Palgrave's *Golden Treasury*. Amy Lowell's response was oral and thus harder to substantiate; but apparently she was far more enthusiastic than Aiken, asserting that this young poet had "the modern spirit." Still, the venture could not be dubbed a success until Bynner or Ficke had fallen victim to the deadly verses of Roppel, "bard of the rushing Catatonk." Months passed with no word from either of the *Spectra* founders, so at last Cowley and Foster turned to other enterprises.

It was not until 1918 that the full story became widely known among literary circles, but by then Bynner himself was willing to admit that the master hoaxers had indeed succeeded from the very first. In fact, Bynner had so admired the work of Earl Roppel that he had circulated the poems among the English Department of the University of California at Berkeley where the academicians made frequent comparisons to Robert Burns. Music professor Arthur Farwell even set one of the poems to a stirring tune and led a chorus of 3,000 voices in singing the "best patriotic song-poem" ever produced in America. It started like this:

> Flag of our country, strong and true,
>   The sky is rosy with your bars;
> But as they fade it turns to blue
>   And radiant with your stars.

§ | *S.I.N.A.* One of the most successful hoaxes of modern times was the product of writer Alan I. Abel, who invented an organization known under several acronyms as a variation of S.I.N.A. (Society against the Indecency of Naked Animals). Abel began the hoax on Jack Paar's "Tonight" show in 1959 and in a short time managed to fool hundreds of newspapers, *Life* magazine, CBS, NBC, ABC, and a number of professional journals. He hired pickets and an answering service, published leaflets, and created G. Clifford Prout, whose fictional $400,000 bequest kept the society operating. Apparently this nonexistent money had some effect, since several off-shoots of the national organization did in fact spring up throughout the country. The purpose of these assemblies is to urge "all good people to clothe their animals with proper covering so that vital areas will not be observed by the naked human eye." S.I.N.A. even has enemies, themselves victims of the hoax, who to this day fume about "those morons who put diapers on horses." Abel, however, has gone on to other careers: under the pseudonym of Julius Bristol he published an article in *Golf Digest* on "revolutionary new putting techniques"—in spite of his never having been on a golf course in his life.

§ | *The Necronomicon.* Just as fantasy writer Robert E. Howard invented the Hyborian Age as a setting for his bizarre tales, so did H. P. Lovecraft concoct the "Cthulhu Mythos" as a background for his own weird stories. Although readers of mainstream literature have never heard of Lovecraft, for decades he has been an underground best seller on college campuses and among certain segments of the science fiction community. Lovecraft frequently mentioned in his stories a book called the *Necronomicon*, supposedly written by the mad Yamanite poet Abdul Alhazred around A.D. 730 and variously translated into Greek, Latin, and a few modern languages. So important is the *Necronomicon* to Lovecraft's plots that the sinister volume itself becomes something of a character in the Cthulhu Mythos. The circumstantial realism of the tales is so effective that collectors for years have tried to locate a copy of the phantom text. The search has been made more frantic by the dozens of rumors and hoaxes that have slithered through the underground for the past forty years: for instance, students at Yale keep the *Necronomicon* indexed in the catalog of their library's rare books room, and certain rare-book dealers offer the book for sale from time to time, no doubt explaining to excited inquiries that they've "just sold" the only known copy to an anonymous buyer. Other writers of weird tales have borrowed the *Necronomicon* for use in their own fiction and have even invented companion volumes such as August Derleth's *Cultes des Goules* or Clark Ashton Smith's *Liber Ivonis*, thus creating a new literary discipline, pseudobiblionomy, the study of books that do not exist. There should be a word of caution for enthused scholars though: Lovecraft reports that Abdul Alhazred died at the hands of an invisible monster conjured out of the *Necronomicon*. He was eaten alive in broad daylight, the victim of his own book.

§ | *Newspaper Hoaxes.* Undoubtedly the champion newspaper hoaxer of the twentieth century was H. L. Mencken, the cantankerous public critic employed by the Baltimore *Sun* in the World War I era and for long afterwards. According to legend, Mencken and rival reporters from two competing newspapers formed a conspiracy of sorts to avoid the unattractive prospects of "over-researching" news stories. As one of the group explained, "Why in hell should we walk our legs off trying to find out the name of a Polack stevedore kicked overboard by a mule?" The three conspirators instead met in a local bar, decided on the stevedore's name, agreed on the particulars of the case, and wrote mutually-supporting stories for their papers.

Nevertheless, Mencken did not reach the acme of his career until publication of the immortal bathtub hoax of 1917. For the *New York Evening Mail* he wrote a long description of the first stationary bathtub ever used in this country, supposedly purchased by the Cincinnati millionaire Adam Thompson in 1842. Besides describing the tub (it had its own pump and drain) Mencken was clever enough to include fraudulent bits of circumstantial realism, such as the thirty dollar installation tax levied on early bathtubs by the state of Virginia. When the story appeared on December 28, 1917, readers took it seriously and included it in speeches, other newspapers, magazines, government publications, and standard reference works. Efforts to kill the story have not completely succeeded even today.

In the nineteenth century newspapers of the West excelled in gulling readers, and one should consult the autobiography of Mark Twain for hoax anecdotes written by the acknowledged master of the times. In the East, though, there occurred two unusually successful hoaxes which are not frequently mentioned today. The first of these appeared throughout the months of August and September, 1835, in the *New York Sun*. The articles ran under the general title "Discoveries in the Moon Lately Made at the Cape of Good Hope," and in them Richard Adams Locke purported to reveal discoveries made by Sir John Herschel in an observatory equipped with an unusually powerful telescope. Locke's description of an alien civilization on the moon alarmed people in a way not approached until Orson Welles's *War of the Worlds* broadcast, and sensing the consequences of discovery he confessed.

Locke's confession did not satisfy another hoaxer however, for Edgar Allan Poe remained convinced that the Moon Hoax, as it came to be known, was stolen from his own story of a trip to the moon called "Hans Phall: A Tale," published in the *Southern Literary Messenger* for June, 1835. Eventually Poe did regain hoaxing supremacy with another story for the *New York Sun*, this one published on April 13, 1844. What is now called the Balloon Hoax first announced itself under these headlines:

ASTOUNDING NEWS BY EXPRESS, VIA NORFOLK! THE ATLANTIC CROSSED IN THREE DAYS! SIGNAL TRIUMPH OF MR. MONCK MASON'S FLYING MACHINE!

In faultless academic jargon Poe described the balloon which made the crossing, gave samples of a journal kept by aeronaut Harrison Ainsworth, and discourses on the complicated navigation of the craft. Nevertheless, frantic reporters and celebrity seekers could not locate Ainsworth or the remarkable craft, and the furor gradually died down. But for Poe the hoax was a success: it made him a small amount of money and gave him for a moment the attention of a reading public that ignored his serious work.

§ | *William F. Mannix.* In 1913 publishers in England and America brought out the authoritative *Memoirs of Li Hung Chang,* edited by William F. Mannix. Scholars confirmed the soundness of the book, and at least as late as 1948 one encyclopedia was recommending it as further, detailed reading on Dr. Li—this in spite of the fact that Chinese historians exposed the text as pure nonsense almost as soon as it was published.

Mannix himself was a known prankster (and worse), but libraries continued to shelve his book for years, and experts refused to admit that they had been hoaxed. The *Memoirs,* in short, became one of the most successful frauds in American literary history; it had its strong defenders even after it became widely known that Mannix had written the entirety of the book in 1912 while serving time in the Honolulu penitentiary for, you guessed it, forgery.

§ | *The Great Debate.* Ben Hecht and Maxwell Bodenheim staged the literary debate of the century in Chicago toward the end of World War I. Considering what happened and what might have happened, *staged* seems the right word to use. Many in the audience had been attracted by the names of the principals and had ignored the topic: thus they could not well object to "Resolved—That People Who Attend Literary Debates Are Imbeciles."

To begin the event, Hecht accepted the affirmative and stalked to center stage where he announced, "The affirmative rests." At this development Bodenheim put on his most surprised and pained expression and shuffled before the audience himself. He surveyed the crowd, glanced back at Hecht, and replied, "You win."

§ | *The Master Forger.* Martin Coneely, alias Joseph Cosey, was born on February 18, 1887, in Syracuse, New York. His unsuccessful career as a petty thief and a dependence on alcohol only slightly retarded progress toward one particular goal: during the decade of the 1930s he reigned as the most successful literary forger in American history.

After a dishonorable discharge from the army, which he later remedied with a forged honorable discharge, Cosey alternated between job and jail for ten years. It was a more or less random visit to the Library of Congress, moreover, that began his spectacular career. From the manuscript division Cosey stole a 1786 pay warrant signed by Benjamin Franklin, then President of Pennsylvania; but when he tried to sell the document to a New York autograph collector, the expert dismissed it as a fraud. There may indeed be a certain poetic justice in the fact that, after a year of careful practice, Cosey was able to sell that same dealer a forged Lincoln signature for more than the asking price of the original Franklin.

Although he was ambitious and in a sense successful, Cosey was by no means the best forger of his times: many of his Franklins, Poes, Lincolns, and Marshalls would not fool a careful amateur who compared real documents to his forged ones. Nevertheless, experts bought enough of his Franklin pay warrants to bankrupt the state of Pennsylvania if they had all been cashed. Cosey's specialty was Abraham Lincoln, whose hand he could imitate well enough to neglect signing many papers, letting the writing itself carry the burden of proof.

The most daring escapade of this career occurred when Cosey stumbled across a ledgerlike book from the nineteenth century with enough blank space in it for him to compose a sort of "Ur-Raven," complete with corrections and cross-outs, in the script of Edgar Allan Poe. The forgery was good enough to send experts on a bidding spree when it was offered at auction by Crown Art Galleries of New York. Some time later Colonel Richard Gimbel, the foremost collector of Poe editions and manuscripts, went to considerable pains to add this "Raven" to his other material, knowing full well that it was a Cosey forgery.

In more recent years Cosey counterfeits have become collectors' items themselves, sometimes bringing more than authentic manuscripts.

§ | *The Irving Trust Company.* William Manchester's popular history *The Glory and the Dream* contains the best account of this century's most ambitious literary fraud. In 1972 McGraw-Hill publishers planned to issue a certain bestseller, the detailed biography of reclusive billionaire Howard Hughes. Veteran novelist Clifford Irving had taped what he said were over a hundred meetings with Hughes "in various motel rooms and parked cars throughout the Western hemisphere," and he intended to turn the tapes into the most sensational biography of the decade. In a way he succeeded.

Irving had indeed done his homework. When *Newsweek* ran the facsimile of a Hughes note in 1970, Irving practiced the handwriting until he could imitate it to perfection. Later he was able to supply vice-presidents of McGraw-Hill and Time-Life Inc. the personal, handwritten confirmation of Howard Hughes that the biography in question was authentic, accurate, and approved. Handwriting experts agreed that the missive could not possibly have been faked. With that assurance the publishers launched their publicity campaign in spite of a few speculative jokes about Irving's earlier book *Fake!*, the biography of a Spanish art forger.

Irving's partners in the venture were his wife Edith and a "researcher" named Richard Suskind. When McGraw-Hill paid its advance to Howard Hughes, it deposited the checks directly into a numbered Swiss bank account (320496) registered to "H. R. Hughes," at which time Edith Irving, as Mrs. Helga R. Hughes, immediately withdrew the money and deposited it into another account. In the meantime Clifford Irving and Suskind were frantically researching the life of Howard Hughes in libraries and newspaper morgues across the country. Eventually they produced a manuscript bearing corrections and marginal remarks done in the same handwriting that had fooled experts earlier.

At this point events began to go awry. The real Howard Hughes held a telephone news conference during which he debunked the Irving biography. Nevertheless, Irving held a rival news conference and handled his case with such skill and courage that reporters began mumbling about the eccentricity of the hermitlike billionaire. Finally, though, the scheme crashed with the testimony of Danish Baroness Nina Van Pallandt, a sometime singer and entertainer who'd had an affair with Irving during the time he was supposedly interviewing Hughes throughout the Western hemisphere: she insisted that Hughes never held an interview with anyone.

The results were varied but not unexpected. Irving, Edith, and Suskind went to jail for a short time. Nina Van Pallandt became an instant celebrity flitting from talk show to talk show. McGraw-Hill recovered most of its money but none of its dignity. And for months the publisher's competitors lashed the company with jokes about a local New York bank which had just moved into the first floor of McGraw-Hill's new building, the Irving Trust Company.

§ | *The Recurring Hoax.* Erik Demos has proved that there is indeed a difference between a good book and a good hoax: the hoax survives longer. Demos is the pseudonym of freelance writer Chuck Ross, who, in 1975, submitted an excellent novel entitled *Steps* to four New York publishers. He knew the manuscript was a good one because it had won the National Book Award when it was first published by Random House in 1969. The real author was Jerzy Kosinski, but it was Demos who retyped the book and submitted it to prove a point, that a first novelist has virtually no chance to be published. All four publishers cooperated by rejecting the submission.

A trade biweekly called *Bookletter* carried the story in 1975 and mentioned the "author's" intention of trying again with his second-hand novel. He did, this time in 1977. *Steps* went to fourteen publishers; and all of them turned it down, the most embarrassed of the lot being Random House, the original publisher. One or two others mentioned that the style seemed imitative of Jerzy Kosinski, but the only encouragement came in the form of suggestions to try literary agents. So Demos tried. Twelve agents wouldn't bother with the manuscript. The Knox Burger agency lost it. On February 19, 1979, *Time* ran a short article on the hoax and announced that it was about time for it to recur, saying further that the conspirators were determined to elicit some form of positive response from the publishing community—either a contract or recognition of the novel for what it was. In the meantime Kosinski advises fledgling writers to go into accounting.

Phenomena

§ | *Introduction.* "Phenomena" are historical anecdotes rather than personal glimpses: they are about accidents, strategies, campaigns, and theories. One might say in addition that they are rarely "phenomenal" in the sense of being extraordinary: they are rather curiosities, items fit for an almanac. They are notes on quirks in American literary history.

§ | *The Book of Mormon.* At the heart of Mormonism there stands an extraordinary man, and from the man there came an extraordinary book. The writer was Joseph Smith, born in Sharon, Vermont, in 1805. Even to Mormons, Smith represents an enigma, a figure to be understood by faith rather than by reason; and to those outside the church, his name is virtually unknown. Furthermore, his book was not "authored" at all: Smith claimed only to be the transcriber of divine revelation. Like a latter-day Moses on Mt. Sinai, Joseph Smith encountered on Hill Cumorah the angel Moroni and translated golden tablets into his *Book of Mormon.*

During his childhood both of Smith's parents exhibited clairvoyance, and the boy himself put tremendous energy into the study of things religious. It was not until 1820 though that his mission became clear. In the fevered excitement of local revivals, the troubled youth attempted to sort out his thoughts. At a certain point he was "seized upon by some power which entirely overcame me. . . so that I could not speak." A pillar of light revealed to him God the Father and Jesus, both bidding him to resign from his church and prepare to found a new faith.

Three years later on September 21, 1823, Joseph Smith had a series of visions which made clear his role in the divine order of things. The angel Moroni appeared with this message: on a hill named Cumorah (near Palmyra, New York) were buried golden plates with mystical writings and with the plates were two stones, called Urim and Thummim, which functioned as "spectacles," through which one received power to translate the writing. When the seeker awoke, he went to the hill and uncovered the plates, but he was not permitted to examine them at once.

Actually it was not until 1827 that Smith began his task of translation; but then several others, Oliver Cowdery, David Whitmer, and Martin Harris, were permitted glimpses of the tablets and signed affidavits verifying some of Smith's claims. Mormons today refer to these men as the Three Witnesses. On another occasion eight individuals signed a document stating that they saw plates "which have the appearance of gold . . ., and we also saw engravings thereon, all of which has the appearance of ancient work and curious workmanship." These men today are called the Eight Witnesses.

In July, 1829, Joseph Smith finished his transcription. Although several publishers refused the text, Egbert B. Grandin agreed to print 5,000 copies for a guaranteed $3,000. That done, Smith and his followers set out in March, 1830, to sell a new book and a new religion to the farmers of upstate New York and northern Pennsylvania. They called themselves the Church of Jesus Christ of Latter-Day Saints. In 1844 hostile neighbors of the Mormons jailed Smith and Hyrum, his brother. A mob attacked the jail, and both prisoners were shot to death. Joseph Smith was then thirty-nine years old. One hundred years later his book had followers numbering two million.

§ | *"The Village Blacksmith."* In October, 1839, Henry Wadsworth Longfellow finished a poem which bestowed an immortality on a chestnut tree. The poet wrote to his father that the newly-completed "Village Blacksmith" was a piece praising their ancestor Stephen Longfellow, who had been a blacksmith, then schoolmaster, and then town clerk in Portland, Maine. The poem itself became famous quickly enough but caused no real sensation until thirty-seven years later when a local bureaucrat ordered the "spreading chestnut tree" to be cut down.

At the time of the cutting no one imagined that the real tree had become a national monument. Its being a danger to carriage traffic had absolutely no effect on outraged sensibilities however, and a virtual hurricane of protest blasted through the northeastern United States for months. Luckily, some now-anonymous diplomat had the good sense to save pieces of the tree, and the school children of Cambridge collected enough money to have the wood made into an ornate chair. When he was seventy-two, Longfellow tearfully accepted the birthday gift which bore this inscription:

To the Author of The Village Blacksmith

This chair made from the wood of the spreading chestnut tree, is presented as an expression of grateful regard and veneration by the children of Cambridge, who with their friends join in best wishes and congratulations on this anniversary.

For years the children who called at the Longfellow home saw the chair on display and were encouraged to sit in it. The poet wrote his reply to his young readers and had printed copies available for them at his house:

Only your love and rememberance could
　　Give life to this dead wood,
And make these branches, leafless now so long
　　Blossom again in song.

§ | *William Shakespeare.* In spite of New England's continuing prejudice against "stage-plays, masks, revels" and other "rude and riotous sports," Americans of the eighteenth century set up a Shakespeare industry that saw no real competition until the era of Eugene O'Neill. Efforts to Americanize England's greatest author began in 1786 when Isaiah Thomas made the first printing of Shakespeare in the New World, a few of the Bard's poems added more or less as an afterthought to a book of Mother Goose rhymes. In the next year William Woods published, in Philadelphia, *The Twins: or Which is Which? A Farce in three acts, altered from Shakespeare's Comedy of Errors.* Playbills and advertisements from the early years show that by far the most popular play in this country was *Richard III*; then tastes seem to have shifted more toward *Romeo and Juliet* by the mid-nineteenth century; and still later *Hamlet* and *King Lear* took on the importance they enjoy today.

Perhaps the continuing adulation of Shakespeare and his near monopoly of the American stage had some basis in this country's resentment of England's own "monopoly" of the Bard. Particularly in moments of high nationalistic fever, Americans have always rationalized that Shakespeare was somehow too good to really be British. Many would agree with Peter Markoe that "the noblest Bard demands the noblest stage," namely the

North American continent. When they were suspicious of all other things English, Americans could still muster fondness for,

> Old Shakespeare, a poet who should not be spit on,
> Although he was born in an island called Britain.
>
> (in Dunn's *Shakespeare in America*)

The greatest threat to England's monopoly came in the nineteenth century when the hallowed birthplace at Stratford-on-Avon actually went up for sale. Equal to the occasion was the American showman P. T. Barnum, who intended to buy the home, cut it into pieces, and ship it across the Atlantic to his own museum. News of the impending sale leaked, and the British experienced something like a collective nervous breakdown. Quickly they raised funds of their own, blocked the sale to Barnum, and declared Shakespeare's house a national shrine. But just as the British readied a sigh of relief, the extravagant entrepreneur struck again, this time with the deal of the century. Somehow Barnum slickered the London zoo out of the world's most successful exhibit, Jumbo the elephant, largest land animal of modern times. At that, Shakespeare faded to insignificance: Britain was ready for war.

§ | *Delia Bacon.* For more than a hundred years Shakespeare scholars have tried to erase the work of one woman and have not succeeded. This author was a New Englander named Delia Bacon, and for a time her insistence that Shakespeare was a fraud captured the interest of very influential minds. Her theory held in short that Sir Francis Bacon, in conspiracy with Sir Walter Raleigh, Edmund Spenser, and Sir Philip Sidney, wrote the collected works in a relatively short time and then assigned authorship to the virtually illiterate William Shakespeare.

Because few serious students support the Baconian theory today, it's hard to appreciate the original allure of what can only be called an intellectual craze in the second half of the nineteenth century. An early convert was Ralph Waldo Emerson, who sent Delia Bacon to England for further fact gathering. Another American, Nathaniel Hawthorne, rescued her from poverty in London and even wrote an introduction for her book. In 1857 she published *The Philosophy of the Plays of Shakespeare Unfolded,* which used some 700 pages to outline fully the extent of the Baconian conspiracy.

The plays, she claimed, were not to be understood as mere history or entertainment but represented instead highly advanced political theories built on an elaborate system of codes and symbols. Her own *Philosophy* decoded the plays and explained further that the ignorant William Shakespeare served only as a front to hide the identities of Bacon, Raleigh, Spenser, and Sidney—who stood to lose their lives if the Crown interpreted their true purposes. Mrs. Bacon was absolutely convinced that the grave of Shakespeare contained documents verifying the existence of a conspiracy and explaining in detail the true meaning of the plays. Having arrived at Stratford-on-Avon, she frequented the famous tomb at odd hours of the night, gazing at the stones for long periods as if she could x-ray the grave's contents. Over and over she declared her intentions of opening the tomb; but something, perhaps fear of what she would find, always held her back.

To be sure, many of her contemporaries dismissed Mrs. Bacon's contentions (she was, incidentally, no relation to Sir Francis); but her book did account for the problem of assigning such grand works to such a, well, "ordinary" person. Even today university-level instructors feel obliged to snarl and snort about this theory, usually without any knowledge of its author or origin. Moreover, what seems most phenomenal about the whole controversy is the sheer survivability of a concept that has been "officially" buried scores of times since the 1850s. Delia Bacon never abandoned her argument but neither did she share its immortality: she died in an insane asylum in Hartford, Connecticut during 1858, the victim, some say, of her own diseased imagination.

§ | *Science and Health.* One of the rarest books in American literary history has been systematically destroyed by admirers of the writer. The author herself was unusual in that Mary Baker Eddy remains the only woman ever to have founded a major religion. The ideas of her book, *Science and Health*, became the basis of that religion, The Church of Christ, Scientist; yet the phenomenon began long before the original publication date of 1875.

Throughout much of her youth Mary Baker Eddy experimented with mesmerism, communing with the dead, and various kinds of trance. It was not until she was forty years old, though, that she came under the influence of Phineas P. Quimby of Portland, Maine, a physician she hired to treat her chronic poor health and depression. Quimby's unconventional curing was miraculously successful, and Mrs. Eddy set out to make a careful study of his methods. She came to believe strongly in his contention that mind and spirit control the body and that suggestion can cure disease.

In 1866 Quimby died, and shortly after that Mrs. Eddy nearly followed him: she fell on ice at a streetcorner in Lynn, Massachusetts, and suffered terrific internal injuries. Friends carried her to the home of S. M. Bubier, but the local doctor asserted that she would never walk again and that there was great danger that she would die. In that condition, she later wrote, "I discovered the science of divine metaphysical healing, which I named Christian Science." Mentally she healed herself, arose, dressed, and immediately joined astonished friends in the Bubier parlor.

When she was fifty years old, Mrs. Eddy finished a manuscript outlining the principles at work behind her seeming miracle. Attached to some of Quimby's theories were a carefully worked out theology, numerous Biblical illustrations, and conjectures on the true composition of the universe. Years later there would be bitter controversies over exactly how much of the church's philosophy was conceived by Mrs. Eddy, but what cannot be disputed is the fantastic success of the philosophy. Late in the century Mark Twain commented on the growing number of followers by suggesting that at the current rate in seventy-five years the entire world would be Christian Scientists.

The 1875 edition of *Science and Health* is a remarkable book for another reason, however: it is the only edition which is completely the work of Mary Baker Eddy. The 1,000 original copies were poorly bound, filled with printing errors, and in content given to embarrassing philosophical assertions. All subsequent editions use a text that was completely revised by a man named James Henry Wiggin, an ex-minister and scholar of some note. Soon after 1875 the first editions of the 456-page text began to disappear although the Mother Church in Boston vigorously denied a campaign to "withdraw" the volume. The result of course is that Mrs. Eddy's early work provides a sort of inspiration even today to a rather specialized group of her followers, the wealthy book collectors.

§ | *Theodore O'Hara.* Perhaps the most famous single poem of the Civil War had absolutely nothing to do with the Civil War itself. In 1846 young Theodore O'Hara volunteered for service in the Mexican War, later saw action on the front lines, and was wounded at Contreras. The army shipped him home to Frankfort, Kentucky, for recovery. It was then in 1847 that O'Hara felt particularly moved on seeing the graves of other young Kentuckians who had fallen at the Battle of Buena Vista. On one amble through the Frankfort Cemetery he took time to jot out a rough draft of "The Bivouac of the Dead."

The poem got a polite reception but did not really capture the national mood until some years later. When war broke out between North and South, O'Hara volunteered once more and became a colonel in the Confederate Army. Again he fought on the front lines, and once more he survived. But by the time that O'Hara died in 1867, his poem had become quite a sensation: with an ironic kinship of spirit, families in all sections of the country read the melancholy words and associated them with the recent conflict. In a way, the public appropriation of "The Bivouac of the Dead" gave the verses a life of their own, and soon all connection with the Mexican War faded. Within a few years of Appomattox, visitors to cemeteries throughout the entire nation could see countless times on the tombstone of Yankee and Rebel alike the haunting first lines of O'Hara's poem:

> The muffled drum's sad roll has beat
>> The soldier's last tattoo!
> No more on life's parade shall meet
>> The brave and fallen few.
> On Fame's eternal camping ground
>> Their silent tents are spread,
> And Glory guards with solemn round
>> The bivouac of the dead.

§ | *Little Lord Fauntleroy.* The most successful popular writers have a keen sense of audience: it was said of Frances Hodgson Burnett, for example, that she never wrote a line that a publisher rejected. Certainly she was a phenomenon in her own right, with fifty books to her credit and a controversial lifestyle that bewildered the nineteenth century. After 1886, however, the author lived in the shadow of her own Little Lord Fauntleroy. Never has one character been so loved and so hated by so many different people at the same instant.

Sentimental mothers adopted the engaging little lord as his story appeared in *St. Nicholas Magazine* during 1885, although children were more or less indifferent to the character. The novel version of the next year enjoyed a handsome success, but it was the little earl's appearance on stage that seized the public's fancy: while one London company was playing 680 consecutive performances, there were in the United States almost 400 separate touring companies also doing *Little Lord Fauntleroy.*

The plot is the same one popularized by Alger: Cedric Errol, heir to a British title, travels to England with his mother and eventually wins the heart of his irascible grandfather, the Earl of Dorincourt. In the first meeting between the boy and the earl, Burnett describes Cedric as wearing a "black velvet suit, with lace collar, and with lovelocks waving about the handsome, manly little face. . . ." It was this appearance that translated so readily to the stage, and it was this appearance that became a fashion rage for more than a decade. Even worse for the little boys who were suited up à la Cedric was the image created by producers of the play who, for some reason, insisted on using actresses in the title role (the first movie version, for instance, starred Mary Pickford). In any case, the stage Fauntleroys set the fashion, and clothing manufacturers flooded the market with costumes for boys.

The velvet, the lace, and the lovelocks seem to have been an object of ridicule in America from the first, but the style would not die. Stephen Crane told of purchasing haircuts for two miserable boys in Fauntleroy attire, then of seeing one of the mothers faint at the result, and still later of receiving a box of cigars from one of the fathers. Master Cedric outlived the neighborhood bullies and despairing fathers, though, only as a stereotype: Frances Hodgson Burnett's character became at last merely a name and then only a costume, but the impact was tremendous.

It was well into the twentieth century that Louis Wolheim, then playing the lead in Eugene O'Neill's *The Hairy Ape*, encountered in New York a vision from his childhood. Coming toward him on Lexington Avenue was a tiny Lord Fauntleroy. As the apparition neared Wolheim, a group of boys began to taunt the obviously privileged but nonetheless miserable child. The hair, the hat, the lace, the shoes, the shirt, each got loud and considerable attention from the rowdies. At last one demanded, "Who curled your hair?"

Came the measured reply, "My mother, God damn her!"

§ | *Dime Novels.* The most successful publishing phenomenon in the history of American literature was not *Gone With the Wind* or *Love Story* or any other single work. Collectively, they were called dime novels, although individually they were as likely to sell for five cents or a quarter as they were for a dime; and today anyone can buy even first editions for only a few dollars. While these books were banned in school, damned from the pulpit, and forbidden at home, they nevertheless managed to have astonishing sales from 1860 to around 1910. Indeed, the dime novel supplied the first mass demonstration that the more a work is condemned, the more it is read. In fact, the firm of Beadle and Adams built a publishing empire on these books that nobody wanted, that is, no respectable person over the age of thirty-five.

What started the avalanche of sales was Mrs. Ann S. Stephens's *Malaeska, the Indian Wife of the White Hunter*, published by Beadle and Adams in the summer of 1860. Although it had all the adventure of later dime novels, *Malaeska* was atypical in a number of ways: it was written by a woman; it was aimed at an adult audience; it had been published earlier (serially in *The Lady's Companion*); its characters had at least some depth; and it didn't have a subtitle introduced by the word *or*. But what it did have was a corner on an untapped market; and it sold and sold and sold and sold.

The publishers attempted to satisfy the public demand for adventure by bringing out two new titles a month; and by their fourth month they had reduced success to something like a formula. All over New York and the surrounding area there appeared signs and posters saying merely, "Who is Seth Jones?" And then only when public curiosity had become absolutely painful did the publishers release a new set of posters bearing the lithograph of a tall, handsome hunter in buckskins: "I am Seth Jones," he said. And almost as if it were an afterthought, a mere extension of the poster, they published *Seth Jones, or The Captives of the Frontier*, by an unknown schoolteacher in Red Bank, New Jersey. The effect was astounding. *Seth Jones* sold over 400,000 copies; and the schoolteacher, Edward S. Ellis, earned a fortune beginning a career that would earn him several more fortunes.

Soon the firm of Beadle and Adams became more of a factory than a publishing house, its horde of writers churned out cliffhanger after cliffhanger, each of which was printed on cheap paper and then literally baled up like cotton and shipped out on flatcars. The four or five major publishers of dime novels produced in all some one hundred volumes a year for a solid fifty years, and individual authors such as Horatio Alger could write several hundred books during a career. Alger himself sold over 250,000,000 individual copies of his works. So popular was the dime novel that even the Civil War could not damage sales. Soldiers on both sides grew addicted to the books, and more than one truce was arranged less for the exchange of prisoners than for new titles by Ellis. In time, though, monotony, specialized magazines, and radio killed off the dime novels. "Modern" critics looked down on them as being hopelessly passé, a failed experiment, and an embarrassing lapse of the national taste. Nevertheless, some eighty years after the publication of *Malaeska*, publishers began to use the same Beadle and Adams formulas to reach the same markets which made the dime novel such a sensation. This time though they used a new name: the books were called paperbacks.

§ | *Edward Bellamy.* In 1888 this son of a Baptist minister produced a book whose success spread far outside the influence of the publishing industry. Bellamy's *Looking Backward*, which became the most widely read utopian fantasy in American literary history, has what most critics agree to be a shallow plot: it is the story of Julian West who, falling asleep in 1887, wakes up in the year 2000. What is most engaging in this book is a series of lectures given to West by a character named Dr. Leete, who explains how society evolved into a benign socialistic community.

Although *Looking Backward* proved to be popular enough, no one recognized it as a real phenomenon until "Bellamy Clubs" began sprouting all over the country. Reformers everywhere tried to institute the very changes in government that had been described in the novel, and Bellamy himself gave up pursuit of a career in fiction to devote himself to the social movement he had created. He even wrote another book in 1897 to answer attacks on his schemes: he called this one *Equality*.

A loose organization of Bellamy Clubs called itself the "Nationalist" movement and in fact enjoyed some political success in the last decade of the century. The aims of Bellamy's legion came directly from his vision of the future: government monopoly of business and industry, abolition of money, equality of wealth, and some form of government service by all citizens. Bellamy's ideas were still popular as late as the Depression years of the 1930s when reformers on the left quoted from *Looking Backward* in supporting such real enterprises as the Townsend Plan and the New Deal itself.

§ | *Nellie Bly.* While a reporter for the New York *World*, Ms. Bly convinced Joseph Pulitzer to sponsor a real race between her and the fictional Phileas Fogg, a character in Jules Verne's *Around the World in Eighty Days*. Although the publisher had considerable prejudice against sending a woman to compete with Fogg's supposed record, a sharp business sense forced him to give in. Bly left New York on November 14, 1889. In France she interviewed Verne himself before racing on to Suez, Calcutta, Singapore, and Japan. By the time she reached San Francisco, interest in Nellie Bly was feverish, and sales of the *World* were soaring. Her arrival in New York prompted a gigantic parade on Broadway. Total time for the circumnavigation—seventy-two days, six hours, ten minutes, eleven seconds.

§ | *Charles M. Sheldon.* If Jesus Christ had been an author, what would he have written? There was a man who claimed to know back at the turn of the twentieth century. Far from being a religious crackpot, though, Dr. Charles M. Sheldon was one of the most widely respected clergymen of his time: he spent more than ten years thinking about Jesus's potential reactions to modern America, and in that same period Sheldon accomplished two of the most remarkable literary feats in the history of any nation.

He began in failure. As minister to the Central Congregational Church of Topeka, Kansas, Sheldon grew distressed at his shrinking audience of young people. In the summer of 1890 he responded by junking his old sermons and writing his own novel, a chapter of which he read every Sunday evening. The book was called *In His Steps, or What Would Jesus Do?* and concerned a number of ordinary people who tried to lead their lives for one year "as Jesus would have done."

To say that Sheldon achieved a kind of success would be an alarming understatement. He packed his church. He published his novel serially in a Chicago newspaper. Then when the full novel came out, it turned into what may be the greatest bestseller in American literature. No one can be sure because a flaw in the copyrighting of the book put *In His Steps* in the public domain. The legitimate edition of 1897 actually made Sheldon very little money because many pirated editions appeared at the same time. Estimates of total sales range from a low of 8,000,000 to a high of 40,000,000; but whatever the numbers, they were astronomical.

Sheldon was not so much interested in this completely unexpected success as he was by a debate over one of his characters, a newspaper editor who ran his paper as Jesus would have and at a profit to boot. The only way to settle the issue, it seemed, was to attempt the experiment. He got the opportunity when publisher Frederick O. Popenoe turned over to Sheldon the *Topeka Capital* for one week, lock, stock, and newsprint. The trial run lasted from Tuesday, March 13 to Saturday, March 17, 1900. During that time Sheldon gave himself up to composing what Jesus Christ would have written if He had returned as a newspaper editor. According to the clergyman the task was relatively easy since Jesus would have concerned himself with the inner man rather than with externals. Thus, the *Capital's* society page shrank to virtually nothing; crime reporting and sensational news became mere filler; signed editorials went to the front page; and advertisers for tobacco or alcohol had their money returned—along with their advertisements. It is hard to say whether Sheldon convinced cynical newspapermen to revamp their styles because the editing experiment became a news event in itself, but it does seem that this most unprofessional of writers accomplished in five days his second literary miracle: in that time daily circulation for the *Topeka Capital* rose from an average of 11,223, to 362,684. And on Sunday, March 18, 1900, Rev. Sheldon led his regular morning church service.

§ | *Algonquin Round Table.* This informal literary society grew famous, or rather notorious, in the 1920s because of the explosive wit displayed by the luminaries who lunched daily at New York's Algonquin Hotel. The only rule for membership seems to have been an ability to hold one's own with the likes of Dorothy Parker, Marc Connelly, and Alexander Woollcott.

While the legend surrounding the Table's origin varies, most accounts agree that Woollcott, Franklin P. Adams, and Heywood Broun worked their way from a small table in the hotel's Pergola Room to a larger one in the Rose Room. Soon only the round table in the center of the floor could accommodate the enlarged "membership," but the luncheons themselves became known only as Board Meetings. Since a waiter named Luigi regularly served the table, someone immediately suggested the "Luigi Board." In fact it was only after a caricaturist finished a group portrait that the public began repeating phrases dropped at the "Algonquin Round Table."

Quotations from Monday's lunch frequently became sparklers for newspaper columns written on Tuesday by Woollcott and Broun. Soon the conflicting barbs shot by Parker, Ross, Connelly, et al. became popular enough to qualify, if not as a legitimate movement, then at the least as an amazing phenomenon, with the New York *Times* and the New York *World* giving regular news coverage to the Algonquin wits. On the other hand, there were no nights of the Round Table, just a smaller subgathering known as the Vicious Circle among other things. This was a highly competitive group of poker players consisting of Harold Ross, Woollcott, Adams, and on occasion one or two others; but even these remained faithful to the Hotel Algonquin, perhaps because owner Frank Case sensed the good publicity in reserving a room for them at no charge.

To prove that the Round Tablers could write the wittiest material in the country, members produced in 1922 their own, private Broadway revue called *No, Siree!* Dorothy Parker composed "The Everlastin' Ingenue Blues"; Jascha Heifetz supplied the music; Harold Ross didn't get on stage but played a cabdriver nevertheless. The finest touch came from the drama critics of the Round Table who invited professional actors and actresses to sit in the audience and to review the play for the next day's newspapers (which they did with considerable malice aforethought). The group secured the Forty-Ninth Street Theatre in New York for its one-shot performance and presented on April 30, 1922, what must have been the most sensational private "event" in the history of American drama. It was called an "Anonymous Entertainment by the Vicious Circle of the Hotel Algonquin." One attended by invitation only.

§ | *B. Traven.* Easily the most mysterious writer in American literature is B. Traven, the pseudonym of a man born on May 3, 1882; or May 5, 1890; or 1894; or 1901—probably in Chicago, or San Francisco, or Germany. Before he died in Mexico City on March 26, 1969, Traven had published in thirty-six languages and over 500 editions; yet his identity remained a secret from the time of his first publication in 1926. Various scholars have thought him to be Jack London (who pretended to have died), Ret Marut (a Bavarian socialist), an American black fleeing injustice, a leper, an expatriate of the old IWW, a fugitive Austrian archduke, or ex-President Lopez Mateos of Mexico (who reasonably pointed out in a press conference in 1969 that he was only five years old when Traven's first book was published).

It wasn't until the 1930s that Traven's work began to appear in America through the firm of Alfred A. Knopf, but mysteries multiplied rather than cleared up. In *The Night Visitor and Other Stories*, for instance, textual critics think that they can detect the American rendering of a British translation of a German translation—of something. The reasons for such a convolution have never been explained.

In 1947 Warner Brothers purchased movie rights for *The Treasure of Sierra Madre*, appointing John Huston director. When Traven expressed admiration for Huston in a letter, the studio invited him to become a consultant for the filming. Huston himself travelled to Mexico City and met a man who claimed to be Traven's representative: the latter presented a card reading, "Hal Croves, Translator, Acapulco." The filmmaker and others suspected that Croves and Traven were in fact the same man, but the question has never been settled.

Just before Traven's *The Death Ship* went to press in Germany, his publisher in that country wrote to him for photographs and publicity information. The author replied this way:

> My personal history would not be disappointing to readers, but it is my own affair which I want to keep to myself. I am in fact in no way more important than is the typesetter for my books, the man who works the mill; . . . no more important than the man who binds my books and the woman who wraps them and the scrubwoman who cleans up the office.

§ | *John Clayton.* The single most successful (that is to say marketable) hero in American fiction was, oddly enough, an Englishman named John Clayton, Lord Greystoke. He was the natural son of another John Clayton, Lord Greystoke, and later the adopted son of Kala, a great she-ape who called him Tar-zan, meaning "white skin." He was lord of the jungle and for more than half a century lord of the Saturday matinees and various publishing enterprises. Tarzan appeared for the first time in *All Story* magazine for October, 1912, as Edgar Rice Burroughs's second published work, a novella called *Tarzan of the Apes*. "I did not think it was a very good story," said the author, "and I doubted it would sell." Although now it seems strange that book publishers agreed with him, it is true that one firm after another refused to come out with a hardback version, even A.C. McClurg and Company who eventually took what they considered to be a fool's chance by publishing the work. Tarzan did appeal to the public though, and the demand for new Tarzan adventures sent Burroughs back to the typewriter time and again. In fact, it was this very popularity which created a strange problem: merchandisers of Tarzan by-products simply usurped the character. So powerful was this industry that books became unimportant to the lucrative Tarzan concession: thus fifty years after Burroughs's initial success his corporation had failed to renew copyright on nearly half of his works.

Burroughs followed . . .*Apes* with twenty-five more Tarzan novels which in turn spawned a commercial empire: Tarzan toys, dolls, posters, t-shirts, loincloths, comic books, cartoons, trade designs, jewelry, prints, pencils, notebooks, and movies helped to make the author a wealthy man. The movies were especially important, with Olympic swimmer Johnny Weissmuller as the most popular Tarzan of all. Surely there is not an American under the age of fifty who has not at least once in his lifetime given vent to that most audiogenic of all war cries. Still, the yell is a thing not meant for human lungs and actually was not perfected until the 1940s when MGM technicians combined five separate sound tracks into one tape. The individual sounds were a dog's growl, a note from the G-string of a violin, a warbling soprano note sung by Lorraine Bridges, a hyena cry run backwards, and Weissmuller himself contributing an imitation of earlier Tarzan yells.

One must remember that Burroughs and his creation had been, if not exactly household cries, very popular figures before the Weissmuller films, however. The very first Tarzan movie appeared as early as 1918, and other stars such as Elmo Lincoln and Buster Crabbe had played the ape-man. It was the growing popularity of Tarzan which drove screenwriters and cartoonists to improvization, thus creating a whole new body of "facts" about the jungle lord. Indeed, one measure of the character's continuing appeal has been the continuing fervor with which purists attack the continuing misconceptions about the "real" Tarzan. For instance,

1. Tarzan does not live in a tree house; he presides over his own African plantation.
2. Tarzan does not speak in monosyllables; he is fluent in English, French, German, Swahili, and animal languages.
3. Tarzan does not live in sin with Jane Parker; he was formally married to Jane *Porter* by her father.
4. Tarzan and Jane do not have a son named Boy; his name is Jack, and he is their natural offspring, not an orphan found in the jungle.

And on go the examples.

So strong was the Tarzan character that Burroughs himself sometimes felt trapped in spite of having produced other financially successful books. And he may well have been trapped in a peculiar sense that no one understood until half a century after *Tarzan of the Apes*. When the author died, his Edgar Rice Burroughs Corporation put so much energy into merchandizing Tarzan that it neglected to renew copyright on many of the remaining novels. This slipup meant that by 1962 half the canon of one of America's most popular writers had fallen into the public domain. In a sense Tarzan had become too successful. Once more it became impossible to find any Burroughs novels, partly because the Corporation itself had ignored the author's Martian, Venusian, and Pellucidarian books. It was competition among publishers for these latter titles which sparked a mid-sixties boom in Burroughsiana which has lasted right down to the present day. Of course anyone with the most rudimentary sense of irony can predict what happened: by far the most popular figure in this revival has been, once more, John Clayton, Lord Greystoke.

§ | *Willard Huntington Wright.* Because he wrote successfully without ever becoming a real success, Willard Huntington Wright became a legitimate phenomenon only after creating for himself a new identity and a new career. Today we would call him a workaholic straining to put his considerable urbanity and careful scholarship into such works as *What Nietzsche Taught, Modern Painting, The Future of Painting,* and *Modern Literature*. Wright was a learned critic of language and the arts who could consistently turn out two books a year while holding down editorships on several magazines and newspapers. He collapsed in 1925.

It was immediate hospitalization and prolonged rest that saved Wright from a nervous breakdown. Nevertheless, when his doctor ordered a complete abstinence from reading, the author balked. At last a compromise developed in which Wright agreed to a strict observation of all other rules in return for the privilege of reading light mysteries and detective novels. By the time his strength returned, he had become addicted to the genre and had even resolved to try his own hand at writing a mystery or two. When he left the hospital, he as much as left behind his old identity and began an extraordinary new life as S. S. Van Dine, one of the most popular and successful detective novelists of all time. The key to this new life was his creation of Philo Vance, a new breed of sleuth whose sophistication clearly reflected Wright's own impressive learning. Van Dine and Vance launched their respective careers in 1926 with *The Benson Murder Case* and never lost the public's attention after that. In some ways Vance, Van Dine, and Wright were identical, all three being recognizable for their attention to detail, research talents, and hoard of esoteric facts. So successful was Van Dine's writing that readers frequently mistook the fiction for reality. The ultimate compliment came from a doctor—it would be delightful to think it was the same one who treated Wright—wanting to know more about the Benson case. At the heart of a letter he wrote to Van Dine's publisher is the following:

> Other than texts on medicine these are the most interesting books I have ever found.
>
> The Benson murder appeals most strongly to me. I am very desirous of obtaining newspapers that were printed shortly after the tragedy and read the speculations, theories, etc., concerning the possible murder. . . . For this reason will you answer the following question. What was the exact date . . . on which Alvin Benson was murdered?

§ | *Who Built The Mousetrap?* There are a few authors, such as Benjamin Franklin, Ambrose Bierce, and perhaps the later Mark Twain, who are remembered as much for their sparkling quotations as for their longer works. Certainly the dean of this college was Ralph Waldo Emerson, our country's most quotable quoter. Many of his pronouncements have become part of the national heritage, for instance this one:

> If a man can write a better book, preach a better sermon, or make a better mouse-trap than his neighbor, though he builds his house in the woods, the world will make a beaten path to his door.

A fine monument to self-reliance is this quotation: it sounds so very, well, Emersonian. The problem, though, is that Emerson never wrote these words. And therein lies a story.

It is true that the mousetrap quotation became very popular and that schoolteachers, calendar salesmen, and almanac compilers all assigned it to the Sage of Concord; but scholars have never located the words in any of Emerson's writings. Others suggest that Thoreau was the author, but again the words do not appear in his works. In fact, the earliest known printing of these famous lines occurred in Oakland, California, during 1889. The occasion was the publication of *Borrowings*, a book of quotations compiled by the ladies of the First Unitarian Church of Oakland. There on page thirty-eight sat the mousetrap, credited to Emerson.

While in 1855 Emerson did write a passage very similar to this one for his journal, he does not ever refer to any rodent-catching devices. To settle the furor over exactly who wrote what, the philosopher's son Edward Waldo Emerson reported that his father indeed had not invented the mousetrap, at least not on paper. But the result of this denial was more confusion: suddenly the "real" authors began popping up all over the country. It seemed for a time that every hack writer in America claimed the quotation or had it claimed for him. Especially flustered was Mrs. Sarah S. B. Yule, one of the original compilers of *Borrowings*: in 1912 she remembered getting the quotation from her own commonplace book, having copied it there from "an address given long ago." Of course the critics howled with glee, most charging that Mrs. Yule had simply made up the quotation and tacked Emerson's name to it. So for a time the 1889 edition of *Borrowings* became quite a collector's item among cynics because of what Emerson did *not* say.

In the newspaper controversies over the issue none of the theorists credited Sarah Yule's story with any degree of truth or accuracy, and unfortunately there is no new empirical evidence to settle the matter. Nevertheless, there is a chance not only that she was right but that she heard the quotation from Emerson himself; for in 1871 the great philosopher visited San Francisco (across the bay from Oakland) and lectured not once, but five times. It is entirely possible that he revised his journal entry into the mousetrap anecdote as he spoke extemporaneously. Also possible is that one of his audiences contained a sixteen-year-old girl named Sarah Beach, later Sarah Yule, who copied into her commonplace book the words that no one else remembered. How ironic it would be that the elder Mrs. Yule could not recall exactly how Sarah Beach came by the quotation and that in recovering additional fame for Emerson she pulled down ridicule on herself.

§ | *The Dead Man's Chest.* It's a rare occurrence when a poet writes a phenomenally popular poem and thereby makes himself anonymous, ignored, and willfully forgotten; but that's what happened to Young E. Allison, city editor of the Louisville *Courier-Journal*. The story begins in the 1880s with the years' long success of Robert Louis Stevenson's *Treasure Island* and his allusion to a sea ditty containing the now famous lines, "Fifteen men on the Dead Man's Chest—/Yo-ho-ho and a bottle of rum!" Curiously, though, if one rereads the novel he will see that Stevenson never gives the reader more than a few enigmatic lines. That's what the young American editor did: long after the novel's first publication Allison wrote the "original version" of "The Dead Man's Chest," although he gave it a different title.

To understand the controversy that followed, one must know that Stevenson never quoted more than a couple of the poem's lines for a very good reason: there weren't any more. The novelist had simply made up the words and tossed them into his narrative to add a sea salty flavor. In a letter to Sidney Colvin the author wrote, *"Treasure Island* came out of Kingsley's 'At Last' where I got the Dead Man's Chest—and that was the seed." Now if one goes back to Kingsley, he discovers an interesting fact: the Dead Man's Chest isn't a literal chest at all. It's an island which, along with Rum Island, Fallen Jerusalem, the Dutchman's Cap, and others, makes up a part of the West Indies. Also, by accident Kingsley had miswritten the name: the real island was called Dead Chest Island, but the name Stevenson copied somehow seems more appropriate.

Allison had read *Treasure Island* sometime before 1891, for it was that year in which he scratched out three stanzas "completing" Stevenson's lines. Henry Waller, also of Louisville, added music to the words; and the two persuaded William A. Pond & Company to publish the song they called "A Piratical Ballad." It impressed no one and faded quickly into obscurity. Later Allison revised his lyrics into a poem of five stanzas and published it in the *Courier-Journal* under the title "On Board the Derelict" (later changed to simply "Derelict"). Newspapers in the Midwest and West reprinted the rollicking old sea ballad, but always anonymously, perhaps because Allison's name had been clipped in an early exchange. This time Allison was much more successful with his tale of blood and booty: soon everyone knew the ending of "Stevenson's" ditty:

> Fifteen men on the Dead Man's Chest—
>   Yo-ho-ho and a bottle of rum!
> Drink and the devil and done for the rest
>   Yo-ho-ho and a bottle of rum!
> We wrapped 'em in a mains'l tight,
> With twice ten turns of a hawser's bight,
> And heaved 'em over and out of sight—
>   With a yo-heave-ho
>   And a fare-you-well
>   And a sullen plunge
>   In the sullen swell
> Ten fathoms deep on the road to hell!
>   Yo-ho-ho and a bottle of rum!

In July 1914, a reader queried the New York *Times* about the incomplete song in *Treasure Island*; and two months later there appeared another letter explaining that the words were part of a very old and anonymous sea ballad about pirates in the West Indies and further that the Dead Man's Chest was an island on which a famous English buccaneer had wrecked and buried treasure. Then in the same column the editors reprinted a six-stanza version of Allison's poem. Of course, the researcher was wrong on three counts: the chantey wasn't old; it wasn't anonymous; and there was not an island called the Dead Man's Chest.

On October 4, 1914, a Mr. Walt Mason published a letter in the *Times* in which he revealed his discovery that the poem had been written by one Young E. Allison but that he had been unable to locate information on Allison in any of the biographical cyclopedias of the day. Obviously Mason found nothing for the simple reason that the author was still very much alive and not buried, as everyone assumed, in some dusty record of forgotten poets. But unfortunately Allison had indeed been forgotten. When the poet himself wrote to the New York *Times*, editors dismissed him as a crank; and they refused to publish as well a letter by C. I. Hitchcock detailing the true history of the poem which for twenty-three years had been taken to be both authentic and anonymous. Young E. Allison did not die until 1932, and even then he died without credit for his most famous work.

§ | *The Movies*. It was both fashionable and necessary for many of the writers of the 1930s and '40s to make a pilgrimage to Hollywood. The attraction, simply, was high pay during hard times: even Faulkner and Fitzgerald needed the money in spite of their pretentions to a kind of intellectual slumming. The big production companies, on the other hand, were on the whole careful not to exploit the phenomenon. The result was a lot of fine screenwriting going into such nonliterary films as *A Star Is Born* (Dorothy Parker, 1937), and *Horse Feathers* (S. J. Perelman, 1932).

Of course relations were not always idyllic. In 1946, for example, someone wrote to Raymond Chandler about the movie version of *The Big Sleep*: he wanted to know who murdered the Sternwood chauffeur. Chandler returned a wire saying, "I don't know," and charged the telegram to Warner Brothers. Brother Jack Warner hit the ceiling and asked sarcastically if such communications were really necessary. Perhaps not, but the questioner had just written to the wrong man: after all, Chandler was only the author. The real expert behind *The Big Sleep* was its screenwriter, a chap named William Faulkner.

As a matter of fact, the Chandler illustration points to the curious and seemingly random yoking of authors and screenplays. There have indeed been a few famous writers who've worked on the screenplays of their own books, for instance John Steinbeck (*The Pearl*, 1948), Thornton Wilder (*Our Town*, 1940), Theodore Dreiser (*An American Tragedy*, 1931), and Ayn Rand (*The Fountainhead*, 1949). Richard Wright even acted the title role in an Argentine movie version of *Native Son*. But at other times Hollywood has produced some strange marriages. Did you really think that Hemingway wrote *A Farewell to Arms*? Well, he didn't; for the movies it was Ben Hecht. How about *Watch on the Rhine*—a play by Lillian Hellman? No, Dashiell Hammett wrote this one in 1943. Have you always thought of *To Have and Have Not* as another Hemingway title? Think again: William Faulkner did it in 1945. And who wrote *Gone With the Wind*? The answer, believe it or not, is F. Scott Fitzgerald and Ben Hecht, both major contributors to the script although the former didn't get screen credit for writing a single word and the latter admitted he never read the novel.

§ | *In the War*. Everyone knows of Ernest Hemingway's exploits as an ambulance driver in World War I, but what of other American writers and other wars? How many of their readers know that Malcolm Cowley, John Dos Passos, Robert S. Hillyer, and E. E. Cummings all served in the ambulance corps? That Russell Davenport of *Fortune* magazine had the same job and won the Croix de Guerre twice? That Cummings was tried for espionage in a French court? That Horatio Alger was rejected as unfit for the Union armies?

While the military careers of some writers have passed into legend (Poe, Whitman, Twain) certainly the service of most authors gets little mention in the anthologies and histories; so to help make up for the omissions here's a brief report on some obscure war records:

When Sidney Lanier graduated from Oglethorpe University in 1860, he realized he could not continue his studies; so the promising young musician joined the Macon Volunteers at the beginning of the Civil War. For a time he served along with his brother as a mounted scout in campaigns along the James River. Then in 1864 Lanier took assignment as a signal officer on a blockade runner. He was captured on November 2, 1864. Although Lanier remained confined only four months, the wretched conditions at the Federal prison at Fort Lookout, Maryland, left him gravely ill; and he never fully recovered. His novel *Tiger Lilies* (1867) reflects many of his war experiences.

Raymond Chandler joined the Canadian army in August, 1917, and later fought as an infantry platoon leader in France with the Seventh Battalion of the Canadian Expeditionary Force. In June, 1918, not far from Cambrai, his unit was caught in a German barrage. Chandler was the only survivor.

J. D. Salinger served in counterintelligence during World War II, landing at Normandy with the Fourth Infantry Division and fighting at the

Battle of the Bulge toward the end of the war. His work involved interviewing both civilians and prisoners in hopes of uncovering Gestapo agents.

Noor Inayat Khan came from a background of mixed cultures, but her American mother was Mary Baker Eddy's niece. Her code name during World War II was "Madeleine," taken from a character in one of the many stories she wrote for children. Recruited as a spy in London, she trained as a radiotelegraphist and later joined *Prosper*, the most important and vulnerable underground network in occupied France. An efficient Gestapo captured Madeleine, and she was tortured to death.

During World War I James Thurber trained as a cryptographer along with Stephen Vincent Benét. Later he worked at the State Department as a code clerk and according to Benet became quite adept at solving difficult messages. Thurber's later book *The 13 Clocks* contains characters which are all ciphers from the government's Green Code of the war years. Thurber also spent time in France, during the war and afterwards: he was there in the mid-twenties and did *not* meet Hemingway, Gertrude Stein, Fitzgerald, Dos Passos, or Faulkner.

John Ciardi was a central fire control gunner on a B-29 in World War II.

Richard Eberhart, on the other hand, was a training officer in aerial free gunnery for the Navy and later tutored the son of King Prajhadipok of Siam.

Ralph Waldo Emerson was too old to fight in the Civil War, but when he was nine years old he was turned out of school to help build breastworks of earth to stall a possible British invasion during the War of 1812.

Theodore Geisel (Dr. Seuss) made it to Lieutenant Colonel after serving from 1943 to 1946. He won the Legion of Merit for his work in preparing indoctrination films for U.S. troops.

Frederick Faust was killed in action in Italy on May 11, 1944. He had been the author of some two hundred books and better known as Max Brand, the king of the pulps. He had written his own epitaph:

> Only the young fear death.
> A god has crossed their path, and they are sure
> Of Happiness, if it would but endure. . . .
> The aged speak not of it. At the door
> They stand with cheerful faces to the last
> Like men who on the homeward way have passed
> The steps of darkness many times before.

Robert Lowell tried twice to enlist in the American armed forces and both times was rejected. By the time they did call him up, Lowell had become a conscientious objector.

Edith Wharton was in France at the outbreak of World War I and at first took a job aiding homeless French children. Later she became a full-fledged war correspondent, writing Robert Bridges in 1915, "I was in the first line trenches, in two bombarded towns, etc., etc. —don't proclaim it too soon, for I don't want to be indiscreet."

Joyce Kilmer, the poet who wrote "Trees," was killed in action in World War I.

The frontier humorist Johnson Jones Hooper was secretary of the Confederate Congress.

Erskine Caldwell was in Moscow when Hitler betrayed Stalin, and began the Russian invasion of June, 1941. As one of the few English speaking foreigners in the city, he was immediately "drafted" as a war correspondent and remained one of the only sources of news for months.

Alan Seeger was killed in 1916 while fighting with the French Foreign Legion. His poem "I Have a Rendezvous with Death" appeared in the *North American Review* for October of that same year.

During the War of 1812 Washington Irving became Aide-de-Camp of Governor Daniel D. Tompkins of New York. His rank was full colonel. According to Irving his most heroic action occurred when Tompkins, General and Commander in Chief of all the Militia and Admiral of the Navy of the State of New York, fell off his horse. Irving hoisted him back to his exalted position.

Henry James was prevented from fighting in the Civil War by a mysterious "obscure hurt" which he never explained but sometimes associated with his back. He went to Harvard Law School instead of the army.

Theodore Roethke was classified 4-F in 1942.

Edgar Rice Burroughs, the oldest war correspondent of World War II, was present at Pearl Harbor on December 7, 1941. He watched the bombing of Hickam Field from a nearby beach.

Ambrose Bierce was a sergeant of the 9th Indiana Volunteers during the Civil War and took part in the bloody fighting of Shiloh. The second day of the battle he fought his own men, trying to prevent a general retreat and making every effort to beat them back on line.

Philip Freneau sailed as a privateer in 1775, a risky business if one is captured. He was indeed taken by the British in 1778 and placed on the prison ship *Scorpion* where he received brutal treatment. When he was exchanged some time later, Freneau immediately joined the New Jersey Militia and served "honorably" for several more years.

In December, 1862, Louisa May Alcott entered the Union Hospital in Georgetown as a volunteer nurse. The sheltered girl who had never seen death or suffering had arrived just in time for the battle of Fredericksburg: soon the hospital was overflowing with torn and dying men. Within weeks she contracted typhoid pneumonia, and authorities sent her back to Concord, Massachusetts, with every expectation of dying herself.

§ | *Titles.* One might think that choosing a title would be an author's easiest chore, and so it is for a few. Harold Frederic, for example, insisted on naming his second novel *Douw Mauverensen* since he'd had that title in mind from the start, but he wondered later why no one bought his book. Other writers agonize for weeks only to offer something like *Gertrude of Wyoming* or Lydia Sigourney's "Monody on the Death of the Principal of the Connecticut Retreat for the Insane." Part of the agony arises because publishers and authors see titles differently: to a writer the title is part of his book while to a publisher it is an advertisement. Usually there is a compromise, but a settlement may take some time. In 1878, for instance, George Washington Cable wrote to his publishers suggesting *Jadis* for the title of his latest work. The publisher said no. Cable next tried *Prose Idyls for Hammock and Fan.* No? well, how about *The Old Regime; Hammock and Fan; Creoles et Creoles; A Peculiar People; Half Hours for Hammock and Fan; Odors of Cypress & Orange; Under the Cypress & Orange; Clusters from a Creole Vine; Creole Burrs & Blossoms; A Gallery of Creole Antiques?* They agreed at last on *Old Creole Days*.

The experts say good titles work by association (after a taste of Pope's *Dunciad* who could resist the American *Porcupiniad?*), by a crafty incongruity (ever read the "Social Life of the Newt"?) or by delayed response (did you think twice about *No Matter from What Angle You Looked at It, Alice Brookhasen Was a Girl Whom You Would Hesitate to Invite Into Your Own Home?*). No doubt this is all true, but a greater truth is that fine titles are as likely as not to come from accidents. A case in point would be the book by William Burroughs originally styled *Naked Lust*: Jack Kerouac nevertheless misread a manuscript as *Naked Lunch*, and Burroughs liked the "new" title better.

There have been enough titles abandoned in American literary history to fill, well, an entire book. But while it's a phenomenon of no particular interest to authors and publishers, few readers have seen a title slagheap. Here's a sampling of original titles followed by the more famous published versions:

(The Inside of His Head)	*Death of a Salesman*
(The Exorcism)	*Who's Afraid of Virginia Woolf?*
(O Lost)	*Look Homeward, Angel*
(The Poker Night)	*A Streetcar Named Desire*
(Among the Ash-Heaps and Millionaires)	
(Trimalchio in West Egg)	
(Trimalchio on the Road to West Egg)	
(Gold-Hatted Gatsby)	
(Under the Red, White, and Blue)	
(The High-bouncing Lover)	*The Great Gatsby*
(The California and Oregon Trail)	*The Oregon Trail*
(A Word Out of the Sea)	"Out of the Cradle Endlessly Rocking"
(In the King's Arena)	"The Lady or the Tiger?"
(The Bride and Her Brother)	*Member of the Wedding*
(Army Post)	*Reflections in a Golden Eye*
(Tomorrow Is Another Day)	*Gone with the Wind*
(Journal)	*Two Years Before the Mast*
(Letters from Prison)	*Soul on Ice*
(Farther Off from Heaven)	*The Dark at the Top of the Stairs*
(The Pathetic Family)	*Little Women*
(The Year of the Rose)	*The House of Mirth*
(Something That Happened)	*Of Mice and Men*

(The Highlands of Africa)	*The Green Hills of Africa*
(The Iron-Bound Bucket)	*Mr. Roberts*
(The Drunkard's Holiday)	*Tender Is the Night*
(The Education of a Personage)	*This Side of Paradise*
(The Fawn)	*The Yearling*
(Facts)	*Time Magazine*

§ | *Gladiator.* Some literary phenomena become successes because of their packaging, or repackaging in the case of Philip Wylie's *Gladiator.* When this novel appeared in 1930, it attracted no particular attention except among a few science fiction readers. Still, there was something appealing about this tale of a contemporary Hercules, a man who could bend steel bars in his bare hands or deflect bullets with a shrug. Author Jerome Siegle saw the possibilities for the further development of such a character but produced nothing significant until he hit upon a collaboration with Joe Schuster, a cartoonist from Cleveland, Ohio. Their response to the Wylie material was to re-present it in the form of a comic strip, borrowing some of the dialogue and adding a few tricks to the hero's repertoire. The effect was magical. By the late 1930s their hero had become one of the most marketable commodities in the publishing business: they called him Clark Kent or, at other times, Superman. Only Philip Wylie and a few others remembered him as the modern gladiator named Hugo Danner.

Anecdotes

§ | *Edward Albee.* In 1961 Albee worked in New York on the play which later became his most widely-recognized success. As he wrote he recalled the phrase which would become the title:

> There was a saloon—it's changed its name now—on Tenth Street between Greenwich Avenue and Waverly Place. . . and they had a big mirror on the downstairs bar in this saloon where people used to scrawl graffiti. At one point back in about 1954 I think it was—long before any of us started doing much of anything—I was there having a beer one night, and I saw "Who's Afraid of Virginia Woolf?" scrawled in soap, I suppose, on this mirror. When I started to write the play it cropped up in my mind again. And of course, Who's Afraid of Virginia Woolf means who's afraid of the big *bad* wolf—who's afraid of living life without false illusions.

§ | *Louisa May Alcott.* Only since World War II have scholars known that Louisa May Alcott, the genteel author of *Little Women*, maintained for years a secret identity as A. M. Barnard, writer of blood and thunder tales for the cheap fiction factories of the day. Although she grew up in the Concord of Emerson, Thoreau, and the Transcendentalists, the Alcotts themselves were poor; and Louisa May attempted to earn extra money by hiring herself out as a companion to an elderly woman named Richardson in nearby Dedham, Massachusetts. This "companionship," however, included shoveling snow, chopping wood, and housecleaning; so the future author quit in disgust after seven weeks, returning the four dollars given to her by the Hon. James Richardson.

It is not clear exactly when Alcott began earning money as a writer of lurid tales, but we do know that throughout 1855 she brought in fifty dollars by teaching, another fifty from needlework and twenty dollars from the sale of certain suspicious stories. Perhaps her first gory masterpiece came in 1854 with the publication of "The Rival Prima Donnas" (one singer has another crushed to death) in *The Saturday Evening Gazette*. In any case, long before she conceived *Little Women*, Louisa May Alcott, or rather A. M. Barnard, had published "Behind a Mask" and "The Abbot's Ghost" in gaudy outlets such as *Frank Leslie's Illustrated Newspaper*. In 1867 appeared *The Skeleton in the Closet* and *The Mysterious Key*, both as dime novellas. Nevertheless, scholars did not see behind the mask of Louisa May Alcott herself until Madeleine Stern and Leona Rostenberg discovered letters to publishers clearly linking the writer to her pseudonym. In 1943 the Bibliographical Society of America published Rostenberg's revelations about the career of A. M. Barnard, and much more recently Stern has edited and published two volumes of the stories. Only after she was well established as a gothic writer did she attempt the shift resulting in *Little Women* and her most popular books.

"Stick to your teaching, Miss Alcott," had said publisher James T. Fields at the beginning of her career; "you can't write."

§ | *Sherwood Anderson*. Everyone knew that Horace Liveright was a womanizer, enough of one to get into real trouble with his wife; and Sherwood Anderson didn't help matters any. In *A Story Teller's Story* Anderson recalled meeting the publisher in New Orleans:

> He was then, and, for that matter, until the end of his life, a very handsome man, tall and erect, his hair just touched with gray. He walked with an easy swing and when I saw him that day in New Orleans, he was accompanied by a very beautiful woman.
>
> There was an absurd mistake made. Already I knew Horace Liveright, had been with him on several occasions in New York. He was the publisher of my friend Theodore Dreiser and of another friend Eugene O'Neill. He was with a beautiful woman and I had seen him with many beautiful women.
>
> "Meet my wife," he said and "Oh yeah?" I answered.
>
> There was an uncomfortable moment. It *was* Mrs. Liveright. I was sunk and so was Horace.

§ | *William Cullen Bryant*. Reflections on the transitory nature of life prompted the seventeen-year-old Bryant to compose his most famous work, "Thanatopsis." Rather than seeking publication, though, the young poet tossed his poem into a drawer of his father's desk. It was not until six years later that the elder Bryant discovered the composition and offered it to Richard Henry Dana, then editor of the *North American Review*. Dana, with good reason, suspected a hoax: to think that a seventeen-year-old could have written a poem so superior in quality to the productions of most mature poets of the day called for a real leap of faith. It was some weeks before Dana became a believer, but he did finally publish "Thanatopsis" in the *Review* of September, 1817.

§ | *Erskine Caldwell.* Although times were hard for everyone in the 1930s, they were particularly hard for young men and women doubtful of their starts as professional writers. With little hope of financial reward, Erskine Caldwell sent his early manuscripts to *Scribner's Magazine*, forcing himself to compete with the best authors of the day. On one occasion he hand delivered a packet of his short stories to a senior editor there and sequestered himself in New York's Manger Hotel to await the reaction.

The verdict did not come until the second day; and when the phone did ring, it nearly shattered Caldwell's nerves. But it was good news. *Scribner's* agreed to take "The Mating of Marjorie" and "A Very Late Spring," and the editors were willing to negotiate a purchase price. How about two-fifty?

This opener caught the author off balance; but Caldwell knew how to horsetrade and carefully took the emotion from his voice as he suggested he'd really expected a bit more for two stories. Okay, okay, came the reply: they'd go to three-fifty, but not a cent higher. Still the author was unsatisfied. Even by Depression standards three dollars and a half seemed small reward for the effort that went into his writing.

The incredulous editor explained as kindly as he could that the offer had in fact been for three hundred and fifty dollars.

Oh, replied Caldwell, that'd be just fine.

§ | *Truman Capote.* In mid-November, 1959, two men murdered in cold blood the family of Herbert William Clutter, a farmer who lived near Garden City, Kansas; and the *New Yorker* magazine made what seemed to be an absolutely bizarre choice of reporters to cover the story. Author Truman Capote swept into Garden City wearing a Dior jacket and towing an "assistant." The jacket was a flamboyant pink velvet, and the assistant was a subdued relative of his, later to make a name for herself as the author of *To Kill a Mockingbird*. Her name was Harper Lee.

Not only did Capote astonish his literary cronies by overcoming the initial suspicions of his New York lifestyle, but within a short while he became a guest in the home of Alvin Dewey, chief investigator in the case for the Kansas Bureau of Investigation. When the two murderers were apprehended, he became their friend too. Months later the one called Perry asked Capote to be a witness at his execution. Moments before the hanging he reputedly kissed Capote and cried, "I'm so sorry." The author passed out. Within a relatively short time the story of the Clutter murders appeared in a new literary form, nonfiction structured like a novel. Within fewer than ten years of the original publication collectors had already begun to scramble for first editions.

§ | *Willa Cather.* A relative with considerable insight saved Cather's first known composition, a four-page exposition of the superiority dogs have over cats. The first few lines of "Dogs," as they appear in manuscript, are printed below:

> *Dogs*
> The dog is a very intelligent
> animal. Some of them are
> very valuable & expensive, the
> Pug is sometimes worth one or
> two hundred dollars and the
> St. Bernard $1000.00.
> The nature of most dogs is
> kind, noble and generous.
> O! how different from the
> snarling, spitting, crul cat. (sic)

§ | *Bennett Cerf.* There was delicate negotiating to do when Random House decided to bring out an anthology of plays based on the Theatre Guild's great successes. Cerf went first to this playwright and then to that, saving the worst for last—George Bernard Shaw. Without his *St. Joan* the anthology would be worthless. It was Shaw's acid tongue and reputation as a sharp businessman that made Cerf quake; but when the two actually began talking, the author was surprisingly cordial and direct. "I'll give it to you if you pay me twice as much as you gave O'Neill."

"Isn't that pretty babyish?" countered Cerf.

But Shaw held the line. "All right; it's babyish. Do you want it or don't you?"

And so Cerf agreed. Just as the publisher was about to leave, Shaw piped up once more demanding even more money if a book club should choose the anthology for one of its selections. Here Cerf chuckled to himself, sensing a moral victory. Since no American book club would touch such a thing, the publisher readily agreed to double the contract if the book was chosen.

In 1936 *The Theatre Guild Anthology* appeared, and immediately Book of the Month Club made it one of its major selections. Shaw got four thousand dollars. Later Cerf heard of Shaw dismissing another negotiator, this one for a motion picture deal, by insisting, "There's no use in our talking about it because, obviously, you're a great artist and I'm just a businessman."

§ | *Raymond Chandler*. Rather than take a contemplated trip to Tangier with Helga Greene in 1958, Chandler allowed his mind to be changed by Ian Fleming. The famous British spy novelist suggested Capri instead. Even more attractive was the offer of the *Sunday Times* to pay all expenses if, on the way, Chandler stopped in Naples to interview Lucky Luciano, who had been deported from the United States some time before. The meeting did take place with America's premier crime writer apparently striking up something of a friendship with America's premier criminal. The article that followed was entitled "My Friend Luco," and in it Chandler pleads the innocence of the notorious gangster, calling him a scapegoat. The *Sunday Times*, on the other hand, did not share the author's high opinion of his host; and the article itself has never been officially published.

§ | *Richard Henry Dana*. Four publishing houses had rejected *Two Years Before the Mast* when Harper and Brothers made an unenthusiastic offer for the book in 1839, and even then the author's father balked at plans to produce a tiny first printing of one thousand copies. So negotiations began which delayed actual publication until September, 1840. The Danas wanted a wider circulation for the book; the Harpers feared heavy losses because of the depressed book market. Finally they reached an odd compromise: the publishers agreed to bring out young Dana's *Journal* (the original title) in the Harper Family Library and at the same time as a cheaply printed School District Library Book for the State of New York. Of course the book became an immediate success, and collectors today are happy to pay the handsomest of prices for what is surely the ugliest book in their libraries. In 1853, a fire destroyed the records of Harper and Brothers, so no one knows the total sales for what was one of the most popular books of the nineteenth century. There is some justice, though, in the fact that a number of years ago the firm of Harper and Row bought a single first-edition copy of *Two Years Before the*

Mast at an amount more than double that paid to Dana for all book rights in 1840.

§ | *Emily Dickinson.* Having published only seven poems in her lifetime, Dickinson left instructions that her remaining poetry be destroyed after her death. The decision to ignore these wishes resulted in incredibly complicated maneuverings and a bitter family feud which were not fully unravelled until the 1960s.

In 1886, Emily's sister Lavinia apparently sought the advice of close friend and neighbor Mabel Loomis Todd. The latter, in turn, contacted editor Thomas Wentworth Higginson; and all parties agreed on the publication of *Poems of Emily Dickinson* in 1890. The 115 poems of this first book received enough attention to justify the publication of *Poems: Second Series* in 1891 and *Poems: Third Series* in 1896. Throughout most of this period, however, Mabel Loomis Todd carried on an adulterous relationship with Austin Dickinson, brother of Emily and Lavinia and husband to Susan Gilbert Dickinson. There is even evidence to suggest that Lavinia knew of the affair.

In any event, Lavinia abandoned her reserve in 1895 when the foolish Austin actually willed a certain piece of land and part of his father's estate to Mrs. Todd. The outraged Lavinia sued for recovery of the property and won. Of course the embarrassed Todds left Amherst, but along with them went a camphor box containing a number of unpublished poems by Emily Dickinson. The bulk of the unpublished poetry nevertheless went to Emily Dickinson Bianchi, niece of the poet and Susan Gilbert Dickinson's daughter. Mrs. Bianchi's poems appeared in 1914 as *The Single Hound*, in 1929 as *Further Poems*, and in 1936 as *Unpublished Poems*.

Meanwhile, Mrs. Todd passed the camphor box along to *her* daughter Millicent Todd Bingham, and presumably its contents were published in 1945 as *Bolts of Melody*. Professor Thomas H. Johnson of Harvard University began his attempts to reconcile the descendants of all parties after World War II and succeeded after a fashion: in 1951 Belknap Press of the Harvard University Press published the first authoritative collection of Emily Dickinson's works called *The Poems of Emily Dickinson*. But to no one's surprise *Poems* did not settle the matter. From time to time a previously unpublished Emily Dickinson poem gets itself "discovered," most often by an advocate of one side or the other; and one can only wonder about the existence of other camphor boxes.

In her own day Dickinson was known as a good cook, not a good poet. In fact, according to family tradition, her father would not touch any bread unless it had been personally baked by Emily. Below is Emily Dickinson's own recipe for gingerbread:

1 Quart Flour
1/2 Cup Butter
1/2 Cup Cream
1 Table Spoon Ginger
1 Tea Spoon Soda,
1 Salt.
Make up with molasses—

§ | *Theodore Dreiser*. Still current among publishers is the story of Horace Liveright's ill-fated luncheon with Dreiser at the Ritz-Carlton in March, 1926. The two had come together with others to discuss motion picture rights for *An American Tragedy*, a book which the author felt had no future with the movies. Liveright, on the other hand, had a faith in the book which the author lacked. Apparently he extracted a promise from Dreiser to divide any movie rights quite generously if the publisher could place the novel with any studio. Suddenly Paramount executives took an interest in *An American Tragedy* and agreed to buy motion picture rights for eighty-five thousand dollars, and immediately Liveright scheduled a meeting at the Ritz to iron out details.

Of course Dreiser was overjoyed to learn of his new wealth and according to some onlookers began scribbling on the tablecloth figuring how he would spend the money. It was at this point that Liveright made the mistake of recalling the earlier agreement about dividing the movie rights. Dreiser mumbled something about "the usual ten percent"; and Liveright began to insist that the sum was much higher, reminding Dreiser of his own belief that they would not sell the book at all. The author followed with more protestations about "his" money, but Liveright refused to back down. Enraged, Dreiser snatched up his steaming coffee and hurled it in the publisher's face.

Reportedly, Liveright turned to the young Bennett Cerf of Random House and managed to say, "Bennett, let this be a lesson to you. Every author is a son of a bitch."

§ | *Ralph Waldo Emerson*. The great sage of Concord declined tragically in his final years, and the once powerful mind dimmed at last. Tradition has it that Emerson at times lost himself in trances or forgot the names of his friends. One of the most touching stories from this era concerns the death of Longfellow in 1882. At the funeral were all the major literary figures then living and with them Emerson himself who had gone to considerable hardship to pay his last respects. The great philosopher stopped at the casket, and those present sensed his struggle to recall more about the dead friend than what came to mind. Later he betrayed himself with a pathetic confession: "The gentleman we have just been burying was a sweet and beautiful soul, but I forgot his name."

§ | *William Faulkner*. The most famous words ever written or spoken by William Faulkner have nothing at all to do with literature: they were his farewell address to the United States Post Office branch at the University of Mississippi. There are so many variations of this tale that it seems clear that no one really knows what happened. What cannot be disputed is that the young author did not make a very good postmaster. Although he had been hired as the only postal employee serving the entire university community, he did not allow official duties to interfere with card games or his own writing. Of course, complaints resulted, some charging that he wrote a book (*The Marble Faun*) when he should have been sorting mail. In any case, a surprise visit from a postal inspector interrupted an otherwise pleasant hand of bridge, and Faulkner was forced to submit his resignation on October 31, 1924. Someone reportedly asked the author how he felt on leaving his domain; and Faulkner replied, "You know, all my life I probably will be at the beck and call of somebody who's got money. But I'll never again be at the beck and call of every son-of-a-bitch who's got two cents to buy a stamp."

Later on one of Faulkner's neighbors is supposed to have cornered him in the drugstore of Oxford, Mississippi. She had just bought his latest book and required certain information.

"Mr. Faulkner," she said, "I want you to tell me something before I read your new book. Do you think I'll like it?"

"Why yes," replied the author, "I think you'll like that book. It's trash."

§ | *Edna Ferber*. Although she never broke into the ranks of the major American authors, Ferber achieved unquestioned success in her own time with titles like *Giant* and *Showboat*. Still, there were those prejudiced against the writer because of her Jewish background, and Ferber developed quickly a fierce pride in her heritage and a withering putdown for people who insulted her. Once she confronted a female member of the cocktail circuit who had just offered some sort of "Oh, I-didn't-know-you-were-Jewish" remark. Without pause Ferber shot back, "Only on my mother and father's side."

She was not a particularly religious woman, but neither was there a question of her commitment. Among her papers was found this private dedication to her autobiography *A Peculiar Treasure*: "To Adolf Hitler who has made of me a better Jew and a more understanding and tolerant human being, as he has of millions of other Jews, this book is dedicated in loathing and contempt."

§ | *F. Scott Fitzgerald.* Although Maxwell Perkins fought long and frequently with his seniors to get Fitzgerald published by Charles Scribner's Sons, the distinguished editor had few character traits in common with the flamboyant author. A revealing contrast between the two lifestyles turns up in Perkins's understated account of an automobile accident in which Fitzgerald drove them into a pond. It seems that in July of 1923, Perkins, Ring Lardner, and Fitzgerald met in a New York speakeasy to discuss certain of Lardner's short stories. When the meeting broke up, the obviously uneasy Perkins could not avoid being driven home by the obviously drunken Fitzgerald: the latter roared off in the general direction of Long Island with the former trying to control what remained of his New England reserve and dignity.

The ride ended with Fitzgerald zooming off the road, down a hill, and into a dark body of water, variously identified as a lily pond, a sewage treatment plant, or the Atlantic Ocean. In time Perkins managed to laugh about the incident and then to turn it into a favorite anecdote of his own, telling his wife and others, "Scott . . . was saying what a good egg I was, and what a good egg Ring was, and what a good egg he was, and then, without thinking, as though it was something one good egg did to another good egg he just drove me into the damned lake."

§ | *Julian Hawthorne.* He had been the bright child of a remarkable father and had the additional advantage of growing up in the shadow of some of the greatest authors in American literature, or perhaps that was the problem. Julian Hawthorne remained forever in the shadow of Nathaniel Hawthorne. When he matured, Julian felt obliged to compete with or at least to imitate his father and wrote a number of short pieces for magazines and pulp publishers. But any comparison between the two writers proved embarrassing. Still, Julian did achieve a fame of sorts. Shortly before Mark Twain's death, the younger Hawthorne sold Clemens shares in a nonexistent silver mine. In fact, the fledgling confidence man managed to sell three-and-a-half million dollars worth of stock without ever paying a dividend before authorities caught up with him. In 1913, Hawthorne was indicted for mail fraud, and he served one year in the Atlanta Penitentiary.

§ | *Nathaniel Hawthorne.* Two literary societies dominated campus life at Bowdoin in the 1820s, the Peucinian and the Athenean. While members of the former were often politically conservative and products of elite families, Hawthorne and his fellow Atheneans came from slightly more humble stock and held to more liberal politics. In 1824, for instance, Peucinians supported the election of John Quincy Adams, and their campus rivals favored Andrew Jackson. It is no secret that Hawthorne's lifelong involvement in the Democratic party sprang from connections in the Athenean society; but what is not so commonly known is that Hawthorne did not cultivate what certainly would have been an interesting friendship because of the division between the two clubs. In fact, while he was at Bowdoin, Henry Wadsworth Longfellow, member in good standing with the Peucinian society, had no reason to suspect that he had anything at all in common with his classmate Nathaniel Hawthorne.

§ | *Ben Hecht.* In 1921, Ben Hecht, not yet at the height of his literary fame, was writing a column called "One Thousand and One Afternoons" for the Chicago *Daily News*. Readers frequently suggested anecdotes for the author to revise into full stories, but Hecht required an assistant to check the facts in each case and to search out new material. He called editor Harry Justin Smith with his request for a legman, allegedly saying, "Don't get me a reporter. A reporter doesn't react to anything but the mangled body of a society leader. Get me a very naive fellow who will notice everything. . . ."

Hecht got his wish and then some. The assistant seemed to have no judgment at all about the public interest or about newsworthy items. He was far too naive. Day after day he distracted Hecht with trivia and displayed no talent for writing whatsoever. Finally, after five weeks, the columnist could stand it no longer and had the young man fired since "nothing he writes makes any sense." So the former assistant to Ben Hecht had to satisfy his journalistic ambitions in another fashion, but within a few years he did achieve a success of sorts: his name was Henry Luce, founder of *Time* magazine.

§ | *Tom Heggen*. Of all the novels to come out of World War II, probably the funniest was Heggen's *Mr. Roberts*. The publishers at Houghton Mifflin were enthusiastic about the book and went to some considerable pains arranging for the kind of publicity they wanted to greet this new author. In return, they expected Heggen to do advertisements for himself. Thus in 1946, he journeyed to New York where he was paired with another new author, John Dos Passos, and launched on the luncheon circuit to spread good will and amusing anecdotes.

Heggen did not do well at the first stop.

He walked stiff-legged with fear into the ballroom of New York's Bellevue Hotel, where some ladies at the head table had saved him a place. He sat but ate nothing. Finally he heard someone, as though far away, introducing him; and Heggen dutifully stalked toward the speaker's platform. Once there, his throat swollen shut, his mind blank, his eyes glassy, he stood suffering for several minutes. At last one of his table companions offered to get him started by asking, "Mr. Heggen, perhaps you can tell us how you wrote your book."

At that the words returned. Tom brightened and piped, "Well, shit, it was just that I was on this boat. . . ."

§ | *Lillian Hellman*. Toward the end of World War II Lillian Hellman made a good will visit to Russia, travelling from Alaska, across Siberia, and finally to Moscow on board an American C-47 which was being flown by a Russian crew. American officials considered the trip a particularly dangerous one, and it is true that the author nearly died; but her misadventure had nothing to do with the war, the subzero temperatures, or the hazards of flying. In fact, it was a gentle and courteous translator who almost killed the American author.

At one of the many stopovers in Siberia, Hellman twisted her ankle on the ice; and in his haste to display some marvels of Soviet medicine the young translator rushed her to a new clinic some distance away. Although there was no doctor, two nurses on duty diagnosed the injury for what it was and insisted that there was really little to be done. At one point Hellman asked for a laxative, and the translator redoubled his prodding of the nurses into some sort of action. After long argument and longer consultation with a Russian-English dictionary, he secured a bag of salts which was to be dissolved in water, after which one would have no more worries. It turned out that he was almost right. Hellman dissolved the salts, drank off the potion, and immediately collapsed. For the two weeks of the flight she remained semiconscious and usually strapped down to boxes in the cargo hold of the plane.

After an eternity they arrived in Moscow with Hellman a bit better and now able to stand. The polite officials knew that she had been dangerously ill, so there were no speeches at the airport; instead her friend Sergei Eisenstein quickly escorted her to a hotel. Again Hellman collapsed, and a doctor from the American embassy diagnosed a pneumonia so grave that he administered his first shot of a new, still-unproved drug called penicillin. Gradually she recovered and found time to recount what she remembered of the events to Sergei Eisenstein, who spoke fluent English. It was Eisenstein who pieced together all that had happened, realizing first that there was no word for laxative in Russian and later that the salts had been for soaking the twisted ankle.

§ | *Ernest Hemingway.* The Hemingway yarns are magnificent, but constant retelling has made many of them clichés. Perhaps the most famous of these is the putdown of F. Scott Fitzgerald in "The Snows of Kilimanjaro," as it was first published in *Esquire.* Referring to the latter's adulation of wealthy society Hemingway wrote,

> He remembered poor Scott Fitzgerald and his romantic awe of them and how he had started a story once that began, "The very rich are different from you and me." And how someone had said to Scott, Yes they have more money. But that was not humorous to Scott. He thought they were a special glamorous race and when he found they weren't it wrecked him just as much as any other thing that wrecked him.

If Fitzgerald did not appreciate the original remark, he was even more upset to see it published in one of Hemingway's stories. He wrote to Hemingway asking him at least to change the character's name if ever he brought out the story in an anthology. For his part Hemingway did change the name for *The Snows of Kilimanjaro and Other Stories*, and "Scott Fitzgerald" became merely "Julian." The remark would have been less stinging, too, if Fitzgerald had known that it was not original with Hemingway, that in fact the same figure of speech had been used against Hemingway himself.

It all came about some time earlier when the author lunched with a writer named Molly Colum. Remarking on his own literary fame, Hemingway joked that he was becoming well known among the rich. Colum bested him with, "The only difference between the rich and other people is that the rich have more money." Hemingway remembered the line; and when the occasion arose, he used it to blast poor Fitzgerald. The shot was effective, but Hemingway didn't mention who fired first.

§ | *George Moses Horton.* This slave, born on a plantation in North Carolina, could not read and write until after his first book was published. As a child he created poetry based on Methodist hymns; and when his master moved close to Chapel Hill and the University of North Carolina, young George impressed the community with his poetic talents. Soon he was earning small sums by dictating love poems to students who would then mail the verses home to their girlfriends. In time Horton became a porter at the university and paid for himself using earnings from his compositions. After the Civil War he moved to Philadelphia and lived there from 1865 to his death (conjecturally, 1883). His published works include *The Hope of Liberty* (1829, reprinted in the North as Abolitionist propaganda), *Poetical Works* (1845), and *Naked Genius* (1865).

§ | *Washington Irving.* A nonexistent love affair caused Irving the most embarrassing moments of his life. What happened, or didn't happen, began during the author's trip to Italy in 1804. Apparently he saw but did not meet a lovely young woman named Bianca, wife of a Frenchman living in Genoa. It was there that he somehow came by Bianca's handkerchief and saved it as a souvenir. Sometime later, though, Irving lost the token and further erred by mentioning the loss to his friend Hall Storm. The devilish Storm of course hurried the news to Bianca herself, who, lo and behold, mailed Irving a bit of her hair in a heart-shaped locket. Three years later Irving still revelled in his "victory" and carried the lock and locket everywhere he went.

June, 1807, found the young writer in Richmond, Virginia, ostensibly as a lawyer in the spectacular trial of Aaron Burr, but in reality spending much of his time in the company of actor friend Thomas A. Cooper and enjoying what he could of Southern congeniality. Irving's fatal misstep occurred when he lent Cooper a pair of trousers. It was not until Cooper returned to Baltimore that he found in one of the trouser pockets a beautiful locket and some curls of a woman's hair. The mischievous actor sent rumors to every gossip mill operating and in a spare moment dispatched these lines to Irving:

> Receive these inquiries, dear friend, in good part,
> And since you have locked the fair hair in your heart,

Ne'er trust, of the girl who your fancy bewitches,
Such an emblem of love in another man's breeches.

§ | *Thomas Jefferson.* While he was president of the University of Virginia
the former President of the United States made a point of inviting each
student to Sunday dinner on a rotating basis. If there was anything
remarkable about these meals and the discussions which followed, surely it
would have come in the schedule of 1826; but Jefferson died on July 4, and
with him died the possibility of a notable encounter, a famous conversation
that might have been. Student number 136 on Jefferson's list for that year
was Edgar Allan Poe.

§ | *Orrick Johns.* No one remembers Ferdinand Pinney Earle or *The Lyric
Year* or the one-legged poet Orrick Johns, but people do remember Edna
St. Vincent Millay: she was the loser in a poetry contest sponsored by Earle
for the *Lyric Year*, an anthology of verse appearing in 1912. Orrick Johns
was the big winner. He had written a poem called "Second Avenue" aimed
at making "human greed despise itself"—for which pains he got $500.
Nevertheless this handsome check hardly compensated for the abuse Johns
received over the next years. Readers hated him for winning over the
nineteen-year-old Millay.

Actually his poem was adequate stuff: it's just that Johns had a poor
sense of timing. He sometimes got carried away in the heat of the moment.
For example, during a Greenwich Village party in the winter of 1914, Johns
and his cronies managed to stay warm only with liberal doses of booze and by
burning all the furniture in the room. According to legend, as the last chair
went up in flames, the obliging Johns snatched off his wooden leg and tossed
it into the fireplace. No one remembers how he got home.

§ | *Edith Newbold Jones.* Some critics claim that one can see the seeds of her
later writing in the very first lines of the very first novel by Edith Newbold
Jones: " 'Oh, how do you do, Mrs. Brown?' said Mrs. Tompkins, 'If only I
had known you were going to call I should have tidied up the drawing
room.' " The novel was never published because of adverse reaction by
readers of the manuscript: for instance, the novelist's mother, a member of
fashionable New York society, sniffed that "one's drawing room is *always*
tidy." That seemed to settle that. Still, Miss Jones was only eleven years old
when she wrote those words, and later the intercession of a family friend
named Henry Wadsworth Longfellow helped her get some poetry published

in the *Atlantic*. Still later she returned to the writing of fiction and enjoyed some considerable success, but not as Edith Jones. In the interim she had married a fellow named Wharton.

§ | *George Lyman Kittredge*. The legendary Kittredge dominated American literary scholarship for years. While he reigned as Professor of English at Harvard, few people dared to offer a differing opinion on Shakespeare or Chaucer since even his slightest frown could send mere assistant professors scurrying for cover. Stories about Kittredge are legion, but the one which best captures his style involves the answer to a mercifully anonymous body who questioned his credentials. Asked why he never finished his Ph.D., Kittredge did not thunder a reply, but merely looked puzzled and mused, "But who would examine me?"

§ | *Sinclair Lewis*. One of the most telling anecdotes concerning "Red" Lewis deals with a night he spent at the home of publisher Bennett Cerf in the autumn of 1948. After dinner Robert Haas telephoned inviting everyone to join him and his recently arrived guest William Faulkner. Cerf happily agreed but had to call back declining the invitation after Lewis insisted it was "his" night, not to be shared with anyone. Early in the evening, though, Lewis retired to the guest room because he was leaving for Italy the next morning. The Cerfs remained downstairs making conversation as best they could. Suddenly Lewis called out with considerable urgency, and the startled publisher dashed to the stairway thinking that some disaster was in the offing. When Cerf cried out himself, Lewis calmly replied, "I just wanted to be sure you hadn't slipped out to see Faulkner."

An atmosphere of animosity surrounds much of what is remembered about Lewis. For instance, in 1931, the editor of *Cosmopolitan* invited both Lewis and Theodore Dreiser to a formal dinner honoring Russian novelist Boris Pilnyak. Few guests knew that Dreiser had been accused of plagiarizing certain passages he had used in a book on Russia. But Lewis knew and attempted to torture Dreiser by greeting him with a loud raspberry and later standing at the table to say, "I am glad to meet Mr. Pilnyak, but I do not care to speak in the presence of a man who has plagiarized three thousand words from my wife's book on Russia."

Witnesses reported that after the meal Dreiser shoved Lewis into an anteroom and insisted on an apology. The latter replied with something else insulting, and Dreiser smacked him hard across the face. When Lewis came back with words like *liar* and *thief*, Dreiser punched him again. For a few days newspapers made much of the "fight" between America's paramount men of letters, but at last the incident achieved its true level with the publication of a parody titled "The Slap Heard 'Round the World.' "

Easily the most amusing among a whole series of ugly incidents was Yale's bumbling refusal of Lewis's Nobel Prize medal. The story goes that the author, somewhat the worse for drink, burst into the Sterling Memorial Library in New Haven loudly insisting that he was the world-famous writer, Sinclair Lewis, come to donate his Nobel medal to the university. The assistant librarian who spoke with him, however, thanked the foundering apparition for its magnanimity but politely refused the "medal." Somehow Lewis steered his way out of the building and roared off, nursing a hatred for Yale that lasted for years.

§ | *Abraham Lincoln.* When officials organizing the dedication of a national cemetery in Pennsylvania invited the President to attend the ceremonies, no one expected Mr. Lincoln to accept. No one wanted him to. Advisors feared an assassination attempt; bureaucrats felt he was needed in Washington; and, worst of all, program organizers worried that he might take too much time from the keynote speaker, Edward Everett. Lincoln did insist on saying a few words however. The day before the dedication found him suffering from a relapse of smallpox, but he managed to jot a few revisions into a speech he had written earlier. On November 19, 1863, Everett delivered the speech he had memorized: it took him more than two hours and flowed in the style of the very best oratory of the day. When Lincoln rose to speak, he hardly seemed to notice the single piece of paper in his hand. It was as though he were in a trance or exhausted by his illness. In all he spoke less than two minutes. Photographers got few pictures and complained that they had not had time to set up their tripods. Neither were the newspaper reporters of the day happy: they agreed that his Gettysburg address had been vastly inferior to Everett's and inappropriate to the occasion.

§ | *Henry Wadsworth Longfellow.* The frontispiece of many Longfellow volumes featured a portrait of the poet remarkable for its sad eyes and handsome beard. There is a story behind the growing of the beard, but it is not a happy one. On July 9, 1861, Longfellow's wife, Fanny Appleton Longfellow, attempted to seal an envelope containing locks of her children's hair. By accident the wax taper she was using lighted the frilly summer dress she wore at the time, and in a moment flames sprang up on all sides. Longfellow rushed in from another room and tried to extinguish the fire with his bare hands, but it was no use. Fanny died the next morning and was buried on the couple's wedding anniversary. Longfellow himself received burns to his face so severe that he later grew a beard to hide the scars.

When he studied at Bowdoin, Longfellow began his first serious work with poetry, writing there some of the most famous of his early pieces such as "Sunrise in the Hills" and the "Hymn of the Moravian Nuns." The latter poem is a real curiosity because it is at the same time based on a real incident and an embarrassing misconception. Longfellow came by his inspiration through the *North American Review*, where he read that the battle flag of Count Casimir Pulaski had been embroidered by the Moravian "nuns" in Bethlehem, Pennsylvania. Of course Moravians have no nuns at all and in fact represent an extreme Protestant reaction to Catholicism. Nevertheless, images of the convent took over the poem; and Longfellow wrote beautifully and skillfully of the "sisters' " mysterious rituals, of smoking censers, of ceremonial garments and flickering candles.

As a general rule Longfellow was much appreciated and greatly admired by the students at Harvard while he was teaching there. The university had hired him as its first professor of modern languages and expected him to institute a vigorous routine of lecture and evaluation. That he did, examining each of his students once a month throughout the year. The course of study itself was a formidable thing to behold, certainly enough to terrify modern collegians. Printed below is Longfellow's schedule for his first twelve lectures:

1. Introduction. History of French Literature.
2. The Other languages of the south of Europe.
3. The History of the Northern, or Gothic, Languages.
4. Anglo-Saxon Literature.
5. and 6. Swedish Literature.
7. Sketch of German Literature.
8, 9, and 10. Life and Writings of Goethe.
11. and 12. Life and Writings of Jean Paul Richter.

§ | *H. P. Lovecraft.* This writer of the macabre was in many ways as bizarre as some of his fictional creations. A recluse of many years, Lovecraft suffered from an incredible ailment which forces mammals to assume certain reptilian characteristics. This *poikilothermia*, or inability to maintain a constant body temperature, forced the author to wear layers of clothing even on very hot days. Below seventy degrees Lovecraft's skin became painfully sensitive, his body rigid, and his breath came in gasps. Several times in winter he collapsed outside his house in Providence, Rhode Island, and was rescued by strangers; on other occasions he could be observed in summer happily strolling along Florida sidewalks wearing his favorite wool overcoat.

§ | *James Russell Lowell.* When he wrote his memoirs, William Dean Howells recalled his first trip east to seek connections in the forbidding literary establishment. In Cambridge, Massachusetts, he secured an invitation to the home of James Russell Lowell, then at the height of his influence and reputation. Contrary to what the nervous young writer expected, Lowell proved to be a genial host; but the great man did have his eccentricities. When it came time to leave, Howells, who had been careful to observe all the proprieties, headed for the front door; but instead of ushering him toward the tree-lined street, Lowell took the arm of his guest and set off across the back lots of Cambridge. When they came to a board fence, Howells hoisted himself over with what little grace he could muster. Lowell, on the other hand, made an enthusiastic leap—straight into the side of the fence. A second time he tried to bound across, and again he fell back. Apparently determined to jump either over or through the obstruction, he tried once more with renewed energy. This time he made it, landing more or less intact near the astonished Howells. "I commonly do that the first time," was all he offered; and Howells continued along the shortcut no longer insecure in the presence of his literary hero.

§ | *Carson McCullers.* Anecdotes about this colorful writer and her family are nearly without number and always fascinating. On one occasion her mother, Marguerite Smith, took a bus to New York to visit the famous daughter. On the way Mrs. Smith sprang into conversation with an aristocratic-looking woman who had mentioned a fondness for reading. The conversation, though, became embarrassingly one sided, the subject being Carson's remarkable skills as a literary artist. Only later did the second woman let it be known that her father had also been a writer. Mrs. Smith paused now to ask her new friend's name. "I am the Countess Tolstoy," came the answer.

Perhaps most famous among her own friends was Carson's tale of innocently moving into a whorehouse on Thirty-Fourth Street in New York. Allegedly she suspected nothing until the "landlady" attempted to arrange a meeting between the author and a gentleman caller.

When she was travelling in France in 1947, McCullers insisted that her ignorance of French was no handicap. Nevertheless, pantomine did not help when a courteous young man shot a stream of incomprehensible syllables at her. Carson merely smiled and nodded from time to time. Days later publicity appeared proclaiming, "The Sorbonne of The University of Paris is honored to announce that Carson McCullers, American novelist, will speak on the comparison of French and American literature. . . ." The writer controlled her panic long enough to arrange a ruse with her friend, Professor of Comparative Literature John Brown, who, along with Professor René Lalou, undertook the actual lecturing while Carson sat on stage between the two smiling and nodding from time to time. By all reports her "lecture" was received graciously and enthusiastically.

§ | *H. L. Mencken*. Perhaps the greatest tribute to the effect of Mencken's pen came with this unanimous resolution of the Knights of the Ku Klux Klan of Little Rock, Arkansas, adopted September 7, 1925:

> WHEREAS, One H. L. Mencken is the author of a scurrilous article recently published in the Baltimore Sun, describing the Klan parade in Washington, D. C., August 3, in which he viciously slurs and insults the good women and the patriotic men who marched in that parade to the number of more than 100,000, declaring that there was not an intelligent or comely face among them, that they looked like a gang of meat cutters and curve greasers on a holiday and many other slanders and insults too vile and indecent to be repeated, therefore be it:
> RESOLVED, by the Knights of the Ku Klux Klan of Arkansas, a State which the said Mencken has in times past slandered as a "land of morons," that we condemn in the strongest possible language the vile mouthings of this prince of blackguards among the writers of America, to whom virtue, patriotism and democracy are only a subject upon which to expend the venom of a poisonous pen; that we further condemn the *Baltimore Sun* for heaping insults upon the good men and women of America, and that we commend the course of the Baltimore Chamber of Commerce in protesting against the calumny too degrading and false to come from the heart of one who is not himself a moral pervert.
> RESOLVED FURTHER, That copies of this resolution be sent to the *Baltimore Sun*, *National Courier*, Baltimore Chamber of Commerce and H. L. Mencken.

§ | *Marianne Moore*. In October, 1955, Moore received a carefully worded letter from David Wallace, head of the Ford Motor Company's Special Products Division requesting that the distinguished poet invent a name for a revolutionary automobile then on the drawing boards. What Ford wanted was another word like *Thunderbird* to conjure up "some visceral feeling of elegance fleetness, advanced features and design." Within a week she replied with "The Ford Silver Sword" (according to Moore the name of a flower growing only on Mt. Haleakala at elevations between 9,500 to 10,000 feet).

The company answered with a diplomatic request for other suggestions sending along sketches of the proposed body style to help Moore with her ideas. Wallace wasn't sure he was being taken for a ride so to speak until the second or third exchange of letters when Moore began suggesting names like "The Pastelogram," "Mongoose Civique," and "The Utopian Turtle-Top." With more and more ridiculous names pouring in, the problem suddenly became how to turn her off. It was more than a year later that Wallace ended the correspondence with this letter:

> Dear Miss Moore:
>
> Because you were so kind to us in our early days of looking for a suitable name, I feel a deep obligation to report on events that have ensued.
>
> And I feel I must do so before the public announcement of same come Monday, November 19.
>
> We have chosen a name out of the more than six thousand-odd candidates that we gathered. It fails somewhat of the resonance, gaiety, and zest we were seeking. But it has a personal dignity and meaning to many of us here. Our name, dear Miss Moore is—Edsel.
>
> I hope you will understand.
>
> > Cordially,
> > DAVID WALLACE
> > Special Products Division

§ | *Eugene O'Neill.* Authors and alcohol have made legendary combinations. In fact, any list of really heavy drinkers would have to include quite a few American writers: Poe, Bret Harte, Joaquin Miller, Fitzgerald, Hemingway, Ambrose Bierce, Dreiser, Sinclair Lewis, Faulkner, Crane, Sherwood Anderson, Upton Sinclair, Edna St. Vincent Millay—and Eugene O'Neill. It was a liquor-induced blackout, though, that was indirectly responsible for O'Neill's first success as a playwright. After a particularly heavy drinking bout he regained consciousness one morning in 1909 to find himself in bed with a strange woman. He roughly inquired her identity, and she replied, "I'm your wife. You married me last night." O'Neill escaped in something akin to disgust and signed on for seven months of sea duty. It was this long voyage that gave him the background for his famous *S. S. Glencairn* group, the one-act plays that started his successful career as a dramatist.

§ | *Dorothy Parker.* Although nearly everyone can recite Dorothy Parker's famous lines about men making passes at girls who wear glasses, too few really appreciate her as the sharpest wit of our century, perhaps because her best lines were spoken rather than written. Her early career was a tortuous route through varying successes and failures punctuated, it seems, at every turning point with some dramatic witticism. 1926 was not a very good year for Dorothy Parker, and some very good quipsters turned against her. In October, for instance, Ernest Hemingway astonished guests at the apartment of Archibald MacLeish by making tasteless jokes about her recent suicide attempt. "Here's to Dorothy Parker," he is reported to have said. "Life never became her so much as her almost leaving it."

Hemingway also contributed a poem on the same occasion. It concerned his lending a typewriter to Dorothy and her neglecting to return it, an allegation which was not true. No one could understand Hemingway's attack on his former friend, least of all Dorothy Parker; but when she made plans to leave France for New York, there was Hemingway at the docks to see her sail on the *Rotterdam*. Dorothy had maintained a hurt silence to this point; but as the farewell parties scrambled to shore, Hemingway took up his joke once again. He stood on the dock shouting up to Dorothy at the ship's rail: what would he do now without a typewriter? Apparently not giving a thought to her depleted finances, Dorothy picked up her own newly purchased typewriter, leaned over the side, and heaved it at the docks. Without a word, she had crushed Ernest Hemingway.

§ | *Edgar Allan Poe*. Throughout much of 1841, Dickens's *Barnaby Rudge* appeared serially in this country, both in official copies and in "extras" pirated by American publishers. In any case, the British author enjoyed a popularity that intrigued Poe, who undertook to solve the murder in *Barnaby Rudge* before it appeared in print. Poe's solution went to the *Saturday Evening Post* and appeared with some fanfare in the edition of May 1, 1841. A year later, when he visited Philadelphia, an astounded Dickens reported that Poe had indeed deduced the ending of the novel before it was even written.

In 1831, Edgar Allan Poe was dismissed from the United States Military Academy at West Point. Because an officer's commission represented the only secure income for a military man, Poe applied to West Point knowing that he would probably never make enough money in the outside world and hoping that as an army officer he would have both financial security and free time to write. Since he was already an army veteran, having risen to the rank of sergeant major, the daily regimen meant nothing to him; but what did complicate matters was relations with his stepfather John Allan. During the Christmas holidays of 1830, Allan ended a bitter quarrel with Edgar by writing that he did not wish to hear from his stepson again.

Poe wrote one final letter asking only for permission to withdraw from the Academy, a formality which would allow him to collect $30.35 in travel money. When Allan did not reply, Edgar merely stopped going to classes and spent the time working on his poetry. On January 23, 1831, the officer of the day ordered Poe to attend church, and the cadet refused. Later in the week he refused other direct orders to attend class. When on January 28, he offered no defense to the court martial board judging this conduct, Poe was found guilty of refusing to obey orders and dismissed from the Academy effective March 6, 1831.

Contrary to what one might expect and in stark contrast to his treatment by John Allan, many officers and cadets at West Point admired Poe and to some extent appreciated his poetry. One small kindness that became significant was the superintendent's permission for Poe to take subscriptions for a new book of poems. The price was a bit steep at seventy-five cents; but Poe gratefully dedicated the volume to "the U.S. Corps of Cadets," and in return he got enough money to survive a bitter transition to civilian life.

§ | *William Sydney Porter.* Most readers know that O. Henry served a prison sentence for embezzlement, but few realize that he had actually beaten the rap and only later turned himself in. William Sydney Porter, as he was known then, wrote copy for a Houston paper at the same time that he worked as a teller for an Austin bank, apparently helping himself to extra cash. Although bank officials accused him of embezzlement, Porter made a daring escape to Honduras where he lived in safety for some time. When he heard of his wife's illness, though, he returned to Texas, went to prison, and began writing short stories that made him famous. Today he lies buried in the cemetery of Asheville, North Carolina, a few feet away from the grave of Thomas Wolfe.

§ | *Ezra Pound.* During World War II Pound made propaganda broadcasts for Mussolini's government. While he was in Italy, he advised American soldiers to cease fighting for the corrupt league of Jewish bankers that controlled world commerce—and so on and so forth. Although Pound's words had little effect, General Mark Clark vowed to personally "shoot the traitor Ezra Pound" the moment he was captured. The poet wasn't shot, but he was captured and hustled off to Washington to stand trial for treason. Pound himself insisted that his defense be based on grounds that one who has renounced citizenship cannot be a traitor; his lawyer, however, sensed a better tactic and pleaded Pound insane. The trial judge agreed, and the poet was declared mentally incompetent to face the nineteen counts of treason against him. The prisoner then entered St. Elizabeth's Hospital for the criminally insane, which for a time became a sort of center representing the best poetic thinking in the Western world. Appeals to the government led by Robert Frost, T. S. Eliot, and Ernest Hemingway finally succeeded in 1958 when Pound was released as "permanently and incurably insane" but probably harmless.

§ | *E. A. Robinson.* It took thirty-five years and the intervention of a President of the United States for this famous poet to get his first recognition. Although Robinson read Shakespeare at age seven and wrote decent poetry at eleven, the poems published later in his first book got so little attention that the author had to take work as a time checker for a construction company. Luckily, though, a teacher named Henry Richards introduced one of his Groton pupils to Robinson's *Children of the Night*; and the student in turn mailed the book home—to the White House. In March, 1905, Theodore Roosevelt praised the book and offered Robinson a post in the New York Customs House. The President reviewed the poems in an issue of *Outlook* and the professional critics howled: Robinson was obviously an inferior talent; and, besides, what did Teddy Roosevelt know about poetry? While it may be true that the President's kind words actually hurt Robinson in some circles, the poet finally did achieve fame with *The Man Against the Sky* in 1915, thirty-five years after he had begun his career. In 1921 Robinson's *Collected Poems* collected the first Pulitzer Prize ever awarded a volume of poetry.

§ | *Theodore Roosevelt.* Although there are dozens of anecdotes detailing the origin of the term *Teddy bear*, few people know that Roosevelt despised the stuffed animals bearing his name. He issued statement after statement condemning the popularity of these cuddly toys, ending one diatribe with the following words: "Take away the little girl's dolly and you have interfered with the nascent expression of motherhood. . . . You have implanted the race suicide where it will work the most harm—in the very heart of the babies themselves." Not content with crude disclaimers, Roosevelt actually hired a young newspaperman to ghostwrite for Dr. Leonard K. Hirshberg some Spocklike articles on baby and child care. Not until later did the ghostwriter become famous under his own name, H. L. Mencken.

§ | *Harold Ross.* During World War I, before he became head man at the *New Yorker* and a dictator in the Eastern literary establishment, Harold Ross served his time as low man for the interservice newspaper *Stars and Stripes*.

But because Private Ross was one of the founders, he was low man in a very special sense of the term. Among his coworkers were Sergeant Alexander Woollcott, Captain Franklin P. Adams, and Captain Grantland Rice, along with Captain Guy T. Vickniskki, the officer ostensibly in charge. Ross had his own ideas on how to run a newspaper and didn't defer for a moment to those who outranked him. Vickniskki, on the other hand, couldn't see yielding to a private; so from time to time he simply had Ross arrested and then instituted his own editorial policy.

As circulation for the paper expanded, so did the private war between Vickniskki and Ross. The final battle began as a skirmish over refund policy to soldiers returning home. But because the dispute involved large sums of money, it went for resolution to the American high command. When officers there sided with Vickniskki, Ross and fourteen cohorts mutinied, claiming that *Stars and Stripes* had started as a newspaper printed for the common soldier by the common soldier and that they would refuse to surrender the principle. Principles, though, did not move the top brass. What did move them was the discovery that without Ross's mutineers the army simply couldn't publish the paper, which by 1918 had a circulation greater than that of the New York *Times*. The result was one of the most amazing surrenders in the history of the United States Army. Major Mark S. Watson, formerly of the Chicago *Tribune*, replaced Vickniskki as "overseer" of operations. But well before the greater Armistice of November 11, 1918, Private Harold Ross, lowest-ranking enlisted man on the staff, accepted his post as unquestioned editor-in-chief of *Stars and Stripes*; and apparently with no thought to the incongruity of his situation, he spent the remainder of the war ordering officers to their various assignments.

§ | *William Saroyan.* When Saroyan traveled east from California for the first time in his life, he came to New York with every intention of making himself into a best-selling author. Rather than being impressed with his first Broadway show (*Ceiling Zero*), he sneered that he could write a better play than that in twenty-four hours. He came close to living up to some of his boasts when in 1939 he produced not one, but two smash hits, *My Heart's in the Highlands* and *The Time of Your Life*. For the latter play he declined the 1940 Pulitzer Prize in drama.

§ | *Gertrude Stein.* In her student days at Radcliffe College, Stein took a course under William James. According to legend, for her final examination she wrote, "My dear Professor James, I really do not feel like taking an examination today."

James studied the paper, returned it with a *B*, and replied, "My dear Miss Stein, I sometimes feel that way myself."

The delightful reminiscences of Bennett Cerf, published under the title *At Random*, are a source for hundreds of anecdotes about American writers. In his book he makes an amusing and instructing confession regarding Gertrude Stein. Although he tried hard not to interfere with the work of his authors while he was president of Random House, the writing of this particular author Cerf found especially puzzling. Printed below is his "Publisher's Note" to Stein's *The Geographical History of America or the Relation of Human Nature to the Human Mind*:

> This space is usually reserved for a brief description of a book's contents. In this case, however, I must admit frankly that I do not know what Miss Stein is talking about. I do not even understand the title.
>
> I admire Miss Stein tremendously, and I like to publish her books, although most of the time I do not know what she is driving at. That, Miss Stein tells me, is because I am dumb.
>
> I note that one of my partners and I are characters in this latest work of Miss Stein's. Both of us wish we knew what she was saying about us. Both of us hope too that her faithful followers will make more of this book than we were able to!

§ | *Frank R. Stockton.* The latter part of the nineteenth century found this little-remembered man one of the most popular writers in the country, his famous short story "The Lady of the Tiger?" having brought him an acclaim that most authors could only imagine. In 1885, Stockton answered the thousands of requests for a solution to the original story by publishing another tale called "The Discourager of Hesitancy." In the latter a delegation from a distant town petitions the king of the first story for some word about which door the young man in "The Lady or the Tiger?" had chosen. The monarch replies with a new yarn in which a handsome prince must guess which of forty beautiful maidens he had just been tricked into marrying (while blindfolded). As the prince surveys the faces before him, one woman smiles, and one frowns. The Discourager of Hesitancy, a huge slave with a gleaming sword, steps forward, raising his blade; but at the last second the prince chooses correctly. The king now addresses the delegation saying, in short, that whoever guesses the maiden chosen by the prince will also hear the ending of "The Lady or the Tiger?"

Of course "The Discourager of Hesitancy" answered nothing and outraged many readers. Publishers too began to show less patience with Stockton: increasingly he received rejections for his stories, many asking why he didn't write another piece like "The Lady or the Tiger?" The point of course is that Stockton could not compete with his earlier success, and he died in relative obscurity.

In 1868, Mary Mapes Dodge started a new magazine called *Hearth and Home* to which Stockton contributed stories and, when he was desperate, recipes, dressmaking hints, notes on patent medicines, home decorating ideas, and articles on vermin control. You might want to try his recipe for "Cold Pink," a creation which brought him two dollars from the magazine:

> Take up all the white meat left over from Thanksgiving Turkey, and chop it up very fine. Pour a thin cranberry sauce over the cold meat. Mix well, put in a china form and set it away to get cold. When cold, serve.

§ | *Harriet Beecher Stowe.* With one book Mrs. Stowe established her career and sparked a conflict that blazed into civil war. But it was with a single book too that she extinguished her career and almost ruined the *Atlantic Monthly.* It happened this way. Mrs. Stowe wrote an article entitled "The True Story of Lady Byron" in which she presented Lord Byron as a profligate and pervert guilty of incest and other suggested dark doings. For proof she quoted passages from *Don Juan* and *Cain.*

Although he was suspicious of her accuracy and her motives, William Dean Howells agreed to publish Mrs. Stowe's piece since "the world needed to know just how base, filthy and mean Byron was, in order that all glamor be forever removed from his literature. . . ." The article appeared simultaneously in the *Atlantic* and *Macmillan's* and met with outrage—against Mrs. Stowe—in both America and England. Circulation for the *Atlantic* plummeted, and the publishers lost tremendous sums. In response to demands for proof the author quickly produced a book called *Lady Byron Vindicated* in which she expanded her original article without offering any substantiation for her charges: if anything, the book enhanced Byron's reputation as a romantic figure. For Mrs. Stowe, on the other hand, the controversy was disastrous: after 1870 she faded from public life and lived her remaining twenty-six years completely in the shadow of her earlier work.

§ | *Henry David Thoreau.* The Harvard of Thoreau's day offered little to inspire a future Transcendentalist. Although much has been circulated about his eccentricities as a student, the truth seems to be that a curriculum weighted heavily with Latin, Greek, and mathematics quashed much of Thoreau's individuality. Nevertheless, he did sign up for one seminar which offered potential relief: it was a course in German taught by a young professor named Henry Wadsworth Longfellow. For some reason, though, Thoreau stopped coming to class after only a few meetings: apparently he got as little inspiration from Longfellow's German as from Professor Cornelius Felton's Greek. Actually, it was insects that fascinated the student Thoreau, as evidenced by the great number of bug-treatises he read: librarian Thaddeus William Harris once remarked that Emerson's influence ruined the budding entomologist.

§ | *James Thurber*. Realism and attention to detail characterized Thurber's practical jokes while he was a writer on the *New Yorker* staff. General editor R. E. M. Whitaker once used too much red ink on galley proofs submitted by the famous humorist. Playing the part of an enraged lunatic, Thurber roared into the editor's office screaming obscenities and brandishing a toy pistol. When he took aim, Whitaker passed out.

In any case, Thurber's most elaborate caper involved fellow writer E. B. White and a daring bank robbery in Ardsley, New York. Gangsters stole White's Buick and used it in the holdup, and the car was recovered only after a fierce shoot-out with police. Of course detectives wanted to interview White as a matter of routine, but Thurber got wind of events and went out of his way to make White nervous before the police arrived. The interview did not go well. White grew even more jittery, and so did the cops. By an incredible stroke of bad luck White had written the date of a dentist's appointment on a memorandum sheet in his office; and, as one would guess in such an instance, it was the exact date of the bank robbery. The devilish Thurber found the memo and before the police arrived scribbled *der tag* beside the date. Wary detectives actually questioned White a number of times, and on each occasion Thurber would call into the office using the best and loudest gangster imitation emphasizing words like *caper*, *dough*, and *hideout*. Only after days of torment did White recover his shot-up car.

§ | *Mark Twain*. One of the most tragic ironies of Clemens's late life was the death of his daughter Jean during the Christmas season of 1909. Ever since the notorious "rumors-of-my-death-have-been-exaggerated" quote issued from England, newspaper reporters had badgered Clemens wanting to know if he were dead "yet," knowing that he would be good for a snappy reply. On December 23, 1909, Twain asked his youngest daughter to contact the Associated Press with the following: "I hear the newspapers say I am dying. The charge is not true. I would not do such a thing at my time of life. I am behaving as good as I can. Merry Christmas to everybody!" On December 24, Jean herself was dead: taken with an epileptic seizure, she drowned in her morning bath.

There is still some question about what really happened in 1877 when Mark Twain spoke at the famous birthday celebration for John Greenleaf Whittier. Assembled in the East Room of Boston's Hotel Brunswick were sixty of the century's most important literary figures gathered to honor the seventy-year-old Whittier and to toast the twentieth anniversary of the *Atlantic*. By all reports the guests received Clemens cordially, but their reaction changed to horror as the speaker unraveled his tale of three deadbeats named Longfellow, Emerson, and Holmes. In Twain's burlesque the three wastrels barge into the hut of a Nevada miner, drink up his whiskey, help themselves to his food, and otherwise insult his hospitality.

Years later Twain and his friend William Dean Howells recalled their own horror on realizing that the audience was not laughing and that a silence "weighing many tons to the square inch, was broken only by the hysterical and blood-curdling laughter of a single guest. . . ." Henry Bishop, the speaker who followed Clemens, experienced stage fright that amounted to panic: on facing those "awful deities" at the speaker's table, he collapsed.

Actually the evening was not the catastrophe that Twain pictures in his autobiography. Most Boston newspapers reported both laughter and applause for the speech, while editors who disapproved tended to publish small town papers in New England and the Midwest. Nevertheless, Clemens made elaborate apologies to everyone involved, getting only kind replies for his efforts. Longfellow himself wrote, "A bit of humor at a dinner table is one thing; a report of it in the morning papers is another. One needs the lamplight, and the scenery."

§ | *George Washington.* This enterprising young book salesman once sold two hundred copies of *The American Savage: How He May Be Tamed by the Weapons of Civilization* throughout the vicinity of Alexandria, Virginia. He later made good in politics.

§ | *Walt Whitman.* While it is true that Whitman himself contributed much to the Whitman legend, modern readers contribute even more by misinterpreting features of the poet's life. It's probably a mistake, for example, to read *Leaves of Grass* as a kind of homosexual manifesto or to point to Whitman's being fired from a government post as evidence of clear homosexual involvement in his own day. The true story is much less sensational and much more ambiguous. Because of the poet's service as a hospital corpsman during the Civil War, a member of Lincoln's cabinet secured for Whitman a minor political appointment in the Indian Bureau. When Secretary of the Interior James Harland located *Leaves of Grass* hidden in a desk, he was so outraged by the general sensuality that he had the author fired. Whitman's friends were themselves outraged by Harland's action. William Douglas O'Connor counterattacked with a combative pamphlet called "The Good Gray Poet" (the source of Whitman's sobriquet), and Whitman received a "transfer" to the Office of the Attorney General where he worked until age fifty-three. *Leaves of Grass* finally did live up to Secretary Harland's worst expectations: in 1881 it was officially banned in Boston.

§ | *Tennessee Williams*. Young Thomas Lanier Williams launched his writing career in 1927 when at age sixteen he published his first piece in *Smart Set*. The topic for his essay was "Can a Good Wife Be a Good Sport?" His answer was no. During the next year Williams published what must now be another collector's item in *Weird Tales*: the title of this one was "The Vengeance of Nitrocris." In 1938 the New York Group Theatre held a contest to identify the best young playwrights under the age of twenty-five, and once more Williams displayed considerable originality: he gave his birth date as March 26, 1914, a solid three years off the true mark of March 26, 1911. The lie seems to have been a fortunate one, however; the three sketches called *American Blues* won Williams a special award, one hundred dollars cash, and the confidence to continue writing plays.

§ | *Thomas Wolfe*. Wolfe had had far too much to eat and perhaps a little too much to drink one evening in 1934 when he insisted that he and Max Perkins work off the effects of their meal with a long walk. The pair ended up in Brooklyn Heights not far from the apartment where Wolfe had written *Of Time and the River*. Taken with the inspiration to show off his historic site, the author seized Perkins and set off toward a brownstone some distance away. On arrival they found the apartment door locked and Wolfe without his key, so the two scurried back outside and up the fire escape to the very top floor of the building; there they broke in through one of the apartment windows.

What the editor did not know was that Wolfe had moved to a new residence several weeks before. Unaware of his danger, Perkins took his tour and settled leisurely into a chair while Wolfe poured stiff drinks of someone else's whiskey. Moments later the new tenants returned home. Perkins and the wife panicked at the same time: she ran screaming for the police and he tried desperately to become invisible. Wolfe, on the other hand, rose magnificently to the occasion by offering the husband a drink, turning on the Southern charm, and striking up a literary conversation. Perkins later wrote, "Tom treated him as though he were the editor of the *Atlantic Monthly*. He asked his advice on how to write short stories and begged for help on his next book." When the police arrived, they found three friends trading stories and discussing in detail the works of Thomas Wolfe. So taken was the writer with the whole affair that he later produced a long account of the incident, which he wanted included in *Of Time and the River*. Wolfe's editor, though, was the same Perkins who had nearly died of fright on the infamous night in question: he said no.

Chronology

1588 Thomas Hariot writes the first account of a survey of what is now the United States, called *A Briefe and True Report of the New Found Land of Virginia*. It is not brief, not true, and not about Virginia.

1620 William Bradford's "dearest consort" drowns in the Atlantic, perhaps a suicide.

1636 John Winthrop secretly sends word to Roger Williams that he is about to be arrested, thereby giving Williams just enough time to escape to Rhode Island.

1637 Thomas Morton publishes *New English Canaan* detailing the events Nathaniel Hawthorne will use two hundred years later in "The May-Pole of Merry Mount."

1638 A man named John Harvard leaves his 320 volume library to a struggling college in Cambridge, Massachusetts. The administrators are very grateful.

1639 The first regular bookseller in the American colonies, Hezekiah Usher, opens business in Cambridge, Massachusetts.

1640 *The Bay Psalm Book*.

1650 *The Meritorious Price of Our Redemption* by William Pyncheon becomes the first book banned in America. Officials have it "burned in the marketplace by the common executioner."

1653 John Eliot publishes the first book in an Indian language, *Catechism in the Indian Language*.

1655 Legal documents in Massachusetts requiring signatures of women reveal an illiteracy rate of more than 50%, the papers being signed with an X.

1662 Michael Wigglesworth publishes *The Day of Doom*, on a percentage basis perhaps the all-time bestseller in American literature.

1665 At Accomac, Virginia, three settlers are fined for performing the first play in America, *Ye Bare and Ye Cubb* (even though Virginia had no law against play-acting).

1670 The first section of what becomes famous as the House of the Seven Gables is built in Salem, Massachusetts.

1675 Cotton Mather enters Harvard at age twelve.

1690 On September 25 Benjamin Harris's *Publick Occurrences* becomes the first newspaper published in America. It is closed down four days later because Harris has no license to print.

1692 Cotton Mather's *Wonders of the Invisible World*, provoked by the Salem witch trials, defends Puritan beliefs about witchcraft.

1693 The charter of William and Mary College is granted.

1697 Samuel Sewall publically recants his role as a special commissioner in the Salem witch trials by standing silently in the Old North Church while his diary entry for January 14 is read aloud.

1700 The first antislavery document published in America is written—*The Selling of Joseph* by Samuel Sewall.

1704 The first permanent newspaper in America is founded by John Campbell, *The Boston Newsletter*.

1708 Ebenezer Cook publishes a very popular, rollicking satire called *The Sot Weed Factor. . . :* 252 years later the same title becomes a best-seller for John Barth.

1714 The first play known to have been composed in America, *Androboros*, is acted: it is written by Robert Hunter, governor of New York.

1727 Cotton Mather publishes "Boonerges: A Short Essay to Strengthen the Impressions Produced by Earthquakes."

1728 William Byrd surveys the Virginia-North Carolina border.

1732 *Poor Richard's Almanac* begins.

1734 Jonathan Edwards begins the Great Awakening. His uncle by marriage, Joseph Hawley, cuts his own throat.

1737 The *New England Primer* published this year contains the first known printing of "Now I Lay Me Down to Sleep."

1742 James Ralph gains a new first for American letters by being mentioned in Pope's *Dunciad* (second edition).

1751 Benjamin Franklin publishes *Experiments & Observations on Electricity*.

1754 What may be the first American cartoon appears in the *Pennsylvania*

Gazette—a snake divided into seven parts with the caption, "Join or Die."

1757 John Trumbull, later one of Connecticut Wits, passes Yale's entrance examination at age seven: his mother does not allow him to enroll until he is thirteen.

1759 Thomas Godfrey writes *The Prince of Parthia*, the first play by an American to be acted on a professional stage (in 1767).

1767 To increase understanding between the red man & white, publishers and politicians in New York City invite ten Cherokee chiefs to view a production of *Richard III*. There is no record of the reaction.

1770 A lawyer named Thomas Jefferson argues in a Virginia court for the freedom of a mulatto slave on grounds that "under the law of nature all men are born free": the judge is so incensed by such rhetoric that he immediately decides against Jefferson.

1773 *Poems on Various Subjects* published by Phillis Wheatley, the slave of Bostonian John Wheatley, who recognizes her talent after teaching her to write.

1774 A bestseller in the colonies is Goethe's *Werther* which sets the pattern for future bestsellers by being condemned by all authorities even as publishers capitalized on its morbid, romantic theme at the same time.

1775 Patrick Henry gives his "liberty or death" speech while his wife is chained, insane, in the basement of their house.

1776 Benjamin Franklin is selected Postmaster General. One hundred fifty years later the Post Office will be banning from the mails his "Speech of Polly Baker" and his "Letter to a Young Man on the Proper Choosing of a Mistress."

1779 For the first time George Washington is referred to as the "father of his country" on the title page of a Pennsylvania German (not Dutch) newspaper called *Der Ganz Neue Verbesserte Nord-Americanische Calendar*.

1782 Use of scarlet letters to punish those who commit adultery is discontinued throughout New England.

1783 Webster's *Spelling Book* begins phenomenal sales: it averages nearly a million copies a year for the next one hundred years.

1786 The first American production of *Hamlet* takes place at the John Street Theatre in New York: it is called "moderately successful."

1789 Six-year-old Washington Irving is patted on the head by his namesake when his nurse accosts the President in a New York shop and presents the boy.

1790 The first book is copyrighted in America: it is *The Philadelphia Spelling Book* by John Barry.

1791 The British arrest Thomas Paine for treason after publication of *The Rights of Man*: English poet William Blake smuggles him to France before he comes to harm.

1794 *Charlotte Temple* becomes one of the first bestsellers in this country after it flops in England. It has never gone out of print.

1799 Henry Lee speaks words forever connected to Washington—"First in war, first in peace. . . ."

1800 The Library of Congress is founded April 24.

1806 James Fenimore Cooper is expelled from Yale for "too much pleasure seeking."

1807 New York City is first called "Gotham" by Washington Irving in one of the *Salmagundi Papers*.

1809 The first American humor book, *The History of New York by Diedrich Knickerbocker*, is published. It is the first American book to be widely recognized in Europe.

1811 Joel Barlow is sent to negotiate a treaty with Napoleon, is caught up in the retreat from Moscow, and dies of the hardships.

1815 *The North American Review* begins.

1817 Edward Everett receives in Göttingen the first Ph.D. granted to an American.

1818 In a letter regarding female education Thomas Jefferson cautions against the reading of a relatively new form of fiction, the novel, saying, "When this poison infects the mind, it destroys its tone and revolts it against wholesome reading."

1819 The sinking of the *Essex* becomes especially interesting to a famous American author thirty-five years later: it is rammed by a maddened whale.

1820 Felix Walker, representing North Carolina's Buncombe County, halts a vote in Congress to make a pointless speech "for Buncombe." His peers begin to use the word to refer to any nonsense, and eventually it is shortened to the modern *bunk*.

1821 Sequoya (1779?–1843) invents the characters of the Cherokee language.

1826 *The Last of the Mohicans*.

1828 Noah Webster becomes the "father of his country's language" by publishing his *American Dictionary of the English Language*.

1830 Sarah Josepha Buell Hale publishes *Poems for Our Children* containing the first known printing of "Mary Had a Little Lamb."

1831 The Georgia Senate offers $5,000 for the capture and conviction of William Lloyd Garrison, publisher of the Boston *Liberator*, a militant abolitionist paper.

1832 President Adams publishes his poetry in a 108-page book: he remains the only President to be a published poet.

1833 Edgar Allan Poe wins a fifty-dollar prize in a contest sponsored by the Baltimore *Saturday Visitor* for his "MS Found in a Bottle," called by some the first science fiction story.

1834 Richard Henry Dana leaves on the voyage which eventually becomes *Two Years Before the Mast*.

1836 Poe marries his thirteen-year-old cousin Virginia Clemm.

1837 Washington Irving invents a cliché, "the almighty dollar," in his book *The Creole Village*.

1838 Emerson gives the Divinity School Address and is not invited back to Harvard for thirty years.

1839 Nathaniel Hawthorne receives appointment as measurer of salt and coal for the Boston Custom House, a $1,500-a-year position.

1841 George and Sophia Ripley found Brook Farm: Hawthorne stays a year; the major Transcendentalists are in and out.

1842 Dickens visits America for the first time and hates it.
       Whitman publishes a temperance novel called *Franklin Evans, or the Inebriate*.
       Richard T. Greene and Herman Melville desert the *Acushnet* at "Nukehiva." Greene becomes Toby in Melville's *Typee*.

1843 Poverty-stricken Edgar Allan Poe offers the editors of a Philadelphia magazine a new poem he is working on: they reject the composition but out of sympathy take up a collection of fifteen dollars for him. Later the poem becomes known as "The Raven."

1844 Margaret Fuller becomes the first professional book review editor in America, hired by Horace Greeley for the New York *Tribune*.

1845 March 5 in New York City a young man named Ellery Channing writes to a friend about the possibility of living alone at a pond close to his home. Later in March the friend agrees and asks permission to build a hut on the lot of his friend and employer Ralph Waldo Emerson.

1846 Thoreau arrested for refusal to pay poll tax.

1848 At the age of twenty-nine young James Russell Lowell publishes all in the same year *Poems: Second Series*, *The Biglow Papers*, *The Vision of Sir Launfal*, and *A Fable for Critics*.

1850 Margaret Fuller dies in a shipwreck off Fire Island; the body of her child washes ashore; hers is never found.

1851 The *New York Times* is born—one cent a paper.

1852 *Uncle Tom's Cabin*.

1853 Hawthorne appointed consul to Liverpool.

1854 Premiere of the most popular play in American literary history, *Ten Nights in a Barroom*. It stays in production for more than one hundred years and has four movies made from the script between 1909 and 1931.

1855 John Bartlett first publishes a book called *Familiar Quotations*.

1856 The text of William Bradford's *Of Plimmoth Plantation*, apparently stolen by British soldiers during the Revolution, is discovered in the personal library of the Bishop of London and is published for the first time.

1860 Henry James suffers a mysterious "obscure hurt" at Newport which keeps him out of the Civil War.

1861 As a reward for writing a campaign biography of Lincoln, William Dean Howells is given an appointment as a consul to Venice.

1863 Samuel Clemens, working in Virginia City, Nevada, hears of the death of Isaiah Sellers, a writer of little note who wrote under the pseudonym of Mark Twain. Clemens decides to carry on the name.

1865 William Cullen Bryant refuses to support construction of a memorial to Poe in Baltimore on the grounds that Poe had no element of goodness in him.

The "Jumping Frog" story arrives too late for *Artemus Ward; His Travels* and so appears for the first time instead in *The Saturday Press* of November 18.

1866 Horatio Alger is removed from his pulpit at the First Unitarian Parish of Brewster, Massachusetts for the "abominable and revolting crime of unnatural familiarity with boys."

1867 Emily Dickinson begins her famous "withdrawal" which eventually leads to a sort of solitary confinement in her house at Amherst, Massachusetts.

1868 Christopher L. Sholes patents a new machine called the "typewriter."

1869 Edward Everett Hale writes one of the first science fiction stories, a three part serial called "The Brick Moon."

1871 The original draft of the Emancipation Proclamation burns in the Chicago Fire.

The *Atlantic* pays Bret Harte $10,000 for his entire literary production of the following year: he writes nearly nothing.

1872 Charles Dudley Warner and his next door neighbor agree to write a book together on post-Civil War corruption: he and Mark Twain produce *The Gilded Age* the following year.

1873 The Comstock Act is passed forbidding the mailing of obscene literature.

1875 The first monument to Poe is erected in Baltimore.

1876 *Tom Sawyer* banned from the Denver Public Library, not allowed in the children's section of the Boston Public Library.

1878 William Cullen Bryant dies after a fall in Central Park (New York) while attending a tribute to the Italian patriot Mazzini.

1880 *Ben-Hur* becomes a runaway bestseller.
Uncle Remus born.

1881 John R. Anderson realizes that President Garfield will probably die from his assassin's shots and decides to capitalize. He asks Horatio Alger how soon a biography of the President can be put together from scratch. Alger says a couple of weeks. They agree on a partnership.

1882 Longfellow dies and is the first American memorialized in Westminster Abbey.

1885 Henry Adams's wife commits suicide.
Huckleberry Finn banned from the Public Library of Concord, Massachusetts.

1886 A book salesman named McConnell gives free perfume samples to go with his books. Soon he realizes that the perfume business yields more money than the book business, and he founds the California Perfume Company. Fifty years later he changes the company name to Avon in honor of Shakespeare's birthplace and his former occupation.

1887 *The Tribune Book of Open Air Sports*, edited by Henry Hall, becomes the first book set by linotype.

1889 Thomas Wentworth Higginson advises Mabel Loomis Todd against publishing the works of an obscure poet named Emily Dickinson. The poems are "too crude in form," he writes.

1890 Eccentric millionaire Eugene Schiefflin takes as a project the bringing to America of every bird species mentioned in Shakespeare. In this year he imports the very first starlings into the United States, and Americans have cursed his name since.
Stephen Crane joins Delta Upsilon fraternity.

1891 An international Copyright Act is passed by Congress.

1892 Robert Frost secretly marries Elinor Miriam White, his covaledictorian of Lawrence High School, Lawrence, Massachusetts.

1893 Ford's Theatre, where Lincoln was assassinated, burns to the ground—twenty-two die in the fire.

1895 Robert Frost publicly marries Elinor Miriam White, his covaledictorian of Lawrence High School, Lawrence, Massachusetts.

Sixty-year old Mark Twain, completely bankrupt and more than $100,000 in debt, begins a world-wide lecture tour to recover his funds and respectability: he eventually repays one hundred cents on the dollar.

1897 O. Henry begins a five-year jail sentence for embezzlement.

1898 *The Turn of the Screw.*

1899 Hart Crane and Ernest Hemingway are born the same day, July 21.

1900 Doubleday publishes *Sister Carrie* and immediately withdraws it because Mrs. Doubleday violently objects to publication.

1901 James Thurber, playing at William Tell, is blinded in one eye by an arrow shot by his brother William.

1902 *The Virginian*, by Owen Wister, perhaps the first cowboy novel, is reprinted fourteen times in eight months.

1903 The worst theatre fire in U.S. history at the Iroquois Theatre in Chicago. As fire breaks out during the play, "Mr. Bluebeard," an actor, persuades many to remain seated; the result is 602 dead, 1000 injured. The fire burns itself out in less than fifteen minutes.

1904 Ida M. Tarbell writes the first major expose of what becomes known as the muckraking school, *The History of the Standard Oil Company.*

Four-year-old Thomas Wolfe goes to the St. Louis World's Fair with his mother.

1905 Running on the Socialist ticket, eighteen-year-old Jack London receives 500 votes in his bid for the mayor's office of Oakland, California.

1906 The Pure Food and Drug Act becomes law because of Upton Sinclair's *The Jungle.*

Teddy Roosevelt coins the term *muckraker.*

Sinclair Lewis works for a month as a janitor at Upton Sinclair's utopian community Helicon Hall.

1907 Ezra Pound is fired from the faculty of Wabash College for having a woman in his rooms.

Eugene O'Neill is expelled from Princeton, according to legend, for throwing a beer bottle (or brick) through President Woodrow Wilson's window.

1908 Sarah Orne Jewett advises an unknown young writer to go it alone and concentrate on improving her skills. The advice pays off for Willa Cather who begins her string of successes within four years: *O Pioneers!*, *My Antonía*, *Death Comes for the Archbishop*, *The Professor's House*, etc.

1911 Edith Wharton writes her best book, *Ethan Frome*, in French. It has to be translated into English before it makes her reputation in Britain and America.

1912 Ernest Hemingway appears in his seventh-grade class play, *Robin Hood*.

Sherwood Anderson abandons his family.

1913 Ambrose Bierce disappears in Mexico.

Sinclair Lewis is fired from the San Francisco *Bulletin* for incompetence: in 1930 he becomes the first American to win a Nobel Prize in literature.

1914 Ezra Pound writes to Harriet Monroe, "An American called Eliot called this P.M. I think he has some sense. . . ."

The "flashback" is more or less invented by Elmer Rice and used for the first time in his play *On Trial*.

1915 Anthony Comstock dies: in his career as secretary for the New York Society for the Suppression of Vice he has destroyed more than 160 tons of books and pictures.

1916 Jack London dies November 22.

1917 Columbia College trustees receive first nominations for the Pulitzer Prize.

E. E. Cummings is tried and sentenced for espionage in a French court.

1918 Faulkner enlists in the Royal Flying Corps (in Toronto) and first adds the *u* to his name.

George Lincoln Rockwell and Mickey Spillane are born on the same day, March 9.

The Little Review begins the first publication of James Joyce's *Ulysses* (in installments).

1920 Editors of *The Little Review* are fined $100 for obscenity because of publication of James Joyce's *Ulysses*.

Scott marries Zelda in St. Patrick's; the following Saturday he publishes *This Side of Paradise*.

1921 E. A. Robinson's *Collected Poems* wins the first Pulitzer Prize for poetry.

1922 Erskine Caldwell is arrested for vagrancy in Bogalusa, Louisiana.

1923 Edgar Rice Burroughs becomes the first author to incorporate himself.

1924 *Billy Budd* published for the first time.
Hart Crane is fired from an advertising agency for being redundant.

1925 Langston Hughes serves as a bus boy at the Wardman Park Hotel in Washington, D.C.

1926 The world's first science fiction magazine, *Amazing Stories*, is published by Hugo Gernsback—first issue is April 5.
Sinclair Lewis turns down the Pulitzer Prize.
Book of the Month Club begins.

1927 T. S. Eliot becomes a British subject.

1928 Claude McKay becomes the first black to write a bestseller, *Home to Harlem*.

1929 Heavyweight Champion Gene Tunney, a serious reader of Shakespeare, lectures on the bard at Yale and makes page one of the *New York Times*.
The phrase "the Greeks had a word for it" originates as the title of a play by Zöe Akins. The "word" is *hetaera*, which is a high-class whore.

1930 Gwen Bristow writes the first real mystery novel, *The Invisible Host*, in collaboration with her husband; the book grows out of their fancied plots to murder their neighbor who had a "raucous radio."

1931 A poem by Francis Scott Key called "The Defense of Fort McHenry" (first published in 1814) is designated the National Anthem by an act of Congress.

1932 Eugene O'Neill's *Strange Interlude* opens across the street from a near-bankrupt restaurant in Quincy, Massachusetts. The long play with its 8:30 intermission saves the restaurant from going under: the owner's name is Howard Johnson.

1933 Hemingway goes on his first African safari.
Sara Teasdale commits suicide.
Gertrude Stein writes her own autobiography as seen through the eyes of her secretary, *The Autobiography of Alice B. Toklas*.

1934 Wallace Stevens becomes Vice President of the Hartford Accident & Indemnity Company.

1935 Thomas Mann's daughter, Erika, marries W. H. Auden, although the two have never met.

1936 *Gone with the Wind.*

1937 A huge manuscript, the poems of Edward Taylor, is unearthed in the Yale Library. They are published now for the first time.

1938 Clyde Brion Davis finally writes it—*The Great American Novel*.
      October 31—broadcast of Orson Welles's *War of the Worlds*.

1939 *The Grapes of Wrath*.
      Archibald MacLeish appointed Librarian of Congress.

1940 Scott Fitzgerald dies, and the Catholic Church refuses to allow him to
      be buried on consecrated ground at the Catholic cemetery in Rock-
      ville, Maryland, (with his family) because he dies a nonbeliever.
      Richard Wright, his wife, and child leave 7 Middagh Street in
      Brooklyn because the black superintendent refuses to fire the furnace
      for another black man.

1941 Sherwood Anderson dies in Panama from complications arising from
      biting a toothpick which a Washington hostess had used in her hors
      d'oeuvres.

1942 Steinbeck's *The Moon Is Down* appears simultaneously as a novel and as
      a play; both are successful.

1943 The same year that Carson McCullers publishes her famous "A Tree.
      A Rock. A Cloud." her sister Rita wins an O. Henry Memorial
      Award for "White for the Living."

1944 Publishers return to an old gimmick, soft covers for books, or
      "paperbacks"—the beginning of a revolution in the publishing
      business.

1945 Events of August 6 prompt John Hersey to begin a factual account:
      Hiroshima becomes a sensation the next year, but his later works do
      not live up to the early reputation.

1946 *The Iceman Cometh*.

1947 Mike Hammer makes his first appearance in *I, the Jury*.
      Zelda Fitzgerald dies in a fire at the Highland Sanitarium in North
      Carolina.
      William Styron is fired from McGraw-Hill for flying paper airplanes
      into his boss's office.

1948 Allen Ginsberg expelled from Columbia for writing profanity and
      anti-Semitic phrases in his dormitory.
      Ross Lockridge (*Raintree County*) commits suicide.

1949 August 11—in going to see a movie (*A Canterbury Tale*) Margaret
      Mitchell is struck by a car on Peachtree Street in downtown Atlanta;
      she dies August 16.

1950 Three ex-F.B.I. agents publish *Red Channels*, an enlargement of their
      earlier *Counter-Attack* (1947): both are lists of writers, actors, an-
      nouncers, etc. who have "communist affiliations." Together these are
      known as "the blacklist." The McCarthy era begins.

Faulkner's 1949 Nobel Prize is not announced until the announcing of the 1950 awards.

1951 The McCarthy hearings send Dashiell Hammett to jail because Hammett doesn't reveal names of contributors to the Civil Rights Congress; in truth Hammett does not know a single contributor but refuses to say so.

1952 Marianne Moore wins the National Book Award, the Pulitzer Prize, and the Bollingen all in the same year.

1953 The Iceman comes for O'Neill; his wife Carlotta allows no one but herself to attend the funeral.
Lawrence Ferlinghetti founds City Lights, the first all-paperback bookstore in the United States.

1954 Hemingway's plane crashes while on a hunting trip in Africa; he cannot go to pick up his Nobel Prize in October.
Walden is banned from U. S. Information Service Libraries because it is too "socialistic."

1956 *Peyton Place.*

1958 Ezra Pound is released from St. Elizabeth's Hospital, after an appeal to the government led by Robert Frost, as incurably insane but probably harmless.

1959 Lorraine H. Hansberry becomes the first black to win a New York Drama Critics Circle Award for *A Raisin in the Sun.*

1960 Sinclair Lewis Year—proclaimed by Governor Orville Freeman of Minnesota.

1961 Robert Frost is supposed to read a long poem about the arts and sciences for JFK's inauguration, but because of glare and wind he cannot read and instead recites from memory "The Gift Outright."

1962 Faulkner dies.
Steinbeck receives the Nobel Prize.

1963 Sylvia Plath dies. Robert Frost dies. William Carlos Williams dies. Van Wyck Brooks dies. Theodore Roethke dies. Clifford Odets dies.

1964 Edmund Wilson makes *Esquire's* "Dubious Achievements Awards" for refusing to pay his income tax for ten years and then writing a book in which he complains about the I.R.S.'s attempt to collect.

1965 T. S. Eliot dies.

1966 *In Cold Blood.*

1969 A Texan pays the highest known sum for a single broadsheet, $404,000, for one of the sixteen known copies of the Declaration of Independence.

1970 William L. Hamling adds 546 nudie pictures to the government's official report by the Presidential Commission on Obscenity and Pornography and sells 100,000 copies of the "unofficial" report. He is arrested, fined $87,000, and given four years in the slammer.

1971 *The New York Times* begins publishing the *Pentagon Papers*, the government's secret history of the war in Southeast Asia.

1972 James Dickey plays Sheriff Bullard in the film version of *Deliverance*.

1976 Seventy percent of this year's *Congressional Record* is made up of "speeches" inserted by Congressmen who never actually gave the speeches in Congress. *The Record* is 51,000 pages long and costs $10,000,000 to publish.

Bibliography

Adams, Franklin Pierce, comp. *F.P.A.'s Book of Quotations*. New York: Funk & Wagnalls Company, 1952.

Adams, Henry. *The Education of Henry Adams*. Edited by Ernest Samuels. Boston: Houghton Mifflin, 1973.

Alcott, Louisa May. *Behind a Mask: The Unknown Thrillers of Louisa May Alcott*. Edited by Madeleine Stern. New York: William Morrow & Company, 1975.

Allen, Gay Wilson. *Walt Whitman Handbook*. Chicago: Packard and Company, 1946.

Allen, L. David. *Science Fiction Reader's Guide*. Lincoln, Nebraska: Centennial Press, 1974.

Altick, Richard D. *The Art of Literary Research*. New York: W. W. Norton & Company, 1963.

————. *The Scholar Adventurers*. New York: The Free Press, 1966.

Andrews, Peter. "Books to Avoid Reading." *Horizon*, 16, No. 1 (1974), 112.

Armour, Richard W. *American Lit Relit: A Short History of American Literature*. . . . New York: McGraw-Hill, 1964.

Arvine, Kazlitt. *The Cyclopaedia of Anecdotes of Literature and the Fine Arts*. Boston: Gould and Lincoln, 1851.

Atlas, James. *Delmore Schwartz: The Life of an American Poet*. New York: Avon, 1977.

Baker, Carlos. *Ernest Hemingway: A Life Story*. New York: Charles Scribner's Sons, 1969.

Ballou, Ellen. *The Building of the House: Houghton Mifflin's Formative Years*. Boston: Houghton Mifflin, 1970.

Bartlett, John. *Familiar Quotations*. 14th ed. Boston: Little, Brown and Company, 1968.

Bauer, Andrew. *The Hawthorn Dictionary of Pseudonyms*. New York: Hawthorn Books, 1971.

Benét, Laura. *Famous American Humorists*. New York: Dodd, Mead, 1959.

Benét, William Rose. *The Reader's Encyclopedia*. 2nd ed. New York: Thomas Y. Crowell Company, 1965.

Berg, Andrew S. *Max Perkins: Editor of Genius*. New York: Dutton, 1978.

Bittner, William. *Poe: A Biography*. London: Elek Books, 1962.

Blair, Walter, et al. *American Literature: A Brief History*. Glenview, Illinois: Scott, Foresman and Company, 1974.

Blake, Nelson M. *Novelists' America: Fiction as History*. Syracuse: Syracuse University Press, 1969.

Bleiler, E. F., ed. *Eight Dime Novels*. New York: Dover Publications, 1974.

Blotner, Joseph. *Faulkner: A Biography*. 2 vols. New York: Random House, 1974.

Bode, Carl. *Mencken*. Carbondale: Southern Illinois University Press, 1969.

Brasch, R. *How Did It Begin?*. New York: Pocket Books, 1969.

Brooks, Cleanth, R. W. B. Lewis, and Robert Penn Warren. *American Literature: The Makers and the Making*. 2 vols. New York: St. Martin's Press, 1973.

Burke, W. J. and Will D. Howe. *American Authors and Books, 1640 to the Present Day*. New York: Crown Publishers, 1943.

Burlingame, Roger. *Of Making Many Books: A Hundred Years of Reading, Writing and Publishing*. New York: Scribner, 1946.

Burnam, Tom. *The Dictionary of Misinformation*. New York: Thomas Y. Crowell Company, 1975.

Cameron, Kenneth Walter. *Lowell, Whittier, Very and the Alcotts Among Their Contemporaries: A Harvest of Estimates, Insights, and Anecdotes from the Victorian Literary World and an Index*. Hartford: Transcendental Books, 1978.

————. *Transcendental Log: Fresh Discoveries in Newspapers Concerning Emerson, Thoreau, Alcott and Others of the American Literary Renaissance Arranged Annually for Half a Century from 1832*. Hartford: Transcendental Books, 1973.

————. *Whitman, Bryant, Melville and Holmes Among Their Contemporaries: A Harvest of Estimates, Insights, and Anecdotes from the Victorian Literary World and an Index*. Hartford: Transcendental Books, 1976.

Carr, Virginia Spencer. *The Lonely Hunter: A Biography Of Carson McCullers*. Garden City, New York: Doubleday & Company, 1975.

Cerf, Bennett. *At Random: The Reminiscences of Bennett Cerf*. New York: Random House, 1977.

Chase, Richard. *The American Novel and Its Tradition*. Garden City, New York: Doubleday & Company, 1957.

Churchill, Allen. *The Improper Bohemians: A Re-creation of Greenwich Village in Its Heyday*. New York: Dutton, 1959.

————. *The Literary Decade*. Englewood Cliffs, N. J.: Prentice-Hall, 1971.

Clapp, Jane. *International Dictionary of Literary Awards*. New York: Scarecrow Press, 1963.

Clemens, Samuel. *The Autobiography of Mark Twain.* Edited by Charles Neider. New York: Harper & Row, 1959.

———. *Mark Twain in Eruption.* Edited by Bernard DeVoto. New York: Harper & Brothers, 1940.

Conrad, Barnaby. *Famous Last Words.* Garden City, New York: Doubleday & Company, 1961.

Cowley, Malcolm. *And I Worked at the Writer's Trade: Chapters of Literary History, 1918–1978.* New York: Viking Press, 1978.

Dardis, Tom. *Some Time in the Sun: The Hollywood Years of Fitzgerald, Faulkner, Nathanael West, Aldous Huxley, and James Agee.* New York: Charles Scribner's Sons, 1976.

Davenport, Marcia. *Too Strong for Fantasy: A Personal Record of Music, Literature & Politics in America & Europe Over Half a Century.* New York: Avon, 1967.

Davidson, Marshall B. *The Writer's America.* New York: American Heritage, 1973.

Davis, Burke. *Our Incredible Civil War.* New York: Ballantine, 1960.

de Camp, L. Sprague. *Literary Swordsmen and Sorcerers: The Makers of Heroic Fantasy.* Sauk City, Wisconsin: Arkham House, 1976.

———. *Lovecraft: A Biography.* Garden City, New York: Doubleday & Company, 1975.

Dekle, Bernard. *Profiles of Modern American Authors.* Rutland, Vermont: Charles E. Tuttle Company, 1969.

Downs, Robert B. *Books That Changed the World.* New York: New American Library, 1956.

———. *Famous American Books.* New York: McGraw-Hill, 1971.

Dupee, F. W. *Henry James.* New York: William Morrow, 1974.

Edmiston, Susan and Linda D. Cirino. *Literary New York: A History and Guide.* Boston: Houghton Mifflin, 1976.

Ephron, Nora. *Scribble, Scribble: Notes on the Media.* New York: Bantam, 1978.

Esquire: The Best of Forty Years. New York: David McKay Company, 1973.

Evans, J. Martin. *America: The View from Europe.* New York: W. W. Norton, 1976.

Exman, Eugene. *The House of Harper: 150 Years of Publishing.* New York: Harper & Row, 1967.

Felton, Bruce and Mark Fowler. *Felton & Fowler's Best, Worst, & Most Unusual.* Greenwich, Connecticut: Fawcett Publications, 1975.

———. *Felton & Fowler's More Best, Worst and Most Unusual.* Greenwich, Connecticut: Fawcett Publications, 1976.

Fields, Annie. *Authors and Friends.* Cambridge: Riverside Press, 1897.

Fletcher, H. George, ed. *A Miscellany for Bibliophiles.* New York: Crastorf & Lang, 1979.

Franklin, Benjamin. *Autobiography and Other Writings.* Edited by Russel B. Nye. Boston: Houghton Mifflin Company, 1958.

Frey, Albert R. *Sobriquets and Nicknames.* Boston: Ticknor and Company, 1888.

Furnas, J. C. *The Americans: A Social History of the United States* 1587–1914. New York: G. P. Putnam's Sons, 1969.

Geismar, Maxwell. *Mark Twain: An American Prophet*. New York: McGraw-Hill, 1970.

Gelpi, Albert J. *Emily Dickinson: The Mind of a Poet*. New York: W. W. Norton, 1971.

Gill, Brendan. *Here at the New Yorker*. New York: Random House, 1975.

Gilmer, Walker. *Horace Liveright; Publisher of the Twenties*. New York: David Lewis, 1970.

"Good Books That Almost Nobody Has Read." *The New Republic*, 18 April 1934, pp. 281–283.

Goodspeed, Charles. *Yankee Bookseller*. Westport, Connecticut: Greenwood, 1974.

Goodstone, Tony, comp. *The Pulps: Fifty Years of American Pop Culture*. New York: Chelsea House, 1976.

Gottesman, Ronald, et al., eds. *The Norton Anthology of American Literature*. 2 vols. New York: W. W. Norton & Company, 1979.

Griffin, Martin Ignatius Joseph. *Frank R. Stockton: A Critical Biography*. Philadelphia: University of Pennsylvania Press, 1939.

Gunn, James. *Alternate Worlds: An Illustrated History of Science Fiction*. Englewood Cliffs, N. J.: Prentice-Hall, 1975.

Gwynn, Frederick and Joseph L. Blotner, eds. *Faulkner in the University*. Charlottesville: University of Virginia Press, 1959.

Hackett, Alice Payne. 80 *Years of Bestsellers,* 1895–1975. New York: R. R. Bowker, 1977.

Haight, Anne Lyon. *Banned Books: Informal Notes on Some Books Banned for Various Reasons at Various Times and in Various Places*. 3rd ed. New York, R. R. Bowker, 1970.

Hale, Edward Everett. *James Russell Lowell and His Friends*. Boston: Houghton, Mifflin and Company, 1898.

Hamilton, Charles. *Scribblers and Scoundrels*. New York: P. S. Erikson, 1968.

Hanaford, Phebe A. *Daughters of America; Or, Women of the Century*. Augusta, Maine: True and Company, n.d.

Harding, Walter. *The Days of Henry Thoreau: A Biography*. New York: Alfred A. Knopf, 1965.

Harding, Walter and Michael Meyer. *The New Thoreau Handbook*. New York: New York University Press, 1980.

Hart, James D. *The Oxford Companion to American Literature*. 4th ed. New York: Oxford University Press, 1965.

——. *The Popular Book*. New York: Oxford University Press, 1950.

Heard, J. Norman and Jimmie H. Hoover. *Bookman's Guide to Americana*. 6th ed. Metuchen, New Jersey: Scarecrow Press, 1971.

Hellman, George S. *Washington Irving, Esquire, Ambassador at Large from the New World to the Old*. New York: A. A. Knopf, 1925.

Hemingway, Ernest. *A Moveable Feast.* New York: Charles Scribner's Sons, 1964.

Higginson, Thomas Wentworth. *Contemporaries.* Upper Saddle River, New Jersey: Literature House/Gregg Press, 1970.

Hoffman, Daniel. *Poe, Poe, Poe, Poe, Poe, Poe, Poe.* Garden City, New York: Doubleday & Company, 1972.

Hoffman, Hester R. *The Reader's Adviser.* 10th ed. New York: R. R. Bowker, 1964.

Holbrook, Stewart Hall. *Lost Men of American History.* New York: Macmillan, 1946.

Howells, William Dean. *Literary Friends and Acquaintances: A Personal Retrospect of American Authorship.* New York: Harper & Brothers, 1902.

Hoyt, Edwin P. *Horatio's Boys: The Life and Works of Horatio Alger, Jr.* Radnor, Pennsylvania: Chilton Book Company, 1974.

Hubbell, Jay B. *The South in American Literature.* Durham: Duke University Press, 1954.

Hyman, Robin. *The Quotation Dictionary.* New York: Macmillan, 1965.

Jones, Howard Mumford and Richard M. Ludwig. *Guide to American Literature and Its Backgrounds since 1890.* 4th ed. Cambridge: Harvard University Press, 1972.

Kane, Joseph Nathan. *Famous First Facts.* New York: H. W. Wilson Company, 1964.

Kaplan, Justin. *Mr. Clemens and Mark Twain.* New York: Simon and Schuster, 1966.

Keats, John. *You Might as Well Live: The Life and Times of Dorothy Parker.* New York: Simon and Schuster, 1970.

Kenin, Richard and Justin Wintle. *The Dictionary of Biographical Quotations of British and American Subjects.* New York: Alfred Knopf, 1978.

Killikelly, Sarah H. *Curious Questions.* 3 vols. Philadelphia: David McKay, 1900.

Krutch, Joseph Wood. *American Drama since 1918: An Informal History.* New York: Braziller, 1957.

Kunitz, Stanley J. and Howard Haycraft. *American Authors 1600 – 1900: A Biographical Dictionary of American Literature.* New York: H. W. Wilson Company, 1938.

Lawrence, D. H. *Studies in Classic American Literature.* London: Martin Secker, 1924.

Leggett, John. *Ross and Tom.* New York: Simon and Schuster, 1974.

Levinson, Leonard Louis. *Bartlett's Unfamiliar Quotations.* Chicago: Cowles Book Company, 1971.

Leyda, Jay. *The Melville Log: A Documentary Life of Herman Melville, 1819 – 1891.* 2 vols. New York: Harcourt, Brace and Company, 1951.

Lubbock, Percy, ed. *The Letters of Henry James.* 2 vols. London: Macmillan, 1920.

Lundwall, Sam J. *Science Fiction: What It's All About.* New York: Ace Books, 1971.

Lyons, Robert, ed. *Autobiography: A Reader for Writers.* New York: Oxford University Press, 1977.

McPhee, Nancy, comp. *The Book of Insults, Ancient & Modern.* New York: St. Martin's Press, 1978.

MacShane, Frank. *The Life of Raymond Chandler.* New York: Dutton, 1976.

McWhirter, Norris and Ross McWhirter. *Guinness Book of World Records.* New York: Sterling Publishing Company, 1976.

Manchester, William. *The Glory and the Dream: A Narrative History of America, 1932–1972.* 2 vols. Boston: Little, Brown and Company, 1974.

Matthiessen, F. O. *American Renaissance: Art and Expression in the Age of Emerson and Whitman.* New York: Oxford University Press, 1941.

Mellow, James R. *Charmed Circle: Gertrude Stein & Company.* New York: Avon, 1974.

Meltzer, Milton. *Mark Twain Himself: A Pictorial Biography.* New York: Bonanza Books, 1960.

Mencken, H. L. *A Book of Prefaces.* Garden City, New York: Garden City Publishing Company, 1927.

Milford, Nancy. *Zelda: A Biography.* New York: Harper & Row, 1970.

Miller, Perry, ed. *The Transcendentalists: An Anthology.* Cambridge: Harvard University Press, 1971.

Mott, Frank Luther. *Golden Multitudes.* New York: R. R. Bowker, 1947.

Moskowitz, Samuel. *Explorers of the Infinite: Shapers of Science Fiction.* Westport, Connecticut: Hyperion Press, 1974.

Muir, Frank. *An Irreverent and Thoroughly Incomplete Social History of Almost Everything.* New York: Stein and Day, 1976.

O'Neill, Edward H. *A History of American Biography 1800–1935.* New York: A. S. Barnes, 1961.

Nance, William L. *The Worlds of Truman Capote.* New York: Stein and Day, 1973.

Pattee, Fred Lewis. *Side-Lights on American Literature.* New York: The Century Company, 1922.

Pearce, Roy Harvey. *The Continuity of American Poetry.* Princeton: Princeton University Press, 1961.

Penzler, Otto, et al., comps. *Detectionary: A Biographical Dictionary of Leading Characters in Detective and Mystery Fiction. . . .* New York: Overlook Press, 1977.

Perrin, Noel. *Dr. Bowdler's Legacy.* New York: Atheneum, 1969.

Petersen, Clarence. *The Bantam Story: Thirty Years of Paperback Publishing.* 2nd ed. New York: Bantam, 1975.

Phyfe, William Henry. *5000 Facts and Fancies. . . .* New York: G. P. Putnam's Sons, 1901.

Pohl, Frederik. *The Way the Future Was: A Memoir.* New York: Ballantine, 1978.

Porges, Irwin. *Edgar Rice Burroughs: The Man Who Created Tarzan.* Provo, Utah: Brigham Young University Press, 1975.

Resnick, Michael. *Official Guide to the Fantastics.* Florence, Alabama: House of Collectibles, 1976.

Reynolds, Quentin. *The Fiction Factory, or from Pulp Row to Quality Street.* . . . New York: Random House, 1955.

Richards, Robert F. *Concise Dictionary of American Literature.* New York: Philosophical Library, 1955.

Robertson, Eric Sutherland. *Life of Henry Wadsworth Longfellow.* Port Washington, New York: KenniKat Press, 1972.

Robertson, Patrick. *The Book of Firsts.* New York: Clarkson N. Potter, 1974.

Rodger, William. *Official Guide to Old Books and Autographs.* Florence, Alabama: House of Collectibles, 1976.

Rusk, Ralph L. *The Life of Ralph Waldo Emerson.* New York: Charles Scribner's Sons, 1949.

Sanborn, Franklin Benjamin. *Transcendental Writers and Heroes: Papers Chiefly on Emerson, Thoreau, Literary Friends and Contemporaries with Regional and Critical Backgrounds.* Edited by Kenneth Walter Cameron. Hartford: Transcendental Books, 1978.

Scherman, David E. and Rosemarie Redlich. *Literary America: A Chronicle of American Writers from 1607 – 1952 with 173 Photographs of the American Scenes That Inspired Them.* New York: Dodd, Mead & Company, 1952.

Schick, Frank L. *The Paperbound Book in America.* New York: R. R. Bowker, 1958.

Seager, Allan. *The Glass House: The Life of Theodore Roethke.* New York: McGraw-Hill, 1968.

Sewall, Richard B. *The Life of Emily Dickinson.* 2 vols. New York: Farrar, Straus and Giroux, 1974

Shavin, Norman. *The Million Dollar Legends: Margaret Mitchell and "Gone with the Wind.* Atlanta: Capricorn Corporation, 1974.

Southwick, Albert P. *Wisps of Wit and Wisdom, Or; Knowledge in a Nutshell.* New York: A. Lovell, 1892.

Spiller, Robert E. *The Cycle of American Literature: An Essay in Historical Criticism.* New York: The Free Press, 1967.

Spiller, Robert E., et al., eds. *Literary History of the United States.* 3rd ed. London: Macmillan, 1963.

Stallman, R. W. *Stephen Crane: A Biography.* New York: George Braziller, 1968.

Stegner, Wallace. *The Uneasy Chair: A Biography of Bernard DeVoto.* Garden City, New York: Doubleday & Company, 1974.

Stevens, George. *Lincoln's Doctor's Dog.* Philadelphia: Lippincott, 1939.

Stevenson, Burton Egbert. *Famous Single Poems and the Controversies Which Have Raged Around Them.* New York: Dodd, Mead, 1935.

Stewart, Randall. *Nathaniel Hawthorne: A Biography.* New Haven: Yale University Press, 1948.

Stowe, Harriet Beecher. *A Key to Uncle Tom's Cabin.* London: Thomas Bosworth, 1853.

Thomas, Isaiah. *The History of Printing in America.* New York: Weathervane Books, 1970

Thomas, Ralph. *Handbook of Fictitious Names: Being a Guide to Authors, Chiefly in the Lighter Literature of the XIXth Century, Who Have Written Under Assumed Names; And to Literary Forgers, Impostors, Plagiarists, and Imitators, by Olphar Hamst, esq.* London: J. R. Smith, 1868.

Vedder, Henry C. *American Writers of To-day.* New York: Silver, Burdett and Company, 1894.

Wagenknecht, Edward C. *Cavalcade of the American Novel.* New York: Holt, 1952.

Wallace, Irving. *The Fabulous Originals: Lives of Extraordinary People Who Inspired Memorable Characters in Fiction.* New York: Alfred Knopf, 1956.

————. *The Square Pegs.* New York: Alfred Knopf, 1957.

Wallachinsky, David and Irving Wallace. *The People's Almanac.* Garden City, New York: Doubleday & Company, 1975.

————. *The People's Almanac #2.* New York: William Morrow, 1978.

Wallechinsky, David, Irving Wallace, and Amy Wallace. *The People's Almanac Presents the Book of Lists.* New York: William Morrow, 1977.

Walser, Richard. *Thomas Wolfe Undergraduate.* Durham: Duke University Press, 1977.

Walsh, William S. *Handy-Book of Literary Curiosities.* Philadelphia: J. B. Lippincott Company, 1892.

Warfel, Harry R. *American Novelists of Today.* New York: American Book Company, 1951.

Welty, Eudora. *The Eye of the Story: Selected Essays & Reviews.* New York: Vintage, 1979.

Wheeler, William A. and Charles G. Wheeler. *Familiar Allusions: A Handbook of Miscellaneous Information.* . . . 8th ed. Boston: Houghton, Mifflin and Company, 1896.

Whittemore, Reed. *William Carlos Williams: Poet from Jersey.* Boston: Houghton Mifflin, 1975.

Williams, Tennessee. *Memoirs.* New York: Bantam, 1976.

Williams, William Carlos. *The Autobiography of William Carlos Williams.* New York: New Directions, 1951.

Wilson, Edmund. *Classics and Commercials: A Literary Chronicle of the Forties.* New York: Farrar, Straus, 1950.

————. *Patriotic Gore: Studies in the Literature of the American Civil War.* New York: Oxford University Press, 1962.

————. *The Shores of Light: A Literary Chronicle of the Twenties and Thirties.* New York: Farrar, Straus and Young, 1952.

Winterich, John T. and David A. Randall. *A Primer of Book Collecting.* New York: Bell Publishing Company, 1966.

Young, Thomas Daniel, et al., eds. *The Literature of the South.* Glenview, Illinois: Scott, Foresman and Company, 1968.

Ziff, Larzer, *The American 1890's: Life and Times of a Lost Generation.* New York: Viking, 1966.

Zochert, Donald. *Laura: The Life of Laura Ingalls Wilder.* New York: Avon, 1976.

Index

Composed in phototype Garamond
and Garamond Old Style by Trend
Western Technical Corporation,
Fullerton, California. Printed by
R.R. Donnelley and Sons, Chicago,
Illinois, via offset lithography on sixty
pound Warrens 1854 regular, in an
edition of twenty-two thousand copies,
of which seven thousand are
clothbound.